# 教室英語
# 活用事典

高梨庸雄、高橋正夫、カール・アダムズ、久埜百合 ― 編　［改訂版］

Kenkyusha's Handbook of
## Classroom
## English

研究社

# はしがき

　本書の初版が出たのは1992年7月で，英語の学習指導要領に「コミュニケーション」がキーワードとして入った頃である．学習指導要領で謳われている目標とその目標に向かって指導していく教師の英語力・指導力との間には，(すぐれた教師もたくさんいたが)かなりのギャップがあったのは事実であり，本書はそのような指導体制における教師の拠り所として，少しでもお役に立ちたいという思いから刊行されたものであった．幸い先生方にご好評をいただき，また，教育委員会主催の研修会で使っていただいたりもし，版を重ねて12年が経過したことになる．多くの読者の方に心から感謝申し上げたい．

　その12年間に，ALT(外国人指導助手)も6000人を超え，日本の英語教育は音声面でかなり前進したと言えるであろう．しかし，それはあくまでも一昔前と比べた場合であって，国際的に見て安心できるレベルに達したかと言えば，まだまだ喜べないというのが現実であろう．中国(含む台湾)，韓国など東アジアの国々では，英語が小学校の正課となり，また国家レベルの大学入学試験(英語)に聴解問題が加えられたりと，積極的に制度改革が行われたばかりでなく，国際的な英語力試験でも日本を上回る結果を出している．そのため，日本でも2003年度から「英語を話せる日本人の育成」の一環として，中学・高等学校の英語教員が全員研修を受けることになった．また，小学校に「英語活動」の形で英語が導入され，目下，正課として導入する場合の諸条件の検討に入っている．

　上記のような時代の流れに対応するために，本書を改訂することになった．改訂の主な点は次の4つである．

1. 小学校の英語活動を支援するセクションを新設した．
2. 構成を5部に分けて，ALTに日本の教育を説明するときの参考になるように想定問答集を加えたりなどした．
3. 全般的に内容を見直し，教育機器にコンピュータを加えるなど，古いものは新しいものと入れ替えた．

4. 英語表現をより平易・適切なものに改めた.

　以前は，Classroom English という用語は，「授業中に使う決まり文句」のような印象を与えていたかも知れない．ごく限られた数の教師だけが英語を使って授業を行っていた頃は，一般にはその程度の認識しかなかったであろう．しかし，授業研究が進むにつれて，大切なのは単なる方法論ではなく授業中の「ことばのやりとり」(interaction) そのものであるということが多くの研究で明らかになった．授業中の interaction を分析・整理してみると，「質問」，「指示」，「依頼」，「確認」，「激励」，「注意」など，日常生活で使用頻度の非常に高い言語機能がたくさん含まれていることがわかる．これらの言語機能は，教師対生徒，あるいは生徒対生徒の間で交わされるさまざまな interaction の中にふんだんに含まれており，外国語習得にとって大変貴重なインプットの源になっている．この事典はその貴重な資源を分類整理して編纂したものである．多くの人々に授業で活用していただければ幸いである．

　なお，初版では，岩見一郎，梅山道子，佐野富士子，杉山敏，高梨庸雄，高橋正夫，野呂徳治，吹貝賢一，古川登美子，緑川日出子，渡辺浩行の 11 名が執筆にあたったが，改訂の作業は編者 4 名で行った．

　初版の刊行の際には研究社の浜松義昭，杉本義則，里見文雄の三氏にお世話になり，今回の改訂では特に杉本義則氏に大変お世話になった．心から感謝申し上げる次第である．

　　2004 年 6 月

　　　　　　　　　　　　　　　　　　　　　　　　　　　　編　者

# この事典の使い方

　この事典を効果的に活用していただくために，この事典がどのような構成になっているか，さらに各部，各セクションが，それぞれどのような目的で編纂されたものであるかを以下に説明しておきたい．

## 1. この事典の構成

　この事典は「小学校での教室英語」を冒頭に置いて，その後，「第 I 部　一般的指示」から「第 V 部　教室英語歳時記」までの構成になっている．

　「小学校での教室英語」では，教室英語の例文だけでなく，指導の際の留意点も解説してある．

　第 I 部は「一般的指示」で，通常の授業で，指導過程のどの段階においても，かなり頻繁に使う教室英語を集めている．

　第 II 部は「授業展開」に必要な教室英語をおおむね指導過程に従って配列している．

　第 III 部には，「オーラル・コミュニケーション」の科目内容にそったセクションのほか，「授業のバリエーション」を持たせるために利用価値の高い「歌とゲーム」，「教育機器の利用」を入れ，最後に，最近の評価への関心に配慮し「テスト」を配置した．

　第 IV 部は，ALT (Assistant Language Teacher) がわが国の英語教育に定着し，今後，各地区・各学校の現状に即した一層の活用が求められるので，Team-teaching で必要な表現はもちろんのこと，ALT に日本の教育について説明する場合の質疑応答を想定した "Questions & Answers" も入れて，「ALT との対話」として独立させた．

　第 V 部は「教室英語歳時記」としてあるが，1 年間の行事や季節ごとの生活表現だけでなく，生徒を取りまく社会や学校環境・学校行事，さらには広く教育関係用語を扱っている．第 I 部〜第 IV 部に比べて語彙集としての性格が強いので，"Words & Phrases" 欄を設け，関連するその他の語彙も扱っている．社会や季節が日々少しずつ変化していくわけであるから，

毎週同じ時間帯の授業であっても，まったく同じ授業というのはありえない．毎回少しずつ変化のある，新鮮な授業にするために第Ⅴ部の表現を活用してもらえれば幸いである．

## 2. 各セクションの構成

### (1) 例文

各セクションは，原則として〈基本的表現〉と〈発展的表現〉からできている．各セクションの最初に列挙してある表現が基本的表現であり，中学生でも理解できるようにできるだけ簡潔な表現にしたつもりである．しかし，内容によってはそれが無理であったり，かえって回りくどくなる場合もあるので，必ずしも中学校の言語材料だけに限定はしなかった．〈発展的表現〉は，基本的表現にさらに情報を付加したもの，あるいは表現が2文以上で構成されている場合である．

これらの表現は，授業中の発言を「概念」(notions) や「機能」(functions) によって分類し，各部，各セクションの目的に従って配列したものである．

### (2) Notes

Notes は各セクションの表現に関する留意事項である．語法に関するものもあれば文化に関するものもある．また，その表現が使われるコンテキストについての説明になっている場合もある．

### (3) Student Response

ここでは，そのセクションで扱われている表現を使った場合に予想される生徒の発話を挙げている．生徒の発話は年齢，学習経験，地域差などによって多様であり，ここに載せてあるのは予想される発話のほんの数例に過ぎない．この事典を使用される方々は，教えておられる生徒の実態や教育環境に合わせて，発展的にご使用いただければありがたい．

### (4) Interaction

これは，教師と生徒あるいは生徒間で交わされる教室英語での対話で，各セクションで扱われている「概念」や「機能」にそって展開している．

## 3. この事典の活用法

　この事典は，使用される方々のニーズによっていろいろな利用の仕方が考えられる．

　小学校の先生方は，「小学校の教室英語」を読まれたら，さらに，第 I 部，第 II 部の基本的表現にも目を通されることをお勧めしたい．

　中学・高校教員を目指す教育実習中の学生や新採用教員の場合は，まず，第 I 部，第 II 部の基本的表現に当たる部分を読まれることをお勧めしたい．また，「小学校の教室英語」で取り上げた英語表現は，教室英語の基本表現ばかりなので，それにも是非目を通していただきたい．もちろん，読むだけでなく，積極的に使ってみることが大切である．そのあとは，第 I 部，第 II 部の〈発展的表現〉，及び第 III 部，第 IV 部をご自分の授業に取り入れる形で活用していただきたい．その間，第 V 部の表現のいくつかを，各地域の実情に合わせて料理のスパイスのように取り入れてもらえればありがたい．

　すでに教壇に立たれて数年以上になる方々の場合は，どの程度英語を使って授業を展開しているかについては，かなり個人差が出ているであろう．したがって，本書の利用の仕方も教師の数だけあると言っても過言ではない．拾い読みするだけで十分な方もあるだろうし，第 II〜IV 部を一度じっくり読んでみたいと思っている方もあるだろう．また，第 V 部を勤務先の教育環境に合わせて自分流の語彙集に編集しなおして使う方もあるだろう．どの利用の仕方をされても構わないが，自分の表現として生かして使っていただければ，編者の喜びこれに勝るものはない．

## 4. 諸記号の用法

① [ 　] 　直前の語句と置き換えられることを示す．意味が変わらない場合と，変わる場合がある．

　　例：
- Will you turn [switch] on the light?
- Look at the screen [wall].
- Stand by [in front of] your desk.
- What beautiful handwriting this is [you have]!

② / 類似の表現を列挙する場合.

例: • You are welcome. / Not at all. / Don't mention it.

• Good morning, class [everybody / everyone / boys and girls].

③ ( ) カッコ内の語句が省略可能であることを示す.

例: • (Go) back to your seat.

• Thank you (very much).

• Straighten your desk(s).

④ ☞ 参照ページを示す.

例: ☞ p. 16 （16 頁を参照）

# 目次

- 小学校での教室英語 ................................................ 1
- 第Ⅰ部　一般的指示 ................................................ 23
  1. 移　動 ........................................................ 25
  2. 注　目 ........................................................ 31
  3. 起立・着席 .................................................... 38
  4. 注意・叱責 .................................................... 45
  5. 発　言 ........................................................ 53
  6. ほめる ........................................................ 61
  7. 励まし ........................................................ 69
  8. あやまる ...................................................... 75
  9. 感　謝 ........................................................ 83
  10. 生徒発言への対応 ............................................. 89
  11. 学習活動への指示 ............................................. 99

- 第Ⅱ部　授業展開 .................................................. 103
  1. ウォームアップ ............................................... 105
  2. 復　習 ....................................................... 132
  3. 導　入 ....................................................... 149
  4. 練　習 ....................................................... 170
  5. 教科書本文 ................................................... 197
  6. 終　了 ....................................................... 233

- 第Ⅲ部　授業のバリエーションとテスト ............................. 251
  1. オーラル・コミュニケーション ................................. 253
  2. 歌とゲーム ................................................... 262
  3. 教育機器の利用 ............................................... 270
  4. テスト ....................................................... 283

- 第Ⅳ部　ALTとの対話 .............................................. 295

- 第Ⅴ部　教室英語歳時記 ........................................... 313
  1. 季節・祝日 ................................................... 315
  2. 学校行事 ..................................................... 330
  3. 社　会 ....................................................... 343
  4. スポーツ ..................................................... 346
  5. 生　徒 ....................................................... 350
  6. 教育関係用語 ................................................. 356

はしがき　i
この事典の使い方　iii

# 小学校での教室英語　1

　基本的指示　3
　動きの指示　4
　ゲーム活動　7
　作業・制作活動　10
　演じる活動　13
　なぞなぞ・歌　15
　ビデオ・紙芝居　17
　小学校での授業の進め方　18

# 第I部　一般的指示　23

## 1. 移　動 …………………………………… 25

　a. 席の移動　25
　　ア. 自分の席につく　25 ／ イ. 活動のための席移動　26
　b. 班編成のための移動　27
　c. 黒板 [OHP] のところへ　28
　d. 教室を出る　29
　　ア. 授業の途中で　29 ／ イ. 授業が終わって　30

## 2. 注　目 …………………………………… 31

　a. 板書に　31
　b. 生徒に　32
　c. 教師に　33
　d. 参観者に　34
　e. 図・絵に　35

f. 窓外に　36

## 3. 起立・着席 .................................................. 38
　　　a. 個人で　38
　　　　　ア. 起立　38 / イ. 着席　39
　　　b. 班ごとに　39
　　　　　ア. 起立　39 / イ. 着席　40
　　　c. ペアで　41
　　　　　ア. 起立　41 / イ. 着席　42
　　　d. 全員で　43
　　　　　ア. 起立　43 / イ. 着席　43

## 4. 注意・叱責 .................................................. 45
　　　a. 静かに　45
　　　　　ア. クラス全体に　45 / イ. 個々の生徒に　46
　　　b. 顔を上げて　46
　　　c. 私語の禁止　47
　　　　　ア. 最初の注意　47 / イ.（注意してもやめないので）しかる　48
　　　d. 罰を与える　49
　　　e. いたずらの禁止　50
　　　　　ア. 短い注意　50 / イ. 長めの注意　51
　　　f. その他の注意　52

## 5. 発　言 .................................................. 53
　　　a. 大きな声で（言う・話す）　53
　　　b. はっきりと　54
　　　c. 口を大きく開けて　55
　　　d. 意味を考えて　56
　　　e. 発言を促す　57
　　　　　ア. 答えを促す　57 / イ. 質問を受ける　58
　　　f. 挙　手　59

## 6. ほめる ............................................................. 61

    a. 一般的なほめ言葉　61
    b. 声の質　62
    c. 声の大きさ　62
    d. 努　力　63
        ア．成果に対して　63 / イ．ねぎらう　64
    e. 手書きの文字　65
    f. 向上の度合い　66
    g. 試験の結果　67

## 7. 励まし ............................................................. 69

    a. 希望をもたせる　69
    b. 意欲をかき立てる　69
    c. 積極性を引き出す　71
    d. 好調を持続させる　72
    e. 慰め・同情　72
    f. 生徒の応答を励ます　73

## 8. あやまる ........................................................... 75

    a. 遅刻して　75
        ア．教師が遅れて教室に入る　75 / イ．理由の説明　76
    b. 生徒の釈明に対して　76
    c. 自習にして　78
        ア．自習の予告　78 / イ．理由の説明　78 /
        ウ．予告なしの自習のあとで　79
    d. 宿題が多すぎて　80
    e. 勘違いして　81
    f. 急用で授業を中座して　81
        ア．教師　81 / イ．生徒の発言　82

## 9. 感　謝 ............................................................. 83

    a. 一般的な「ありがとう」　83

b. 手伝いに対して　84
　　　　ア. 手伝いを頼む　84 ／ イ. 生徒が手伝いを申し出る　84 ／
　　　　ウ. 手伝いに感謝する　85
　　c. 黒板などの掃除　86
　　　　ア. 掃除を頼む　86 ／ イ. 掃除に感謝　87
　　d. 花などに対して　87
　　e. プレゼントに対して　88

## 10. 生徒発言への対応 ......................................... 89

　　a. 誤りの訂正　89
　　　　ア. 誤りを指摘する　89 ／ イ. 小さな［大きな］誤り　90
　　b. 場面ごとの誤りの訂正　91
　　　　ア. 音声　91 ／ イ. 文法　92 ／ ウ. 綴り字・句読法　93
　　c. 理解の確認　93
　　d. 任意参加を求める　94
　　e. 指名して反応を喚起　95
　　　　ア. 指名　95 ／ イ. 反応を促す　96 ／ ウ. 助け舟を出して　97
　　f. 無反応の状況で　97

## 11. 学習活動への指示 ......................................... 99

　　a. グループワーク　99
　　b. ペアワーク　99
　　c. 聞くこと　99
　　d. 読むこと　100
　　e. 文　法　100
　　f. 語　彙　101
　　g. 子どもたちの活動　101

## 第 II 部　授業展開　　　　　　　　　　　　　103

### 1. ウォームアップ ..................................................... 105
#### ① 挨　拶 ........................................................... 105
　　a.　挨　拶　105
　　　　ア．普段の挨拶　105 ／ イ．休み明けの挨拶　106
　　b.　生徒の反応に続けて　107
　　c.　時　間　108
　　d.　曜日・月日　110
　　e.　自己紹介　111
　　　　ア．教師から　111 ／ イ．生徒に自己紹介を促す　112
#### ② 出欠・遅刻 ...................................................... 113
　　a.　出席の確認　113
　　b.　欠席［遅刻］の理由　114
　　　　ア．欠席の理由　114 ／ イ．遅刻の理由　115 ／ ウ．注意　116
　　c.　健康チェック　117
#### ③ 天　候 ........................................................... 118
　　a.　晴　れ　118
　　b.　曇　り　119
　　c.　雨　119
　　d.　暖かい　121
　　e.　暑　い　122
　　f.　蒸し暑い　123
　　g.　寒　い　124
　　h.　霜・氷　125
　　i.　雪　125
#### ④ 前日等の話題 ................................................... 126
　　a.　普段の生活　126
　　　　ア．家庭生活　126 ／ イ．学校生活　127 ／ ウ．社会生活　128

      b. 週の始め・休暇明け　129
      c. 週の終わり頃　130

## 2. 復　習 ............................................................. 132

### ① 宿題の提出 ........................................................ 132
      a. 係が集める　132
      b. 列ごとに集める　133
      c. 教卓に出す　134
      d. 授業後に提出　135

### ② 宿題の発表 ........................................................ 136
      a. 口頭で　136
      b. 板書で　137
      c. OHP で　138
      d. 隣の人と宿題チェック　139

### ③ 暗唱文の確認 .................................................... 140
      a. 口頭英作文として　140
      b. 対話形式で　141
      c. １人で　142
      d. 意味を考えて　143
      e. 気持ちを込めて　143

### ④ 前時のテキスト .................................................. 145
      a. 要　約　145
      b. 主人公の行動　146
      c. 対話の理解　147

## 3. 導　入 ............................................................. 149

### ① 重要構文 ............................................................ 149
      a. 意　味　149
        ア. 日本語で意味をとらえさせる　149 /
        イ. 聞いてその文の内容を考えさせる　150
      b. 表現形式　151
      c. 読み方　151

d. 言い換え　153

## ② 演示による導入　……………………………………………154
　　a. 教師の動作　154
　　b. 生徒の動作　155
　　c. 動作の指示　155
　　d. ２つの動作の相違　157
　　e. 役割指定　158
　　　　ア. 状況設定を教師が指定　158 /
　　　　イ. グループ内で生徒同士が役割決定　158

## ③ 新出語　………………………………………………………159
　　a. 発　音　159
　　b. 意　味　160
　　　　ア. 実物で　160 / イ. 絵で　161 / ウ. 英語で　161
　　c. フラッシュカード　163
　　d. 連　語　163
　　e. 同音異義語　165

## ④ 本文・対話　…………………………………………………166
　　a. 要　点　166
　　b. 質　問　167
　　c. 登場人物の相互関係　167

# 4. 練　習　……………………………………………………170

## ① 語と文　………………………………………………………170
　　a. 強　勢　170
　　b. イントネーション　171
　　c. 例　文　172
　　d. ルックアップ・アンド・セイ　172
　　e. 綴　り　174

## ② 文型練習　……………………………………………………175
　　a. 代　入　175
　　b. 語順転換　176

c. 文転換　176
　　　d. 拡　大　177
　　　e. 短　縮　178
　　　f. 結合・完成　178
　③ 動作を伴う練習 ............................................................179
　　　a. CLL（Community Language Learning）　179
　　　b. TPR（Total Physical Response）　180
　　　c. サジェストペディア　182
　　　d. コミュニカティブ・アプローチ　182
　　　e. ジャズ・チャンツ　183
　④ 練習の指示 ....................................................................184
　　　a. 個人，班ごとの切り替え　184
　　　b. ノートの取り方・板書の写し方　185
　　　c. 図・絵などの説明　186
　⑤ 書く作業 ........................................................................187
　　　a. プリントの配布　187
　　　b. ワークブック　188
　　　c. （OHP用）TPシートを使った練習　189
　　　d. 筆記体・活字体　189
　　　e. なぐり書き・丁寧に書く　190
　　　f. ペン・鉛筆　190
　　　g. 色を塗る　191
　　　h. 図を描く　192
　⑥ 黒板での作業 ................................................................193
　　　a. チョークの指示　193
　　　b. 板　書　194
　　　c. 下線を引く　195
　　　d. 消　す　195

## 5. 教科書本文 ..................................................... 197
### ① 読み方 ........................................................ 197
- a. 範　読　197
- b. 教師のあとについて読む　198
- c. テープ［CD］のあとについて読む　199
- d. 音　読　201
- e. 黙　読　202
- f. 個人読み　203
  - ア. 個人の生徒が読む場合　203 ／ イ. 生徒が各自で読む場合　204
- g. ペア読み　205
- h. 斉　読　205
- i. 読む箇所の指定　206
- j. イントネーション　207
- k. 強　勢　208
- l. 発音の訂正　209

### ② 内容把握 ..................................................... 210
- a. 語［句・節・文］の意味　210
- b. パラグラフの大意　212
  - ア. 大意把握の指示　212 ／ イ. 大意把握の具体的方法　213
- c. 指示語の把握　214
- d. 和　訳　215
  - ア. 和訳の指示　215 ／ イ. 和訳をよくしようとする場合　216
- e. パラフレーズ　217

### ③ 文法練習 ..................................................... 218
- a. 書き換え　218
- b. 和文英訳　219
  - ア. 和文英訳の指示　219 ／ イ. 誤りを訂正する場合　220 ／
    ウ. 別訳を検討する場合　221
- c. 穴埋め　221
- d. 文の転換・結合　223
  - ア. 文の転換　223 ／ イ. 文の結合　223

④ **言語活動** ....................................................................224
 a. 聞くこと　224
 b. 話すこと　227
 c. 読むこと　229
 d. 書くこと　231

# 6. 終　了 ..........................................................................233

① **残り時間** ....................................................................233
 a. 短い場合　233
  ア．急いで進む　233 ／ イ．生徒を呼び止めて　234
 b. 長い場合　235
  ア．予定外の活動を入れる　235 ／ イ．早めに終わる　236
 c. 予定の変更　236
 d. 次回の予告　237
 e. チャイム　238

② **宿題の指示** ................................................................239
 a. 教科書の該当箇所　239
  ア．宿題の指示　239 ／ イ．指示の確認　240
 b. 暗唱文の指定　241
 c. 単語の予習・練習　242
  ア．予習　242 ／ イ．練習　242
 d. プリントの配布　243
 e. 小テストの予告　244

③ **終わりの挨拶** ............................................................246
 a. 一般的な挨拶　246
 b. 来週まで　246
 c. 次時まで間が空きすぎる場合　247
 d. 長期休暇の前　248
 e. 時間割変更の予告　249
 f. 後片づけ　249

# 第 III 部　授業のバリエーションとテスト　251

## 1. オーラル・コミュニケーション .......................... 253
- a. 日常会話　253
  - ア. 緊張をほぐす　253 ／ イ. 自分のことを語らせる　254 ／
  - ウ. ペアワーク　255 ／ エ. グループワーク　255
- b. リスニング　256
  - ア. テープ［CD］を利用する　256 ／
  - イ. 教師が音読して聞かせる　256 ／ ウ. 作業を行わせる　257
- c. スピーチ・討論　258
  - ア. 意見を求める　258 ／ イ. スピーチ　258 ／ ウ. 暗唱　259 ／
  - エ. 討論　250

## 2. 歌とゲーム .......................... 262
- a. 歌　262
  - ア. 曲を聴く　262 ／ イ. 歌う　263
- b. ゲーム　263
  - ア. ゲームの開始・終了　263 ／ イ. ゲームの説明　264
- c. チーム分け　265
- d. 順　番　266
- e. 順位決定法　267
  - ア. 得点　267 ／ イ. 勝敗　268

## 3. 教育機器の利用 .......................... 270
- a. 操　作　270
  - ア. テープレコーダー　270 ／ イ. CD　270 ／ ウ. ビデオ　271 ／
  - エ. DVD　271 ／ オ. OHP　272 ／ カ. スライド投映機　272 ／
  - キ. LL　273 ／ ク. CALL　273 ／ ケ. インターネット　274 ／
  - コ. Eメール　275
- b. セットの仕方　276

　　　　ア．カセット・CD　276 / イ．ビデオ・DVD　276 / ウ．OHP　277 /
　　　　エ．スライド　277 / オ．LL　278
　　c. 機器の故障　279
　　　　ア．カセット・CD　279 / イ．ビデオ・DVD　280 /
　　　　ウ．OHP・スライド関係　280 / エ．LL 関係　281
　　d. 聞こえますか・見えますか　282

## 4. テスト ...................................................................................283

### ① 小テスト .....................................................................................283
　　a. 問題配布時に　283
　　b. 机の上を片づける　284
　　c. 辞書の使用　285
　　d. 自己採点　286
　　e. 答案交換　287
　　f. 後日返却　288
　　g. 挙手などによる確認　288
　　h. 正答読み上げ　289

### ② テストの解説 ............................................................................290
　　a. 成績概評　290
　　b. 問題ごとの解説　291
　　c. 個々の解答の仕方でほめる　292

# 第 IV 部　ALT との対話　　　　　　　　　　　　　　295

　　a. スピーチの依頼　297
　　　　ア．自己紹介　297 / イ．日常生活の話　297
　　b. モデル・リーディングの依頼　298
　　　　ア．音読の依頼　298 / イ．音読方法の指示　299
　　c. 板書の指示　300
　　d. 生徒への対応　301
　　　　ア．個別指導の依頼　301 / イ．生徒への指示を依頼　301

e. 授業の流れについて　302
　　　　　ア．活動の中断を求める　302 ／ イ．時間調整　303
　　　f. 指導案作成　304
　　　g. ティーム・ティーチングの評価　304
　　　h. 授業環境の説明　305
　　　i. 小学校での「英語活動」　306
　　　j. 日本の教育事情　309

# 第 V 部　教室英語歳時記　313

## 1. 季節・祝日　315

　　　a. 日本の祝祭日　315
　　　b. 英米の祝日　316
　　　　　ア．米国の祝日　316 ／ イ．英国の祝日　317
　　　c. エイプリルフール　317
　　　d. 花　見　318
　　　e. 梅　雨　318
　　　f. 夏　至　319
　　　g. 七　夕　320
　　　h. 花　火　321
　　　i. お祭り　321
　　　j. 秋　分　321
　　　k. 月　見　322
　　　l. 菊　322
　　　m. 紅　葉　322
　　　n. 木枯らし　323
　　　o. 冬　至　323
　　　p. クリスマス　323
　　　q. 正　月　324
　　　　　ア．挨拶　324 ／ イ．飲食物　324 ／ ウ．遊び　325 ／ エ．飾り　325
　　　r. 梅　325

      s.　節　分 325
      t.　雛祭り 326
      u.　花言葉 326
          ア．誕生花 326 ／ イ．日本の花の花言葉 327

## 2. 学校行事 ........................................................... 330

      a.　遠　足 330
          ア．遠足の前 330 ／ イ．遠足のあと 331
      b.　写生会 331
          ア．写生会の前 331 ／ イ．写生会のあと 332
      c.　校内球技大会 332
          ア．大会の前 332 ／ イ．大会のあと 333
      d.　対外試合 333
          ア．試合の前 333 ／ イ．試合のあと 334
      e.　修学旅行 335
          ア．修学旅行の前 335 ／ イ．修学旅行のあと 335
      f.　弁論大会 336
      g.　文化祭 336
          ア．文化祭の前 336 ／ イ．文化祭のあと 336
      h.　運動会 337
          ア．運動会の前 337 ／ イ．運動会のあと 337
      i.　定期試験 338
      j.　入学試験 338
      k.　生徒会活動 339
      l.　給　食 340
      m.　掃　除 340
      n.　PTA 341
      o.　入学式・卒業式 342

## 3. 社　会 ........................................................... 343

      a.　地　震 343
      b.　災　害 343
      c.　交通事故 344

d. 誘　拐　344
e. 殺　人　344
f. 外国の出来事　345
g. 環　境　345

## 4. スポーツ .................................................. 346
a. 陸上競技　346
b. サッカー　346
c. 野　球　346
d. バレーボール　347
e. バスケットボール　347
f. 卓　球　348
g. バドミントン　348
h. テニス　348
i. スキー　349

## 5. 生　徒 ...................................................... 350
a. 誕生日　350
b. 病　気　350
c. 怪　我　351
d. 選手として活躍　352
e. 入賞・入選　352
f. 好き嫌い　353
g. 趣　味　353
h. 家　族　353
i. 住まい　354
j. テレビ番組　354
k. 友人関係　355
l. 職　業　355

## 6. 教育関係用語 .......................................... 356
a. 教　室　356
　ア. 特別教室　356 / イ. その他　356

- b. 中学校の科目 357
- c. 高等学校の教科・科目 357
  - ア. 国語 357 / イ. 地理歴史 357 / ウ. 公民 358 /
  - エ. 数学 358 / オ. 理科 358 / カ. 保健体育 358 /
  - キ. 芸術 358 / ク. 外国語 358 / ケ. 家庭 359 / コ. 情報 359
- d. 組織(教師・生徒) 359
  - ア. 教職員 359 / イ. 生徒 360
- e. 教務関係 360
- f. 校舎・校庭・運動場 360
  - ア. 校舎 360 / イ. 校庭 361 / ウ. 運動場 362 /
  - エ. 体育館 362 / オ. その他 362

# 小学校での教室英語

Classroom English
in Elementary School

## 基本的指示

| | |
|---|---|
| みんな，いる？ | Is everyone here? |
| 欠席は誰？ | Who's absent today? |
| よく聞いて． | Listen carefully. |
| よく見て． | Look at this. |
| 1枚取って． | Take [Draw] one. |
| 後ろに送って． | Pass them down. |
| 静かに． | Stop talking. |
| 用意はいいですか． | Ready? |
| 終わり． | Time is up. |
| 英語で． | In English, please. |
| 大丈夫？ | Are you okay? |
| 大きな声で． | Louder, please. |
| はっきりと． | More clearly, please. |
| 繰り返して． | Say it again. |
| もう1回． | Try again. |
| 続けて． | Go ahead. Go on. |
| さあ，がんばって． | Come on. Try it. |
| よくできました． | Good job! |
| 拍手！ | Let's give a big hand. |
| これで終わり． | That's all for today. |
| さよなら． | Bye. See you next time [week]. |
| また来週． | Have a nice weekend. |

## 動きの指示

### ア．体を動かして

| | |
|---|---|
| じっとして． | Stand [Sit] still. |
| 動かないで． | Freeze. / Don't move. |
| さがって． | Move back(ward). |
| ぐるっと回って． | Turn around. |
| 前[黒板の方]を向いて． | Face the front [board]. |
| 後ろ向きになって． | Turn around. / Face the back. |
| 私の真似をして． | Do as I do. |
| 言うとおりにして． | Do what I say. |
| こうしなさい． | (Do it) like this. |
| そうでなく，こうです． | Not like that, but like this. |
| 背中[肩]をポンとたたこう． | Tap your friend on the back [shoulder]. |

### イ．ポーズを指示して

| | |
|---|---|
| (右)手を挙げて． | Raise your (right) hand. |
| (右)足を上げて． | Lift your (right) leg. |
| 片足で立って． | Stand on one leg. |
| 両手を前に． | Put both your hands in front. |
| 両手を挙げて． | Raise both your hands. |
| 腕を左右に伸ばして． | Spread your arms wide. |
| 目を閉じて[開けて]． | Close [Open] your eyes. |
| 向かい合って． | Face each other. |
| 友達の手を取って． | Hold your friend's hand. |
| 足首を押さえて． | Hold your ankles. |

膝にさわって．  
(☞ p. 155, 180)

Touch your knees.

## ウ．位置を指示して

| | |
|---|---|
| 位置について，よーい，ドン． | On your mark. Get set. Go! |
| どこでも見えるところに座りなさい． | Sit where I can see you. |
| 黒板の前に立って． | Stand in front of the blackboard [board]. |
| 後ろ向きで立って． | Stand with your back toward me. |
| 廊下に出ていいよ． | You may leave the room. |
| どこでもいいよ． | (You can sit) anywhere you like. |
| 教室の後ろへ． | Go to the back of the room. |

窓[入り口]のところに立ちなさい. | Stand by the window [door].
壁のほうを向いて. | Face the wall.

### エ．順番を決める

最初は誰？ | Who goes [tries, speaks, etc.] first?
一番にやりたい人？ | Who wants to try first?
じゃんけんで決めよう. | Do "janken" to decide the order.
ぐう，ちょき，ぱー. | Rock, scissors, paper — go!
コインで決めよう. | Let's toss a coin.
表，裏？ | Heads or tails?
かわりばんこだよ. | Take turns.
自分の番まで待って. | Wait for your turn.
割り込みはだめ. | Don't butt [cut] in.

## ゲーム活動

### ア．組を作って

| | |
|---|---|
| 3人一組になろう． | Make a group of three. / Find two partners. |
| 2人でやりなさい． | Work in pairs. |
| そこに入れてもらって． | Join that group. |
| そこと仲間になって． | Join another group. / Make a bigger group. |
| 輪を作ろう． | Make a big circle. |
| かよさんの後ろに並びなさい． | Everyone, line up behind Kayo. |
| 列を作って． | Form a line [lines]. |
| 2列に並んで． | Make two lines. |
| 1列に並んで立ちなさい． | Stand in a line. Get in a line. |
| 割り込みはだめ． | Don't jump [cut into] the line. |

### イ．カード遊び

| | |
|---|---|
| カードを配りなさい． | Deal all the cards. |
| 1人に4枚． | Deal four cards for each. |
| ない人，手を挙げて． | Raise your hand if you don't have one. |
| カードは伏せて［表を出して］． | Put your card(s) face down [face up]. |
| 机の上に広げなさい． | Spread the cards out on the desk. |
| 自分のカードは見せないように． | Don't show your cards to your friends. |

| | |
|---|---|
| カードを戻しなさい. | Return the card to the deck. |
| カードを積んでおきましょう. | Stack the deck of cards. |
| カードを切りなさい. | Shuffle the cards. |
| のぞいちゃだめ. | Don't peek. |
| カードは胸のところに. | Hold the card against your chest. |
| 全部そろったら終わり. | You win when you complete your hand. |
| ほしいカードをお願いしなさい. | Ask your friends for the card you want. |
| （生徒同士のカードのやりとり） | "Do you have a 〜 card?" "Yes, I do." "Please give it to me. ... Thank you." "You're welcome." |

### ウ．カルタ・すごろく

| | |
|---|---|
| 机を寄せなさい. | Put your desks together. |
| 机をここに持ってきて. | Move your desk over here. |
| 机を寄せて大きなテーブルにしよう. | Put your desks together to make a big table. |
| 全部片づけなさい. | Put away everything. / Put everything away. |
| 絵カードを机に広げなさい. | Spread all the picture cards on the desk. |
| 文字カードは全部配る. | Deal out all the letter cards. |
| あなたの番ですよ. | Your turn. |
| そこは1回休み. | You lost your turn. |
| 上がりですか. | Did you finish? |

**エ． 競争させて**

| | |
|---|---|
| たくさんポイントを取りましょう． | Score as many as you can. |
| 1 位には 3 点． | Three points for the first to finish. |
| 日本語が入ったら減点． | You lose a point if you use Japanese. |
| 最初に 5 点とったチームが勝ち． | The first team to get five points will win [wins]. |
| 一番点数の多いのはどこ？ | Who [Which team] got the most points? |
| 結局何点だった？ | What's your final score? |
| 一緒に数えよう． | Let's count up the points together. |
| あなたの勝ち． | You won. / You are the winner. |
| おめでとう． | Congratulations. |

(☞ p. 263)

- No luck. Too bad.
- No fighting, please.
- No peeking.
- Don't skip me. Don't cheat.
- My turn?

## 作業・制作活動

### ア．紙細工

|  |  |
|---|---|
| 鳥のところを切り抜きなさい． | Cut out a [the] bird. |
| のり付けしなさい． | Paste [Glue] it on the larger sheet. |
| 2つ折りにして． | Fold it in half. |
| 折り紙を外折り[山折り]に． | Fold the sheet with the colored side out |
| 赤く塗って． | Color it red. |
| 赤鉛筆で線をなぞりなさい． | Trace the line in red. |
| 三角に折りなさい． | Fold the paper into a triangle. |
| 紙を半分に切りましょう． | Cut the paper in half. |
| ごみは落ちていませんか． | No trash around you? / Pick up the litter. |
| それはくずかごに入れましょう． | Put it [them] in the trash can. |

### イ．用具の始末

|  |  |
|---|---|
| はさみを使います． | You'll need some scissors. |
| クレヨンを出しなさい． | Take out your crayons. |
| コンパスをケースにしまいましょう． | Put your compass back into your case. |
| 消しゴムを自動車に見立てます． | (Imagine) your eraser is a car. |
| 何か足りませんか． | What (else) do you need? |
| （のり，はさみなど）なかったら手を挙げて． | Raise your hand if you don't have one [your glue, scissors, etc.]. |

作業・制作活動　11

| | |
|---|---|
| マジックをください． | Pass the marker to me. |
| 全部片づけなさい． | Put everything away. |
| 机の上を片づけて． | Clear up your desk. |
| 物差しはしまって． | Put your ruler into your desk. |
| 仲間で使いなさい． | You have to share it [them]. |
| ナイフには気をつけて． | Be careful with your knife. |

ウ．積み木遊び

| | |
|---|---|
| 赤の積み木を青の積み木に重ねなさい． | Place a red block on a blue block. |
| 積み木を立てて置きなさい． | Stand the block upright. |
| 積み木を横に置きなさい． | Lay the block flat. |
| いえ，もっと大きなもの． | No. Use a big one. [A bigger one.] |

- This is hard.
- It's easy.
- It must be a fish.
- I'll try.
- Two more minutes.
- I made a mistake.
- I'll show you how.

| | |
|---|---|
| 四角ではなく細長い積み木です． | Not a square, but a slender [long / thin] block. |
| それを使って家を作ろう． | Build a house with those blocks. |
| 赤い積み木は屋根にしよう． | Use the red block as a roof. |
| ゆっくりやろう． | No hurry. / Take your time. |
| 時間は大丈夫． | We have plenty of time. / Work slowly. |

## エ．絵・図を描いて

| | |
|---|---|
| このように線を引きましょう． | Draw a line this way. |
| 縦[横]に線を一本． | Draw a vertical [horizontal] line. |
| 線を真っ直ぐに． | Draw a straight line. |
| 点[波]線を引きなさい． | Draw a dotted [wavy] line. |
| 右上[左下]に名前を書きなさい． | Write your name at [in] the upper right [lower left] corner. |
| 画面の下[中央]に川を描こう． | Draw a river at the bottom [in the center] of the picture. |
| 茂みにウサギを3匹描き入れて． | Put [Draw] three rabbits in the bushes. |
| 唇は赤く塗りましょう． | Color the lips red. |
| 海の魚は○で囲みなさい． | Circle the fish in the sea. |
| 魚が描けていなかったら減点1． | Minus one point for no fish. |
| (☞ p. 192) | |

## 演じる活動

**ア．ロールプレイで**

| | |
|---|---|
| お医者さんのつもりで． | You're a doctor, |
| 映画館にいるつもりで． | Imagine you're in a movie theater. |
| | |
| 山田先生のふりで． | Do like Mr. Yamada. |
| 看護師さんになりたい人？ | Who wants to be a nurse? |
| あなたは銀行員． | You will be a bank clerk. |
| 会話に動作をつけましょう． | Let's act out this conversation, shall we? |
| | |
| お母さん役をやって下さい． | You play the role of the mother. |
| あなたから会話を始めて下さい． | You start the dialog. |
| メモは見ないで言いなさい． | Now try without looking at your notes. |

| | |
|---|---|
| もらったら「ありがとう」と言いなさい. | Say "thank you" when you get them. |
| 「どういたしまして」を忘れないように. | Don't forget (to say) "You're welcome." |
| 背景を黒板に描きましょう. | Draw some scenery on the board. |

(☞ p. 158)

### イ．指人形を使って

| | |
|---|---|
| 木の切り抜きはうちわに貼りましょう. | Paste the cutout tree on a fan. |
| 制限時間はありません. | There is no time limit. |
| 指人形で演技しよう. | Let's play with the hand puppets. |
| 人差し指に人形をはめて. | Put the puppet on your first finger. |
| 誰[どの組]が一番上手だった？ | Who [Which group] did it best? |
| どの人形が好き？ | Which puppet do you like best? |
| じゃんけんで決めよう. | Let's decide by *janken*. |
| 右手にウサギさん，左手にカメさん. | Put the rabbit on your right hand and the turtle [tortoise] on your left hand. |

## なぞなぞ・歌

**ア．なぞなぞで**

| | |
|---|---|
| なぞなぞを出します． | Here's a riddle [quiz]. |
| 君のなぞなぞを出して下さい． | Give us your riddle. |
| 簡単ななぞなぞだよ． | It's a simple riddle. |
| ヒントをあげよう． | I'll give you some hints. |
| 3つ目のヒントだよ． | This is the third hint. |
| 5つのヒントでもわからなかったら負け． | You'll lose if you can't find the answer before the fifth hint. |
| わかった人は手を挙げて． | Raise your hand when [if] you know the answer. |

How is it going? Let me see it.

I have a question.

I've got it.

Check this, please.

Not quite.

No way.

| | |
|---|---|
| 知っていても言っちゃだめ. | Don't tell your friends even if you've found the answer. |
| まだわからないの？ | You still haven't got it? |

## イ． 歌を歌って

| | |
|---|---|
| 歌にしようか. | Let's sing a song, shall we? |
| 歌にしたい？ | Do you want to sing? |
| まず曲を聴いて. | Let's listen to the melody first. |
| 聞いたことある？ | Who has heard this song before? |
| 聞いたことがあるでしょ？ | You know the melody, don't you? |
| 歌詞を説明します. | I'll explain the words first. |
| 歌手は誰でしょう. | Who's the singer? / Do you know the singer? |
| テープについて歌おう. | Sing along with the tape. |
| 太郎君，一緒に歌おう. | Join in singing, Taro. |
| ギターに合わせて. | Please sing along as I play my guitar. |
| 「〜」の替え歌だよね. | This is another song [parody] of "〜", isn't it? |

(☞ p. 262)

## ビデオ・紙芝居

| | |
|---|---|
| さあ紙芝居が始まるよ. | Now *kamishibai* time. Please listen. |
| テレビ[紙芝居]の前に集まって. | Go and sit before [in front of] the television [*kamishibai*]. |
| これ面白いよ. | Here's an interesting program [story]. |
| みんな見える？ | Can everybody see? |
| よく見てて. | Watch it carefully. |
| たった2分だからね. | It's only two minutes long. |
| だいたいわかった？ | Did you get the main idea? |
| 誰と誰が出てきたでしょう. | Who are the people in the program? |
| どんな話だった？ | What's the story? |
| ネコさんは何と言っていた？ | What did the cat say? |

Now, let's watch the kamishibai.

It's cool. Nice. Great!

I can't see. Move over, please.

Stop that!

## 小学校での授業の進め方

■ はじめに

　小学校教育課程に，「総合的な学習の時間」が2002年から導入され，その枠の中で英語活動が取り入れられました．各学校で実践されている授業形態は，その地域の実態に合わせて，一様ではありませんが，導入当時の調査で，すでに56％以上の学校が何らかの形で英語活動をしているという数字が出ています．

　授業は，教育委員会が派遣するALT（外国人指導助手）や，地域のボランティアの参加によって行われますが，それだけでは，年間の授業回数を増やすことが難しくなります．せめて週1回子どもたちが英語に慣れ親しむ機会を与えたい，ということになると，どうしても学級担任の教師が英語活動の授業を担当することになります．2000年以来，移行措置の間から英語活動を試行され経験を重ねた先生の間に，自ら英語活動を子どもと楽しもう，とする傾向が強くなっているようにみえます．

　英語指導の研修を受けておられない先生方にとって，どのような英語を使って子どもたちを英語に触れさせようか，自分の英語で大丈夫か，と心配が少なくないようです．

　本事典は，そのような先生方のサポーターとしてお役に立つように，実際に子どもたちに英語で指示を与え，ゲームをし，歌を歌うことができるように，その文例を集めています．

■ 小学校英語活動が目指すもの

　小学校英語の目的，指導内容，さらに指導方法などについては，さまざまな指導書がありますので，それに譲りますが，簡単に，子どもたちが英語に触れて，どんな力をつけていくのか，そのために，どのような活動をするのか，まとめてみます．

　子どもたちは好奇心の固まりで，英語を使おうと積極的に先生やALTの真似をしようとして一生懸命英語を話す人を見つめています．聞き取った英語の音を声に出して，面白がります．日本語の中に英語の外来語がたくさんありますから，話しかけられるとそれを頼りに，大体の意味を類推し，英語を聞くことに苦痛を感じていません．そして，自分で考えたことを伝えようとします．まだまだ未熟な英語ではありますが，この「英語を使いたい」という気持ちを

育てることが大切です．

　そこで，互いに自分のことについて，名前，年齢，今日の日付，季節やお天気，気分，好きなこと，持ち物，住所，得意なこと，やってみたいことなど，目の前に起こっていることを，短くてやさしい英文で語り合います．指導のはじめのころは，このような語り合いはほとんどが指導者の誘導で行われ，子どもたちが正確な英語で応答することは期待しません．

　子どもたちの衣服の色やデザイン，ボタンやポケットなどを話題にして数えてみたり，質問をしながら，子どもたちの反応をみます．また，歌を歌ったり，手遊び歌で体を動かして遊んだり，簡単であまり勝負にこだわらないゲームをしたり，折り紙や塗り絵をしたりもします．このような活動で頻繁に使われるのは，カードやおもちゃ類やチップなどです．絵や実物やおもちゃが英語の意味を伝え，子どもたちの理解を助けます．

## ■「4技能＋1（thinking）」の考え方

　新しい言葉とのはじめての出会いは，その言葉特有の「音」を聞かせることから始まります．「聞いていると，何だかわかるところがある」という経験をさせて，「聞いているとわかる」自信を与えます．

　そして，「聞いていると，真似をしたくなる」という気持ちから，自分でも「英語で何かを言ってみたい，相手に何かを伝えてみたい」と思うようになります．指導する者は，このような子どもの心の動きを誘い出すようにしますが，そこで，子どもにわかりやすい英語を使って聞かせる必要があります．

　英語との触れ合いが深まると，文字の指導に進みたくなりますが，これも，文字のあるものを見ながら英語を聞かせる，「読み聞かせ」の指導技術が必要です．そうして，いつか子どもたちが文字を真似して「写し書き」をしたり，単語を書いて相手に伝達したりすることができるようになります．

　このような指導の過程で，子どもたちに教えたことを完全に覚えさせて言わせようと繰り返し機械的な練習をするのは，無理があるだけでなく，言葉の習得のプロセスに反していますので，気をつけたいと思います．聞こえてくる英語を受け止めて，考え，意味を判断して，間違っているかもしれないけれど応答し，それが求められていたことだったかを自分で考えてみる，そして，さらにコミュニケーションを深めていく，というプロセスを大事にしていきたいものです．「聞く」「話す」「読む」「書く」4つの活動に，常に学習者の「自分で考え判断する」ことがあれば，「英語を使う」ことに深く関わることができるで

しょう．

## ■ 子どもたちと英語で表現活動をするときに使える語彙

　子どもたちが知っている，と思っている英語の語彙は，大人の想像以上のものがあります．果物や料理の名前を考えても，食べものは外来語の宝庫です．スポーツやその用品，動物の名前，衣服の種類とその色，乗り物や文房具の中にも外来語があります．最近は，特に英語を習っていなくても，10くらいまで英語や他の言語で言える子どもは珍しくありません．コンピュータが日常の道具となって，その用語が子どもにも親しみのあるものになりました．25年くらい前に学習を始めたばかりの4年生を対象に語彙調査をしたときでさえ，1200を超えましたから，今，子どもたちが聞いてわかる単語の数は，相当数に上るだろうと考えられます．

　子どもたちに新しい単語を教えようとするのではなく，子どもがすでに持っている語彙を使い，それを梃子にして意思を伝えあい，勘を働かせてとっさの判断でコミュニケーションを図る能力を培うことが，学習を楽しくし，チャレンジングなものにするでしょう．子どもとのコミュニケーションの鍵となる語彙を使って，英語で話しかけることができれば，授業は良いテンポで展開するはずです．

## ■ 子どもたちが英語に慣れ親しみ，使えるようになる授業

　まず，英語で挨拶をしましょう．Good morning, everyone. / Good afternoon, class. 子どもたちが緊張しているか，リラックスして次の言葉を待っているかを瞬時に判断します．声を出して挨拶の返事をするのは無理かもしれませんが，子どもたちの目が返事をしています．回を重ねるにつれて，必ず英語で挨拶をする楽しさを身につけてくるでしょう．

　子どもの様子を見極めるためには，How are you? / Are you OK? / Who is absent today? などと尋ねます．きちんと答を強要しなくても，表情を見ればわかります．元気そうなら Good! 病気で欠席の子どもがいれば，Oh, he is absent. That's too bad. と自問自答です．子どもたちも慣れてくれば，返事をしたくなります．そのころあいを見計らって，答え方のモデルを聞かせて，慣れさせていきます．

　子どもたちは英語活動の直前まで日本語で遊んでいましたから，頭の中は日本語モードです．これを簡単に英語モードに切り替えるときに役立つのが，簡

単に歌える短い歌や，早口言葉です．Shall we sing the ABC song? / Let's sing "Seven Steps". / How about singing "BINGO"? 好きな歌なら，2, 3回繰り返して歌ってくれるでしょう．早口言葉でしたら，Shall we try a tongue twister? Can you say "She sells seashells on the seashore."? と誘いかけます．もたもたして途中でつっかえるのがおかしくて，笑いながら挑戦してくれるでしょう．歌や早口言葉のようなものは，1回の授業で完全に言えるようにしよう，などと張り切らないことが，楽しく練習できるコツです．面白いと思えば，子どもが練習を始めて，いつの間にか上手になってしまいます．

このように，子どもたちを「その気にさせてしまう」のは，学級担任の先生方の特技だと思います．儀礼的に褒めるのではなく，まさに子どもが励ましを必要としているときに，的確に，Very good. / You did it. / Wonderful. / Good job. と元気よく声をかけます．

また，いつも気になる子どもの表情が曇っているときには，Shall we try once more? / Let's sing it one more time. などといって，クラス全体を巻き込みながら，自信を与えていきます．少し上手になったときには，That's better. と大袈裟にならないように褒めると，真実味が伝わるでしょう．

■ "英語らしさ" の獲得

子どもたちと英語で活動するときに，正しい英語の語法を使えるようにと，何度も練習をさせると，きちんと言おうとするあまりに，英語のリズムやイントネーションが不自然になります．それより，ゲームで夢中になっているときに口走る英語のほうが自然で，間違いだらけかもしれないのですが通じてしまうのです．これは母語の日本語を覚えかけた幼児がカタコトなのに十分に意志を通じさせて，楽しい毎日を送るのと同じことです．

先生方が，まだ英語に不慣れだと思われているときは，表情豊かに録音されている視聴覚教材が増えてきましたから，子どもたちと一緒に聞いて，楽しんでください．Let's listen to the CD. / Let's listen to the song [story]. / Let's watch the video. 子どもたちは素晴らしい評論家で，好き嫌いを正直に表し，気に入れば15分でも真剣に見入ったり，聞き続けたりします．そして，同じものを何回でも見たり聞いたりします．そのときに，何が聞き取れたか，わかったか，と問い詰めるより，Did you like it? / Was it fun? / I like that, too. くらいで十分です．それより，視聴の間に見せる子ども表情をしっかり観察しましょう．

## ■ ゲームの目的

　英語活動にゲーム的な要素を入れると，子どもたちの表現意欲も高まり，指導しやすいと思われていますが，「ゲームのようなアクティビティ」をするのであって，「ゲームをして楽しませる」のではありません．勝ち負けのゲームで興奮してはいますが，これで英語が上手になれるのかな，と子ども自身も思いのほか懐疑的です．やっぱり，英語が使えるようになる手ごたえが欲しいようです．

　語彙を増やすため，発音を確認するため，情報伝達のため，さらに複数の情報を伝えるため，とゲームの目的を明確にして準備し，それに沿って楽しいアクティビティを仕組んでいくことが必要です．ルールが複雑だったり，ゲーム自体に時間がかかったりするのは効果的ではありません．また，子ども同士が英語を使って伝達するときに先生の指導が及ばなくなってしまうときがあります．使っている英語がぞんざいになったり，わからないときの支援ができない場合，ゲームそのものに無理があるので好ましくありません．

## ■ 絵本やお話の使い方

　最近，絵本の読み聞かせを取り入れた指導例が増えています．絵本は指導者の英語を補ってくれることもあり，心強い教材です．しかし，物語の文をそのまま読んでも子どもが理解できるものは意外と少ないので，絵本を選択する段階で注意したいものです．まずイラストの訴える力の強いものを選び，そのイラストについて，What is this? / What are these? / Look at this. / What is he [she] doing? / Is he happy? / Is she dancing? と，簡単な文で質問をし，確認していきます．最後のページまでこの調子で語りかけても，そのお話を知っている子どもたちは，すっかりお話の世界に浸っています．日本語で書かれた童話でも，十分にこのような活動に利用できます．

　英語を意思伝達の道具として使ってみる面白さを感じ取らせるためには，指導者が英語を楽しそうに使うことが絶対に必要です．あまり声を張り上げず，ゆっくり語りかける練習をして，授業に備えてください．

〈久埜百合〉

# 一般的指示
# General Directions

第 I 部

# 1. 移動
## Movement

### a. 席の移動　Changing seats

**ア．自分の席につく　Taking one's seat**

1. Sit down.
2. Settle down.
3. Take your seats quickly.
4. Go (back) to your seat.
5. Be seated.
6. Seat yourselves at your desks and be quiet.
7. Let's begin our English class. Is everyone ready?
8. The break is over. Let's start today's English lesson.

〈発展的表現〉

9. Today I'll give you the new seats. / Here's the new seating chart.
10. Will you move to the following seats as I call your names?
11. Sit down in the following order: First, students from No. 1 to No. 6, take your seats in this row. Next . . .
12. There are three courses for today's lesson. If you like Course 1, get together over here. If you like Course 2, go over there . . .
13. Can we start the class? Recently, you haven't been in your seats when I come in. You should sit down when you hear the chimes [bell].
14. I'd like to start the class now. Will you go back to your seats?

**Notes:**　1 の sit down は身体的動作だけであるが，2 の settle down には気持ちのうえでも「落ち着く」の意が入る．4 は席を離れている生徒への指示，1 人の生徒に呼びかけるのなら back が入ることが多い．5 は 1 に比べて穏やかな命

令. 8 は同一教師が前時ホームルームなどをやっていた場合. 9〜11 は席替え. 12 は能力別編成のような場合. 14 は穏やかな注意喚起.（☞ p. 40）

---
**Student Response**

待って，先生　　Wait a moment, please. / Hiroshi went to see the nurse and he will be late. / I left my book in my locker. Can I go and get it?

今日の席は？　Is today's seating as usual, or special? / Where do [should] I sit today?

席替えして　　We want a new seating order. / How about changing our seats today? / Don't you think we should have a new seating arrangement?

---

## イ. 活動のための席移動　Changing seats for activities

1. Stand up and move around.
2. You can stand up now.
3. You are free to move around.
4. Now, you don't have to remain in your seat.
5. You may go to anyone to ask them the questions.
6. Find someone who can answer the questions.
7. Stand face to face with your neighbor [partner].
8. You may ask anyone, anything you like.

〈発展的表現〉

9. Leave your seats and ask these questions to each other.
10. Find three boys and three girls and interview them.
11. Look for others who have the same card as yours.
12. I want to change the classroom formation. Take your desks out of the room and leave only your chairs here.
13. Take your desks to the back of the room and put your chairs in a large circle.
14. Students in these rows, turn round and face the back [look at Mr. Brown]. Others, look at me.

**Notes:** 1〜10 はインタビュー形式の活動．5, 8 など単に命令文で言うよりは may を用いた方が一般的である．11 は matching game．12〜14 はチーム・ティーチングなどでの特別な授業形態．14 は ALT が教室の後ろにいる場合．

> **Student Response**
> 席を離れていい？　May I stand up? / Can we leave our seats now? / Is it free time now?
> 持ち物は？　Shall I take this handout with me? / Do we need to bring our notebooks? / What do we need for this activity?

## b. 班編成のための移動　Group organization

1. Okay, groups [group work].
2. Let's make groups.
3. Okay, get into groups.
4. Let's form groups as usual.
5. Get into groups of three as you like.
6. Work in pairs [threes / fours].
7. I'll divide the class into groups.
8. I want you to form groups. Four persons in each group.

〈発展的表現〉

9. We'll have some tasks for you to work on in groups.
10. If you can't join a group, come to me.
11. There are too many in this group. Hiroshi, join Group 5.
12. Everyone, come here. Then draw lots from this box. There are eight numbers from 1 to 8. If you draw No. 1, come to this corner. No. 2, go to that corner . . .
13. Let's make up groups using a matching game. Find the person who has the same cards as yours. Don't speak Japanese. Don't show your cards to others. There are five different cards. Now, start.

**Notes:** 7, 8 はややかたい表現．10 ではあぶれる生徒も忘れずに．12, 13 のように，くじやゲームで班を決めると公平．(☞ p. 265)

> **Student Response**
> 班活動する？　Will we have a group activity today? / Now, it's time for a group activity?
> あぶれた　I could not join any groups. / Every group is full.

## c. 黒板 [OHP] のところへ　　To the (black)board [OHP]

1. Please come here.
2. Will you go to the board?
3. Come up to the blackboard.
4. Come and stand by the OHP.
5. Who wants to come here?
6. Whose turn is it to come over here?
7. Stand in front of the board. / Stand by the OHP.

〈発展的表現〉

8. Come to the front and write the word [sentence] on the board.
9. Go to the OHP and draw a picture of a cat.
10. Who has not come to the board yet? Oh, you haven't? Okay, will you write it here?
11. Students No. 4 and No. 23, will you both come up to the board?
12. Whose turn is it to erase [wipe / clean] the blackboard?
13. Step aside so that the class can see the sentence you have written.

**Notes:**　11のように在籍番号を氏名の代わりに用いることは英米ではしない。

> **Student Response**
> 私の番じゃない　It's not my turn. / I've already done it. / Someone else's turn.
> 用意ができていない　Wait a moment. / I am not ready yet. / Not yet. Could I do it next week [time]?

## d. 教室を出る　Going out of the classroom

### ア．授業の途中で　During the class

1. Okay, let's go.
2. Let's move, shall we?
3. Let's go to the CALL [multimedia] room. Move quickly.
4. Shall we go to the gym and play a game [the game] there?
5. How about going to the AV room and watching a video?
6. Will these three groups move to the next room?
7. Bring the handouts and your notebooks with you.
8. Everyone, let's go but don't forget your pens and notebooks.

〈発展的表現〉

9. You look sick. You can go to see the school nurse.
10. I forgot the handouts. Could you please go and get them from my office, please.
11. There's no colored chalk here. Would you go and look for a yellow one there — at the back board?
12. Go and ask Mr. Suzuki for some sheets of paper.
13. This projector doesn't work. Can you bring another one from the next room?

**Notes:** 6〜8 はティーム・ティーチングなどで，クラスの一部を他教室に移動させたいとき．10 を go and fetch としないように．fetch には犬に命令するような響きがある．

---
**Interaction**

| | |
|---|---|
| S：教室を出てもいいですか． | Can I go out of the classroom? |
| T：どうしたの． | Why? |
| S：辞書を忘れました． | I left my dictionary in my locker. |
| T：なるほど．他に忘れた人は？取りに行ってきていいよ．急いで！ | I see. Anyone else? O.K. You can go and get it. But hurry back. |

## イ．授業が終わって　At the end of the class

1. Let's go out.
2. You can go out now.
3. Okay, you can leave.
4. You may leave the room.
5. Would you mind leaving the room?
6. That's all for today. You are free to go.
7. O.K. Please find your way out.

〈発展的表現〉

8. The bell is ringing. But give me two more minutes. Please remain seated.
9. Don't make a noise when you leave.
10. The class has finished earlier than usual. So other classes are still working. Be quiet, please.
11. This is the end of the lesson. But wait until the bell rings.

**Notes:**　5は寒い日など生徒が教室から出たがらない場合．7は特に大勢が集合した状況で．8はもう少し時間のほしいとき．9～11は早めに終わったとき．

## 2. 注 目
### Directing Students' Attention

### a. 板書に　To the blackboard

1. Look (here)!
2. This is important.
3. Hiroshi, can you see this?
4. Hanako, read this, please.
5. Look at this and listen carefully.
6. Attention, everyone (, please).
7. Look at this sentence and repeat after me.

〈発展的表現〉

8. Now look at this. Which words are the subject, the verb, and the object?
9. Something is wrong with this sentence. What is wrong?
10. Hanako said this, and Taro said this. Which sentence do you think is better? And why?
11. This is a rather long sentence, but you don't have to worry. Why don't you try to understand it phrase by phrase like this?

**Notes:** 6はクラス全体に注意を促している．注目させるべきものを指しながら言うのが普通．8は文の構造に注目させたいとき．10は複数生徒の発表にずれがあった場合にそれを取り上げて，クラス全体に問題提起するとき．「どちらが正しいか」には Which is correct? より Which is better? が用いられることが多い．11はフレーズごとに意味を確認させたあと，全文の意味を考えさせるとき．

**Student Response**
ちょっとさがって下さい　Could you move back a little?

| | |
|---|---|
| もっと大きな字で | Please write them in larger letters. |
| 黒板が光っている | The board is too bright. / There's a reflection on the board. |

## b.　生徒に　To each other

1. Look!
2. Look at Naomi.
3. Watch her mouth.
4. Face your partner [neighbor].
5. Let's see what Masato has to [will] show us.
6. We'll see how Junko acts out the sentence.
7. Watch the movement of Kumi's hands carefully.
8. Listen to me and keep your eyes on Satoshi.

〈発展的表現〉

9. Everybody, turn to Wataru. He has something in his hand.
10. Move your chairs so that you can sit face to face with your neighbor.
11. Look directly at your partner when you ask him [her] questions.
12. Don't look aside while you are talking to Toshi.
13. Look at your partner's eyes when you are saying the dialogue.
14. It is polite of you to look at the person when you speak English.

**Notes:**　1は生徒を指さしながら．8はある生徒について教師が何かを述べる活動の中で．11～14は対話のとき相手をきちんと見る習慣をつける上でも大切である．

**Student Response**

| | |
|---|---|
| わかりました | Yes. / O.K. / I see. / All right. / Sure. |
| 私ですか | Oops, my turn? |
| どこから？ | From where? |
| すみません | I beg your pardon? / I'm sorry. |

## C. 教師に　To the teacher

1. Look!
2. Here!
3. Look here [at me].
4. Can you hear me?
5. Look at my mouth closely [carefully].
6. Look at my gestures. Guess what I am doing.
7. Tell me what I am pointing at.
8. Will you come and help me, Tomoko?
9. Look directly at me.
10. Don't turn your eyes away.
11. Don't look away from me.
12. Give me all your attention.

〈発展的表現〉

13. Why don't you look at me more closely? You will see something nice on my dress [shirt].
14. Look here and see what is coming out of this box.
15. Look at my face. I am rather unhappy with the test you did yesterday.
16. You can see what I have on [in] my hand, can't you? Let me tell you something about it.

**Notes:** 13 は教師に注目させるテクニックの１つ．ネクタイピンとかブローチとかに気づかせて，それを英語で説明することから授業に入っていく．15 は怒った表情で．16 で手のひらに載せておいても in the hand ということもできる．

--- 

**Student Response**

よく見えない　　I can't see it very well.
花瓶が邪魔　　The vase blocks my view. / I can't see it because of the vase.
持ち上げて　　Will you raise it a little higher, please?

## d. 参観者に　To the observer(s)

1. Today we have guests.（参観者を紹介する動作を伴って）
2. Here is our guest.
3. As you can see, we have lots of guests today.
4. This is Ms. Carol Green from the United States.
5. Many teachers in this city have come to see you today.
6. Turn around and say, "Good morning" to them.
7. Some of your parents are with us today.

〈発展的表現〉

8. We have a special guest from a foreign country. Guess where he [she] is from.
9. We have many parents as our guests. Let's study hard to make them happy.
10. I'd like you all to greet John. He is going to introduce himself. Please listen and ask questions if you want to know more about him.
11. This is Sarah from Australia. She's here because she wants to know what a Japanese school is like.
12. As you see, we have a lot of teachers today. Some of you look very tense [nervous], but just smile at them. Then you'll feel more relaxed.
13. There are a lot of teachers today. Please find the gentleman wearing a red tie and glasses. Then go and shake hands with him.

**Notes:** 4 は formal な場合で，姓もつけて紹介する．11 のように First name だけの場合は informal. 5 は研究授業，7 は父母の授業参観日などで．13 は緊張している生徒をリラックスさせることと，言語活動を兼ねている．

---
**Student Response**

こんにちは　Hello. My name is Noriko. What's your name? / Are you an English teacher, too?

お座り下さい　Please sit down. / Here is a chair (for you).

| | |
|---|---|
| どの学校から？ | Where do you teach? |
| 僕たちの印象は？ | What do you think about this class? |

---- Interaction ----

| | | |
|---|---|---|
| S: | 今日来ているあの人は誰？ | Who is that lady over there? |
| T: | 気になる？ 誰で何をしている人かは自分で尋ねてごらん．それより，あの方に椅子を持っていってくれる． | You're interested in her, eh? You can ask her questions and get some information. By the way, will you bring this chair to her first? |
| S: | はい．何を聞いてもいい？ | O.K. Can I ask her any questions? |
| T: | いいですよ．年齢以外はね． | Sure. Except her age! |

e.　図・絵に　　To the picture(s)

1. Look.
2. There!
3. Look at the screen [wall].
4. Look at the pictures on page 53.
5. Look at the pictures and listen to the tape, will you?
6. Turn around and look at the map at the back of the room.
7. Can you see Mike's cousins in the pictures on page 53?

〈発展的表現〉

8. Can you guess what the name of the tower is?
9. How many students can you see in this picture?
10. Do you know the name of this boy? You'll find out when you read this page.
11. Look for something round in this picture. What is it?
12. Who are the boy and the girl in the picture on page 5?
13. Please look at the picture and tell me something about it.
14. You see, these pictures are in the wrong order. Put them in the right [correct] order.

Notes: 8 以下は絵に注目させて、何かの活動を行う場合の指示. (☞ p.186)

**Student Response**

暗くて見えない　It's too dark.
カーテンを引いて　Could you draw the curtains?
明りをつけて　Will you turn [switch / put] on the light?
目が悪い　My eye sight is not very good.

**Interaction**

| | |
|---|---|
| T: どのページかわかっていますね. | What page are you on, Takuya? |
| S: はい．ここですか． | Is this the page? |
| T: 違います．55ページです．あなたのは52ページじゃない？ | No. You're on page 52. You must turn to page 55. |
| S: あっ，そうだ．すみません． | Oh, I see. I'm sorry. |

## f.　窓外に　Outside the classroom

1. Look out of the window.
2. Let's look outside.
3. It's a beautiful day, isn't it?
4. There's something interesting in the garden.
5. The leaves are getting more and more yellow, aren't they?
6. Oh, it has started to rain. Did you bring your umbrellas with you?
7. Can you see those red flowers over there? They're in full bloom. What do you call those flowers in English?

〈発展的表現〉

8. It has been snowing since yesterday. Everything is white outside.
9. Your eyes must be tired. Look at the tall tree in the distance for a few moments.
10. Such a fine day! It's a shame to stay inside and study, isn't it?

**Notes:** 「見る」で，watch は look よりも比較的長めの注視時間を意味しており，したがって静止しているものよりは，動きのあるものを対象にしていることが多い．

> **Student Response**
> 
> 外に行きたい　Everybody wants to go out.
> 外は寒そう　It must be cold out there.
> 小鳥が来ている　I can see some birds in the trees.

## 3. 起立・着席
### Standing Up and Sitting Down

### a. 個人で　Individual(s)

**ア．起立　Standing up**

1. Stand up.
2. Please stand up, Kimiko.
3. I want you to stand up.
4. I'd like you to stand up.
5. Will [Can] you stand up?
6. Would [Could] you stand up?
7. Please get up.
8. Would you mind standing up?
9. Come on! Out of your seat(s).

〈発展的表現〉

10. Stand and face the class.
11. Stand by [behind / in front of] your desk.
12. How about standing up and telling the class your idea?
13. Why don't you get up out of your chair and come to the front?
14. Please stand up when [while] you introduce yourself.
15. It's your turn to stand up and read the paragraph.
16. It's O.K. You can do it. Please stand (up) and begin.

**Notes:** would, could は will, can よりやや丁寧．8 は丁寧な言い方で，「立って〜しなさい」の文脈でよく使われる．9 は重ねて立つように命じる場合．seats は複数人の場合．10 は顔を皆に向けて．13 は命令というより提案のニュアンス．16 は生徒を励ましている．

> **Student Response**
> また僕？　Me again? / I did it last time. / You always make me do it. Can't you choose someone else?
> 立たなくても　Is it O.K. (for me) to read (while) sitting down? / Do I have to stand up?

### イ．着 席　Sitting down

1. Sit down.
2. Please sit down, Hiroshi.
3. Sit in [on] your seat.
4. You may [can] sit at your desk.
5. Have a seat.
6. Take your seat.
7. (Go) back to your seat.

〈発展的表現〉

8. Thank you. You can sit down again.
9. Will you sit behind Takao?
10. You have to sit at the back of the class.
11. That was very good. Please be seated.
12. This is not your seat. Go back and sit at your own desk.
13. Don't move around. Stay in your own place.
14. Please don't sleep in class. Sit up straight.

> **Notes:**　3は机があるときはsit in，椅子だけのときはsit onと使い分けることもあるが，教室の生徒用のかたい椅子はsit onの感じがより適している．5のhave a seatは相手が複数でもa seat．6はやや formalで教室英語らしい．11はformal．14は姿勢を正して．(☞ p. 25)

## b. 班ごとに　In group(s)

### ア．起 立　Standing up

1. This row.

2. This group, please stand up together.
3. I want this row of students to stand up.
4. I'd like only the back row of students to stand up.
5. The students on the left, will [can] you stand up?
6. Group A, would [could] you stand on the platform?
7. Next group, get up quick!
8. Only boys, would you mind standing up?
9. Now it's your turn. Out of your seats.

〈発展的表現〉

10. Will you stand up and make a circle with your group?
11. All those on the right, stand up and repeat after the tape.
12. It's your group's turn to stand up and perform your drama [do your skit].
13. Why don't you stand up and come to the board?
14. Don't wait. Time is limited. Please go [come] to the board.
15. Would you all do it standing up? Students in the back can't see you.
16. Team A and B, get out of your chairs! Please stand in rows and face each other.

Notes: 1は「立ちなさい」という合図を伴う．14はなかなか立たない生徒を促して．「時間がない」は We haven't got much time. とも表現できる．

**Student Response**

グループがわからない　Which row? / What [which] group am I in?
ちょっと待って　So soon? / We're not ready yet. / Give us more time.
他のグループにして　Why us? Why don't they go first?

## イ．着席　Sitting down

1. This group.
2. Group A, sit down please.
3. Sit in [on] your seats.
4. You may [can] sit at your desks.
5. Have a seat.

6. Take your seats.
7. Okay. (Go) back to your seats.

〈発展的表現〉

8. Move your chairs and sit in groups of four.
9. That was a good performance. Thank you. Please be seated.
10. When you finish it, go back and join your group.
11. Which team can finish and sit down first? Ready?
12. Would you mind sitting in groups of three, please?
13. No, it's not your turn yet. Stay in your places.

**Notes:** 1は手の合図を伴って．11はグループ対抗で競うゲームの開始に．13は「まだ立たないで」．

## C. ペアで　In pair(s)

### ア．起 立　Standing up

1. You, two.
2. Please stand up, both of you.
3. I want you to stand in pairs.
4. This pair's turn, please get up.
5. I'd like you to stand face to face.
6. Will you two stand in front of the blackboard?
7. Yuko and Sachiko, would you stand up and read this dialog?
8. Would you mind standing by [beside / with / near] your partner?

〈発展的表現〉

9. Why don't you stand up and come forward?
10. Would you mind standing back to back with your partner?
11. It's your pair's turn. Get up! Hurry! Don't waste time!
12. Odd number students, get up and stand behind the even number students.
13. How would you like to do this, standing or sitting?
14. After you memorize this dialog, stand up and come here. Let's see

which pair can finish first.

**Notes:** 1は合図を伴って．5はペアで向かいあって．8の would you mind は相当丁寧な言い方．10は背中合わせに．12は奇数番号の生徒が偶数番号の生徒の後ろに立つ．

---
**Student Response**

私のペアは？　I don't have a partner. What shoud I do? / Where is my partner? / Who is my partner?

あとにして　Us first? / We're not ready. How about the next pair?

---

## イ．着席　Sitting down

1. Okay.
2. Thank you.
3. Please sit down, you two.
4. Sit in your seats.
5. You may [can] sit at your desks.
6. Have a seat, both of you.
7. Take your seats.
8. Return to your seats.

〈発展的表現〉

9. Good. Please be seated.
10. Turn your desks and sit face to face.
11. When you finish the dialog, you can both sit down.
12. Let's take turns. The students standing, have a seat.
13. You two stop talking. Please sit apart.
14. Oh, your partner is absent today. Would you mind sitting with me then?

**Notes:** 1, 2は着席させる生徒が自明の場合．13は叱責，「離れて座りなさい」．14はパートナーのいない生徒と教師がペアを組む．

## 3. 起立・着席

### d. 全員で　Whole class

**ア. 起 立**　Standing up
1. Everybody, stand up.
2. All rise.
3. I want all of you to stand up.
4. I'd like you all to stand in rows.
5. Will you get up out of your chairs?
6. Let's all stand up and sing a song!
7. Would you please all stand up?
8. Okay, out of your seats. Let's go!

〈発展的表現〉

9. Shall we stand up and make a big circle?
10. You should all stand up and then line up in alphabetical order.
11. For this exercise it's better standing up than sitting down.
12. We don't need chairs. It's better to stand up.
13. It's time to stand up and play a game.
14. How would you like to sing a song, standing or sitting?
15. Stand up, walk around and talk with each other.

**Notes:**　授業開始時に生徒を立たせることはアメリカやイギリスなどでは行われていない。2 は formal。10 は出席番号順に並ぶ。「五十音順」は強いて言うと、in the order of the Japanese syllabary. 15 は言語活動のときなど.

---
**Student Response**

期待　What's happening? / What do we do now? / Where do we stand?
立ちたくない　Again? / All of us? / I'm tired. / We can do it sitting.

---

**イ. 着 席**　Sitting down
1. Everybody, sit down.
2. Sit in your seats.
3. You may [can] sit at your desks.
4. Have a seat.

5. Take your seats, all of you.
6. All right. Find a seat and sit down.

〈発展的表現〉

7. Sit down quietly when you find the answer.
8. You mustn't sit down until you've finished reading.
9. That's enough. Let's move our desks and sit in rows as before.
10. Bring your chairs and sit in a big circle.
11. After you've finished reading this page, be seated.
12. You have to move. Find [Take] a seat wherever you like except the seat next to you. Do you understand?
13. Don't be so noisy. Settle down, everybody.
14. Please find a seat. Seat yourselves wherever you want.

**Notes:** 12 はフルーツバスケットのゲームでの指示．13. settle down は座るだけでなく，「静かに」の意味も込めて．14 はどこに座ってもいい場合．

---
**Student Response**

もう終わり？　So soon? / I want to have more time. / Too short.
疲れた　Phew! I'm tired.

---
**Interaction**

| | |
|---|---|
| T: では，みんな立って．クラスの人に質問をして，自分のパートナーを見つけよう． | O.K. Let's stand up, everybody. Ask your classmates questions and find your partner. |
| S: 見つかったらどうするんですか． | What do we do when we find our partners? |
| T: いい質問をしてくれましたね．そしたら席について下さい． | Good question. Then you can take your seats. |
| S: Seats って？ | Seats? |
| T: 座っていいってことです． | I mean you can sit down. OK? |

# 4. 注意・叱責
## Warning / Scolding

### a. 静かに  Be quiet

**ア． クラス全体に**  To the class
1. Sssh!
2. Quiet!
3. Hush!
4. Silence!
5. Quiet, please.
6. Everybody, listen!
7. Be silent, everyone.
8. Don't be noisy!
9. Button your lips.
10. Be quiet, will you?
11. Please be quiet.
12. Will you be quiet?
13. Settle down.
14. Please quiet down.

〈発展的表現〉
15. What a noise! Take it easy, everyone.
16. Listen! Listen, everybody. Now I want you to be quiet.
17. Can't you keep silent for a while?
18. Listen, everyone. Be quiet and stay quiet.
19. Can't you hear me? I said, "Be quiet."
20. Why are you making such a noise? Calm down class.
21. Calm down, will you? Let's have some peace and quiet.

22. What's going on [What is all this noise]? I cannot begin the class with this noise.

   **Notes:** 一般に注意・叱責は表現そのものよりもイントネーション，声の強さ，高さ，響き，また表情やジェスチャーによってその程度が違ってくることを考慮したい．3 は中学 1 年生ぐらいまでが対象．16 で呼びかけに my students を用いるのは不自然．

## イ．個々の生徒に　To individuals

1. You're too noisy, Toshiko! I need [want] you to be quiet.
2. Who is making this noise? Is it Tadashi? Tadashi, be quiet!
3. Yamada, close your mouth (and open your textbook).
4. Kenji, don't make such a [so much] noise. I can't hear Kazuko.
5. Akiko, I think you can be a little quieter.
6. There is too much noise [talking] there.

〈発展的表現〉

7. Why are you so excited? You are making too much noise.

**Notes:** 2 の Is it Tadashi? は Is it you, Tadashi? とすると皮肉や強調の雰囲気が出る．5 の can の表現は穏やかな命令としてよく用いる．6 の最後の there で 1 人あるいは一部の生徒を指すことになる．したがってこれを取れば，クラス全体に対する注意となる．日本では「周囲の迷惑を考えなさい」という発想でよく注意するが，英語では，Think of the other students. などの言い方はしない．

┌─ **Student Response** ─────────────────
│ すみません　Sorry. / I'm sorry.
│ 僕じゃないよ[私じゃありません]　Not me. / It's not me.
└──────────────────────────

## b．顔を上げて　Looking up

1. Look up!
2. Faces up!
3. Face forward!

4. 注意・叱責　47

4. Face the front!
5. Look (up) at the (black)board.
6. Look (up) at me.
7. Don't look down. Look up.
8. Let me see your face(s).

〈発展的表現〉
9. Look up here, not at your neighbor [not out the window].
10. Stop writing for a moment and look up at the board.
11. You can't see me with your face down [looking out (of) the window].
12. You cannot read the (black)board with your face down, can you?
13. Look up here now. You can write later what is written on the (black)board.
14. Look up here and watch what I'm going to do.
15. Look up and pay attention to what I'm going to write on the (black)board.
16. Give your attention to what's written on the board.

**Notes:**　9のように注意を喚起するという意味合いでは here などの語句を添える．Look up! という表現だけでは，漠然と「顔を上げなさい」という意味しか持たないことに注意．15 で pay attention to の場合，attention に your はつけない．代わりに give your attention to という言い方がある．

## C.　私語の禁止　No whispering

### ア．　最初の注意　First admonishing
1. No talking!
2. No whispering!
3. Don't talk.
4. Don't whisper.
5. Don't talk, but listen.
6. Stop talking and listen to me.
7. It's my turn to talk(, not yours).

8. I am talking now.
9. What are you talking about? Stop it!
10. Do you need to talk with Kazuhiko now?
11. You can talk with Megumi later [after class], but not now.
12. No whispering is allowed in class!

〈発展的表現〉

13. Why are you still talking? The class has already started.
14. Does your talk have anything to do with this class [lesson]?
15. Stop talking with your neighbors. You're making it hard for others to hear.
16. What are you talking about? If you are not talking about the lesson, you should stop it right now.
17. Do you have a story to share with the class?
18. Do you have something to tell us?
19. It's time for me to talk, not for you. Do you understand?

**Notes:** 8 では I am に強いアクセントを置くことになる。10 はジョークとして用いる。17, 18 はもちろん言い方次第で friendly になったり sarcastic になったりする。イギリスでは話をやめない生徒に対して Have you got verbal diarrhea? とたしなめることもある (You can't stop talking. の意)。

## イ．(注意してもやめないので) しかる　Scolding

1. It's getting noisy again.
2. I told you not to talk with your neighbor.
3. You're still talking. Stop it right now.
4. You were talking and you are still talking.
5. Don't make me say, "Quiet" again.
6. Stop talking! Stop talking! Once more?

〈発展的表現〉

7. Seiko, sometimes you may talk with your neighbors in class, but not so often! (And certainly not now!)
8. You are talking again. If you can't stop, you'll have to leave the

room [stand outside].
9. You two are still talking. What's so interesting? Tell me what you are talking about, of course in English.
10. You haven't stopped talking! I cannot stand it any more. Please be quiet.

**Notes:** 4 では were に強いアクセントがある．6, 8 はユーモアとして言うべき言葉であり，生徒が文字通りに解釈しないように用いたい．

---------- **Interaction** ----------

| T: 静かに．まだ喋ってるのか．一体何喋ってるの． | Be quiet! You two are still talking. What on earth are you talking about? |
| S: … | … |
| T: 何なの．言ってみなさい．怒らないから． | What's so interesting? Tell me. Just tell me. I won't get angry. |
| S: 昨日見たテレビ番組のこと話していたんです． | We've been talking about a TV program we saw last night. |
| T: そうか，すごく面白かったんだね．でも今じゃなくてあとで話しなさい．いいね． | I see. You obviously enjoyed the TV program a lot. But talk about it later, not now. Okay? |

## d. 罰を与える　Punishing

1. Stand up and keep standing.
2. You did it again. Now stand up. Walk to the back and keep standing there for a while.
3. I've had enough. Stand up. Quick! Come over here. Turn around. Look at your friends. And stay standing there.
4. If you don't stop it, you'll get a punishment.
5. Stop it, or you must sing a song in front of your friends.
6. If you do it once more, you will have to answer every question I ask.
7. Which would you like, to be a good student or to do this exercise all

by yourself?
8. Can't you stop talking? Then, one of you, come to the front with your desk, chair and everything.

〈発展的表現〉
9. Do it again, and you'll clean this room all by yourself after school.
10. You didn't listen to me. I see. So you will have some special homework.
11. You know what you did. O.K. You, come to [and] see me after this class. I will talk with you then.

**Notes:** 9以下は与える注意や罰が授業外に及ぶ例である．

## e. いたずらの禁止　No mischief

### ア．短い注意　Shorter warning
1. Sit still.
2. No! Don't do that.
3. Stop it right now!
4. Knock off the chatter [talking].
5. Knock it off.
6. Don't ever do that again.
7. Never do that again!
8. What are you doing?
9. Don't act that way.
10. Don't behave like that.
11. Behave yourself!
12. Don't be mean.
13. Don't make me angry!
14. What are you up to?

〈発展的表現〉
15. I want you to be a good student.
16. You can be a good student, can't you?

17. Don't play with your pencil case.
18. Be more attentive in class.
19. Don't do that! Do as I told you.
20. I'm running out of patience!
21. You're bothering your neighbors!
22. That is not the way to act.
23. Is that how you act at home?
24. Is that any way to behave in class?
25. You're not supposed to behave like that.

**Notes:** 12 は I've noticed it. I think you should stop it. という意味で用いる．15, 16 は言い方によっては皮肉になり，言い方によっては親愛の情がこもる．17 は with のあとにいたずらをしている物が来る．

## イ．長めの注意　Longer warning

1. Stop it and be sure you don't do it again.
2. Stop it, or would you like to stay after school?
3. I think you should stop it. That's enough (of that)!
4. You're doing what you shouldn't. Stop it right now.

〈発展的表現〉

5. Don't do that! / Don't act like that!
6. I'm afraid you're interrupting the class.
7. Do you think it's all right to do such a thing?
8. I'll have none of that in my classroom.
9. Do you have any questions, or are you just talking with your friend?
10. What is the [your] idea in behaving like that? Why don't you work together with your classmates?
11. How would you feel if I did the same thing to you?
12. You don't want me to get angry, do you? I guarantee you wouldn't like it.

**Notes:** 3 で That's enough! はいたずらに対する厳しい注意になる．8 で that はしてはいけない行為を指し，クラス全体に対してしてはいけないことを明確

に指摘する表現. 10 では the [your] idea in の部分を a big idea of と言うこともできる. 12 は大変厳重な注意である.

## f. その他の注意　Others

1. Turn around and face the front.
2. Straighten your desk(s).
3. Put it back where it was. Quick!
4. Put away what you don't need.
5. Find where we are in the textbook. We are on page 45.
6. Clear your desks of everything but your textbook.
7. Get everything ready on your desk. Don't waste any time!

---

**Interaction**

| | |
|---|---|
| T: こら！ 何してるんだ. 何をするかわからないのか. | What are you doing? Don't you know what to do? |
| S₁: すみません. わかりません. | I'm sorry. I don't know. |
| T: わからない？ ちゃんと言ったじゃないか. 聞いてなかったんだな. | Why not? I told you what to do. You were not listening to me. |
| S₁: … | … |
| T: よし. じゃー勇一. 何をしろと言ったかな. | O.K. What did I tell you to do, Yuichi? |
| S₂: すみません. 僕も聞いてませんでした. | I'm very sorry I was not listening to you, either. |

## 5. 発 言
Remarks / Responses

### a. 大きな声で(言う・話す)　Louder

1. Louder!
2. A bit louder.
3. In a big voice, please.
4. Please speak up.
5. Could you speak in a louder voice, please?
6. You can speak louder, can't you?
7. Speak up so that everyone can hear you.
8. I beg your pardon. I couldn't catch what you said.
9. Answer my question with "Yes" or "No" in a loud voice, please.

〈発展的表現〉

10. Don't worry too much about your pronunciation. Just speak out [up].
11. When you say something, you should look up. Then we can hear you (better).
12. If you look down when you are speaking, you can't be heard.
13. You should look at the person you are talking to.
14. Your voice is too low. Don't be shy. Have more confidence.
15. You are speaking in a weak voice. Is anything wrong [Is anything the matter]?
14. I couldn't catch the last word in your sentence. Will you say it again in a louder voice?

　　**Notes:**　1はぶっきらぼうな命令調. 8はやや formal. pardon を動詞として使って Pardon me? という表現もある. いずれも文末は上昇調になる. 10の speak out は「意見などをはっきり，思いきって述べる」ことを意味する．speak up は speak out の意味のほかに，「より大きな声で話す」という意味がある．

> **Student Response**
> 風邪で声が出ない　I can't speak (any) louder because I have a cold. / I've lost my voice because I have a sore throat.
> 発音がわからない　I don't know how to pronounce the word. / How should I pronounce the word?

## b. はっきりと　Clearer

1. Clearly, please.
2. Speak more clearly.
3. Could you say it more clearly?
4. Could you speak loud and clear, please?
5. Say each word more clearly.
6. Try to pronounce your words more clearly.
7. Try to make your pronunciation a little clearer.

〈発展的表現〉

8. Please don't mumble. Try to say each word clearly.
9. You speak too fast. Would you please slow down a little bit?
10. I think you've got the right answer. So try to say it more clearly.
11. I don't think I understand you fully. Will you explain it more simply?
12. I'm not saying your answer is wrong. I just couldn't hear you. So say it once again slowly and clearly, will you?
13. Why don't you say it in a simpler sentence so that the rest of us can understand more easily?

> **Notes:**　3 は音声だけでなく，言い方も clear に，の意．8 はやや formal．9 は発話のスピードに関する指示．10～12 は教師の発問に対する生徒の答えの文についてのコメントを含む指示．

## C. 口を大きく開けて　With the mouth wide-open

1. Open your mouth wide.
2. Speak with an open mouth.
3. Try to speak with your mouth wide open.
4. Try to move your tongue and lips more.
5. Don't hesitate to open your mouth wide when you read aloud.
6. Always check that your mouth is wide open when you read aloud.

〈発展的表現〉

7. If you open your mouth a little wider, your voice can be heard more easily.
8. Now let's read aloud the first paragraph all together. Remember to keep your mouth wide open.
9. Look at my mouth. You notice my lips are moving, don't you? You should do the same thing. O.K.?
10. If you exaggerate the movement of your mouth a little, you can make a clearer sound.
11. When you pronounce the word 'hot', try to lower your jaw and open your mouth wider.

**Notes:** 2の with an open mouth は「大声で」という意味でも使われる．5の Don't hesitate to do ～ はややかたいが，口語でも使われる．4, 9, 10 は発声器官についての指示．11 は個々の単語の発音指導の例．

---
**Interaction**

T: 誰かに本文を読んでもらいましょう．誰がいいかな．
I would like to have someone read the text? Let's see, who should we have?

S₁: 田中さんがいいと思います．
Let's have Tanaka-san read it.

T: それじゃ，田中さん．第1段落を大きな声で読んで下さい．
Well then, Tanaka-san, please read the first paragraph in a loud voice.

| | |
|---|---|
| S₂: はい.<br>T: 読むときは顔を上げて，みんなに聞こえるように．意味もよく考えて． | Yes, sir [ma'am].<br>When you read, try to look up so that everyone can hear you. Also, think about the meaning of each sentence. |

### d. 意味を考えて　With meaning in mind

1. Think about the meaning.
2. Try to keep the meaning in (your) mind.
3. Pay more attention to the meaning.
4. Always try to remember the story.
5. Don't lose the story line when reading [you read].
6. Think about how the hero feels in this scene.
7. Suppose (that) you are in the hero's position.

〈発展的表現〉

8. Always try to keep in mind the meaning of what you are reading.
9. Read aloud the first paragraph, thinking about the meaning of each sentence in it.
10. Your reading will sound more natural if you consider the meaning of the text while you are reading it.
11. We are going to make a pause after each group of words this time, so you need to think about the meaning carefully.
12. Think more about how Della feels in this scene. Then try to read it a little more sadly.
13. Let's do some role-playing (practice). In order to make your conversation sound real, you need to imagine how a person in your role feels.

　　**Notes:**　いずれも本文読解を終えた音読練習の段階での指示．4 の story は「筋」の意味．6, 7, 12, 13 は登場人物の心情面も考えさせて音読させるための指示．7 はやや formal.

> **Student Response**
> どこで区切るか　Where should I make a pause? / I don't know where to make a pause.
> 読むところを間違えた　I read the wrong line. / I forgot where I was reading.

## e. 発言を促す　Stimulating students to talk

### ア. 答えを促す　Encouraging students to answer
1. Ready?
2. Be ready with your answer.
3. Are you ready to answer?
4. I want you to answer my questions.
5. Please read your answer to the class.
6. Answer my questions simply with 'yes' or 'no'.
7. Why don't you try [make a guess]?
8. Will you tell us what you think?
9. Anyone ready with the answer may speak up [out].
10. Anyone who has an answer may feel free to speak.

〈発展的表現〉
11. You are on the right track. Why don't you go on and finish your answer?
12. If you can't find the answer by yourselves, you can talk to each other about it.
13. Even if you are halfway through with the answer, tell me what you've got so far.
14. This question is a little difficult, so you don't have to worry even if you can't get the right answer. Just give it a try.
15. Don't be afraid of making mistakes. The important thing is to try and speak in English.
16. I think your answer is also correct in a sense, but can't you think

about the question in a different [another] way?
17. I will give you some hints so that you may hit upon [can find] the right answer.

**Notes:** 5 は書き留めておいた答えなどを「読み聞かせる」という意味である．11 はかなりくだけた表現であり，生徒が答えを発表している途中における指示．16 は他に see the question differently などの表現も考えられる．

---
**Student Response**

質問がわからない　I can't understand your question. / I don't know what you asked [are asking].

見当がつかない　I have no idea. / I don't have the least idea. / I can't think of anything.

もう少し待って　Would you give me some more time? / I'm still thinking. Can I answer later?

---

## イ．質問を受ける　Eliciting questions

1. Any questions?
2. Do you have any questions?
3. Are there any questions?
4. No further questions?
5. No more questions?
6. Is everything clear now?
7. That was a very good point. Any other questions?
8. Do you understand today's lesson?
9. Don't you have any trouble understanding today's lesson?
10. Feel free to ask whatever questions you have.

〈発展的表現〉

11. If you have any questions about the last lesson, I will answer before we begin today's lesson.
12. Is there anything unclear [you don't understand] about today's lesson? If so, let's clear it up now.
13. Now we have only five minutes left. I will answer whatever ques-

tions you have about today's lesson.
14. Now let's review today's lesson roughly. If you find any part you have missed, let me know and I will explain it to you.

   **Notes:** 10 はややかたい表現．11 は前回の授業でわからない所がなかったかを確認してから，本時の授業に入っている．12～14 は授業の終わりの段階における指示．

   ┌─ **Student Response** ─────────────────────────────
   質問がある　I have a question. / May I ask you a question?
   訳せない　I can't translate this sentence into Japanese. / I don't know the meaning of this sentence in Japanese.
   筆記体が読めない　I can't read your handwriting. / Will you write it in block letters for me, please?
   └───────────────────────────────────────────────

## f.　挙 手　Raising one's hand

1. Hands up.
2. Put your hands up.
3. Raise your hand.
4. Who knows the answer to this question? Hands up.
5. Put your hand up if you know the answer.
6. Are there any volunteers for this question?
7. If there are any questions, just put your hand up and stop me.

〈発展的表現〉

8. If you think this sentence is true, please raise your right hand and if you think it is false, (raise) your left hand.
9. I can't see whose hands are up. Put your hands up straight.
10. Your hands are too low. Raise them higher.
11. Keep your hands up while I count them.
12. O.K. You may put your hands down now.

   **Notes:** 1 は賛成・反対等の意志表示をさせるときによく使われる．2 は複数の生徒に言う場合，片手なのか両手なのか区別しない．7 は机間巡視の際の指示．9,

10 は手の挙げ方について.

---
**Interaction**

T: 本文について何か質問があったら手を挙げて下さい。　　If you have any questions about the text, put your hand up, please.

S: （挙手し）質問があります。　　I have a question.

T: 鈴木君, どこがわからないのですか。　　Yes, Suzuki-kun, what is your problem?

S: 5行目の it が何を指すかわかりません。　　I don't know the meaning of 'it' on line 5.

T: it は前の行の the custom を意味します。　　This 'it' stands for 'the custom' found in the previous line.

S: わかりました。　　Oh, now I see [understand].

# 6. ほめる
Praising

## a. 一般的なほめ言葉　Praise in general

1. Good.
2. Right.
3. Fine.
4. Yes.
5. Great.
6. Splendid.
7. Excellent.
8. Fantastic.
9. Marvelous.
10. Terrific.
11. Beautiful.
12. Wonderful.
13. Super.
14. Superb.
15. Perfect.
16. Impressive.
17. Flawless.
18. Quite right.
19. That's correct.
20. Just right.
21. You've got it.
22. That's exactly the point.
23. That's it.
24. Very good.
25. All right.
26. That's better.
27. That's what I've wanted.
28. An ideal answer.
29. Such a beautiful job.
30. A very good job.

〈発展的表現〉

31. I couldn't have given a better answer myself.
32. That's the best job you've ever done.
33. I didn't expect such a perfect response from you.
34. Nobody could possibly give a better reply than that.

**Notes:**　ここに挙げた語や短い語句は，ほとんどどのような状況でも用いることができる．1〜5はきわめて一般的，6〜17, 28〜30はかなり強意，18〜27は応答の正しさに反応している．31〜34はかなりおおげさなほめ言葉である．

## b. 声の質　Voice quality

1. Your voice carries well.
2. You have a clear voice.
3. What a nice soft voice you have!
4. Your voice is nice [very good].
5. You have a really good voice.
6. You read in a loud, clear voice.
7. That was terrific — really loud and clear.
8. Thank you. That was nice and clear.
9. Good. You speak very clearly.

〈発展的表現〉

10. I like your voice. It's very dramatic.
11. I didn't catch what you said. Will you say it more clearly this time? Thank you. Now I understand.
12. Good reading. You sound in high-spirits today.
13. Your pronunciation is still a little rough, but I like your cheerful tone.

**Notes:** 1は「声がよく通る」の意味. well の代わりに far も使用可. 6〜8は生徒に指名して音読させたあとのフィードバックとして. 13は発音の正確さよりも元気のよさを高く評価したい場合.

## c. 声の大きさ　Loudness of voice

1. Thanks for reading in a loud voice.
2. Now I can hear you.
3. Yes. That's much louder.
4. Good. That's loud enough.
5. Pretty good. That's nice and loud.

〈発展的表現〉

6. I appreciate your loud voice. Then why don't you try to read more

clearly?
7. Reading in a loud voice is the first sure step toward better pronunciation.
8. Your voice is very pleasant to hear. But could you say it more loudly?
9. I can't quite hear you. Why don't you (try to) use the nice big voice that you have when you talk with your friends?

**Notes:** 1~5 は大きな声で生徒が発表したのに対するフィードバック．

---- **Interaction** ----

| S : | (think, through, tenth を不正確に発音する) | /sink/, /sru/, /tens/. |
| T : | th が日本語の s みたいに聞こえるよ．よく見て，/θink/. | Your /th/ sounds like a Japanese /s/. Watch my mouth carefully, /θink/. |
| S : | /θink/. | /θink/. |
| T : | ほらできた．もう一度やってごらん． | That's it. Do it again. |
| S : | /θink/. | /θink/. |
| T : | いいぞ．大きい声できれいに発音できたね．よし．O.K. | Good pronunciation — loud and clear. Very good job. |

## d. 努 力　Students' effort

### ア．成果に対して　To the result of the effort

1. A good job.
2. Nice work.
3. Well done.
4. Good for you!
5. Isn't that a great job?
6. What beautiful work!
7. You did a wonderful job.
8. You did really well this time.

9. You've done that very nicely.
10. I'm glad you did so well.

〈発展的表現〉

11. Your efforts have paid off, haven't they?
12. I am impressed with your work.
13. I bet you did a lot of work for this (masterpiece).
14. I have never seen such beautiful work.
15. That's the best work you've ever done.
16. That's the best work I've ever seen you do.
17. That's a good answer, but not perfect. Think it over again.
18. I know the question was hard for you, but you did very well.
19. I know today's lesson was hard. But you did a good job, class. I'm proud of you.

**Notes:** 4 は「いいぞ，でかした」などの文脈で使われる．11 は努力が報われた場合．paid off の代わりに been rewarded も使用可．13 の masterpiece はかなり強意のほめ言葉であるから，場面によっては sarcastic に響く．17 は成果をほめながらもさらに努力するように促すときの指示．18, 19 は難しいのによく頑張ったとほめる場合．

--- **Student Response** ---
頑張ったんです　I did [tried] my best. / I really tried hard.
ほめられて　Thank you. / I'm happy to hear that.

## イ．ねぎらう　Appreciating the students' effort

1. Thank you for trying.
2. You always work hard.
3. You always try your best.
4. You always put effort into your work.
5. You're such a hard worker.
6. You're very industrious.
7. You must have worked hard on this.
8. You have really been studying hard, haven't you?.

9. I know you worked hard.

〈発展的表現〉

10. I'm happy that you did your best.
11. I'm glad you gave it a try.
12. I like the way you tried.
13. You must have spent a lot of time doing this homework.
14. You survived, didn't you?
15. I'm really impressed by how thorough you were.
16. You're doing very well, but don't work too hard.

**Notes:** 12は努力するその姿勢を評価したい場合．14は難しい試験など何か大きなtaskのあとで．15は課題等をきちんとやる生徒に対してのほめ言葉．

―――――― **Interaction** ――――――

| | |
|---|---|
| T： 間違ってもいいから，思い切ってやってごらん．誰か？ | Don't worry about making mistakes. Just give it a try. Anyone? |
| S： はい．（手を挙げる） | Yes. |
| T： それではケン．やってみよう． | O.K., Ken, go ahead. |
| S： （つまずきながらも訳す） | |
| T： はい，そこまで．ちょっとつまずいたけれど，いい訳だった．よく発表してくれたね． | O.K., stop there. That was a nice translation. Only a few small mistakes. Thank you for trying. You did a good job. |

## e. 手書きの文字　Hand writing

1. Very good.
2. Neat writing.
3. You write very clearly [legibly].
4. Your handwriting is neat.
5. You have beautiful handwriting.
6. You write beautifully [very well].

7. What beautiful handwriting this is [you have]!
   〈発展的表現〉
8. I like your writing.
9. Your writing is easy to read.
10. I wish my writing were as neat as yours.
11. I would like to show you how neatly Chiyoko takes notes. They can be a good model.

   **Notes:** 2 の neat は口語で単に very good の意味もあるので，writing の内容をほめる意味にもなる．6 の very well は文字だけとはかぎらない．11 はノートの取り方をほめる場合．

## f. 向上の度合い　Improvement

1. You're much better.
2. I'm impressed.
3. What an improvement!
4. You've improved a lot.
5. That's much better than before.
6. You've improved so much.
7. You're getting better.
8. You're making progress.
9. You did much better this time, didn't you?
10. I'm pleased with your improvement.
11. A great improvement! That makes me really happy.
12. There has been a great [tremendous] amount of improvement in your work.
    〈発展的表現〉
13. Your grades have improved a lot [considerably].
14. You can really be proud of your improvement.
15. I'm amazed [surprised] at the great [remarkable] progress in your English.

16. You must have studied a lot last night; you've improved a great deal.
17. It would have been even better if you had practiced it a few more times.

   **Notes:** 10〜15 は成績や英語力が飛躍的に伸びた場合．特に 12, 15 は強意であるから，実体を伴わないと奇異に響く．17 は一応努力は認めるがよりよいものを期待していた場合．

## g. 試験の結果　Results of the test

1. Full marks.
2. Perfect answer.
3. You got a hundred percent.
4. You got a perfect score.
5. Your answer is just perfect.
6. Congratulations! You did a good job.
7. You were close (to the top).
8. You almost made it.
9. You got 90 percent on this exam.
10. You did well on that.

〈発展的表現〉

11. This is one of the most difficult tests I have ever given. But your class has done the best of all.
12. You touched on all the key points.
13. You've got the general idea.
14. That's good, but you're still missing some points.
15. You did fairly well, but I still have a feeling that something is not quite right.

   **Notes:** 1 はイギリス英語，2〜5 が米語表現．1〜5 は 100 点満点を取った生徒へのフィードバックとして．8 はあと一歩のところで惜しくも不合格になった生徒に対して．12 は米語表現．13〜15 は一応満足できる答えだが完全という

には何か物足りないことを表したい場合．

> **Student Response**
> 
> よい点だった　I got the top score on the English exam. / I got an A in English.
> 
> 満点だ　I got a hundred percent right. / I got full marks.
> 
> まあまあだった　I did my best. / I did the best I could.
> 
> がっかり　I'm very unhappy. / I'm disappointed with the result.
> 
> 次回頑張る　I'll do better next time.

## 7. 励まし
### Encouragement

### a. 希望をもたせる　Hope

1. Don't give up.
2. You'll do better next time.
3. I know you will do better next time.
4. I'm sure you will pass the test next time.
5. Try it again. I'm sure you can do better this time.
6. Keep trying until you get it right.
7. Everything will be O.K. next time.
8. Don't worry. You can still do it.

〈発展的表現〉

9. No pain, no gain.
10. Every cloud has a silver lining.
11. Look on the brighter side.
12. Soon you'll see the light at the end of the tunnel.

   **Notes:** 9は本来スポーツ選手に対する励ましの表現．10, 11は希望を失わないようにと励ます場合．10は口語的表現ではないが，面白い表現なので説明すると生徒は興味を持つ．12は少しでも希望が見えたときに．

### b. 意欲をかき立てる　Motivating

1. Go for [to] it!
2. Cheer up.
3. Take it easy.
4. Hang in there.

5. Stick it out.
6. Stick to it.
7. I wish you good luck [the best].

〈発展的表現〉

8. Where's your usual get-up-and-go?
9. That's not like you at all.
10. You've made a breakthrough.
11. Where there is a will, there is a way.
12. I know you can do well if you work harder.
13. I know you can do it if you just try.
14. What is worth doing is worth doing well.
15. Come on. If you try your best, you'll never fail in the exam.
16. It's up to you to decide to do this work. It's all in your mind.

**Notes:** 1は「やれ！ やれ！」の感じ．3～6は頑張れと励ます場合．8,9はいつもの元気がない生徒を励ます場合．9は怠惰で不合格になった生徒などに対して．このあと12,13などのコメントが来る．11はやる気が何より大切だと励ます場合．14はやる以上はきちんとやるように励ます場合．16は自分の気持ち次第だと励ます場合．

---

**Interaction**

S： 試験の採点は終わりましたか．
Have you graded [marked] the mid-term exam yet?

T： まだだけど，どうして．
Not yet. Why?

S： 難しくて全然書けなかったんです．
Well, I'm afraid I didn't do so well. It was very tough.

T： そう？ 確かに難しかったね．でも思ったほどひどくないかもよ．まあ，復習はきちんとやっておくべきだったね．
Oh, really? I'm sure it was hard, but it may not have been as bad as you think. Anyway, maybe you should have reviewed more thoroughly.

S： そうですね．次頑張ります．
Yes. I will try my best next time.

## 7. 励まし

### c. 積極性を引き出す　Positive attitude

1. Speak up.
2. Come on.
3. Don't be shy.
4. Give it a try [go].
5. It's worth a try.
6. Go ahead and try.
7. Feel free to say what you think. / Feel free to give your opinion.

〈発展的表現〉

8. Well, it's now or never.
9. Those who hesitate are lost.
10. First come, first served.
11. Don't be afraid of making mistakes.
12. Don't try to say everything perfectly.
13. Don't put off until tomorrow what you can do today.
14. Your answer was not quite right, but I like your positive attitude.
15. You don't have to be perfect. I always make mistakes, too. Even native speakers do.
16. Any questions? There is no harm in asking. This is your last chance.

**Notes:** 7は「遠慮しないで」の意でto以下にさせたい行動などが来る．8, 9, 10, 13はその場で生徒に何かを思い切ってやらせたい場合．11, 12, 15は文法にとらわれず積極的に話すことを奨励する場合．14は積極性をほめたい場合．16は生徒から全然質問が出ない場合．

---
**Student Response**

やってみます　I will do it [try].
自信がない　I'm not sure. / This may be wrong.
恥ずかしい　I'm too shy. / I'm not sure of myself.

## d. 好調を持続させる　Keeping in (good) condition

1. That's it.
2. That's more like it.
3. Keep working.
4. Don't slow down.
5. Stick to your work.
6. You're doing fine.
7. Keep up the good work.
8. That's the spirit.
9. You're on the right track.
10. It looks like you're doing well.

〈発展的表現〉

11. Everything is all right, isn't it?
12. How's everything going with you?  Can you keep up?

**Notes:**　1 はその調子で頑張れの意味で，it の代わりに the way も使用可．2 はだんだん調子が出てきた場合．4 は調子を落とさずに頑張れの意で，スピードのことではない．8 は意欲が出てきた生徒を励ます場合．

## e. 慰め・同情　Sympathy

1. Bad luck!
2. What a shame [pity]!
3. That's a shame [pity].
4. Isn't that a shame [a pity]?
5. That's terrible [awful / too bad].
6. How terrible [awful]!
7. Never mind.
8. Don't worry about it.
9. Don't take it so seriously [hard].
10. Don't look so sad.

11. Don't feel so bad.
12. Don't be depressed [disappointed / discouraged].
13. Sorry about that.
14. I know how you feel.
15. Oh, well, that's life.
16. I sympathize with you.

〈発展的表現〉

17. It could happen to anybody.
18. It could have been a lot worse.
19. If anything can go wrong, it will.
20. No problem. Nobody is perfect.
21. Everyone experiences ups and downs in their life.
22. Don't worry so much (about it). It may not be as bad as you think.
23. I had exactly the same problem when I was a student.

**Notes:** 1〜6は「それは大変ですね」と相手の不運を認める発言で，通常このあとに慰めの言葉がくる．17は誰にも起こりうることだという慰めの表現．15, 20〜23はもっと楽観的になるようにという慰めの表現．

---
**Student Response**
励まされて　Thank you. / You're very kind to say so.
大丈夫　I'm O.K. / Don't worry.

---

## f. 生徒の応答を励ます　Encouragement to speak out

1. You're almost right.
2. You've almost got it.
3. Go on. Have another try.
4. You are already halfway there.
5. You're probably right. I just couldn't hear you.
6. Don't be discouraged. You were almost right.
7. Take it easy. There's no need to hurry.
8. Try again and you may find a better answer.

〈発展的表現〉

9. There's nothing wrong with your answer. But you can say it better.
10. You did a good job. But you can do even better next time.
11. I'm very anxious to know what your second answer is.
12. Could you give us another answer? Maybe you will get it right then.
13. There's no shame in making a wrong guess. You can try again.

**Notes:** 3はおずおずと発言している生徒などに．9〜13はいずれも，生徒の初回の発話は間違いではないが，もっと考えるとさらにいい応答になると励ましている．

## 8. あやまる
### Apologizing

### a. 遅刻して　Being late

**ア．教師が遅れて教室に入る**　Teacher being late
1. Sorry. I'm a bit late.
2. Sorry. Did you wait long?
3. I'm sorry I'm late.
4. I'm sorry to be late.
5. I'm sorry for being late.
6. Oh, you've all been waiting for me.
7. I'm sorry to have kept you waiting.
8. I apologize for being late.
9. I must apologize for being so late.
10. Thank you for waiting for me so long.
11. Whew. I'm five minutes late. Let's get into the book [lesson] quickly.

〈発展的表現〉
12. I'm very sorry I'm late. I missed the bus.
13. I'm sorry for being late. I had something to do (in the office).
14. I'm really sorry for being so late. I was stuck [caught] in a traffic jam.
15. I'm so sorry I'm late. I was not feeling very well this morning. So I went to see the doctor before coming to school.

**Notes:**　遅れて教室に入って，教師が生徒に謝罪するという場面は考えにくいが，状況によっては7～10のような丁寧な言い方もあり得よう．1～4のほうが5より標準的．一般に少しぐらいの遅れのときは I'm sorry I'm late. だけですむことが多いが，ある程度以上の遅れのときは，12～15で示したように，何らかの

理由を詫びと共に述べるのが普通である．

### イ．理由の説明　Explanation

1. I missed the bus [the train / the subway / the express].
2. I missed my usual express [bus].
3. The bus never came.
4. I worked till late last night.
5. I lost one of my contact lenses on the way.
6. I sprained my ankle on the way.
7. I had a headache [stomachache] this morning.
8. I felt sick [dizzy / feverish] this morning.

〈発展的表現〉

9. I felt sick in the train. So I got off and took a rest for a while on the platform.
10. I had a flat tire on my way. And I had to drag [walk / push] my bike to school.
11. I had to drop in at a repair shop to have my bike [car] repaired [fixed].
12. My bicycle was missing. So I had to walk all the way.
13. I realized I forgot my textbook, and returned home.
14. I realized I left my books at home, so I went back to get them.

### b．生徒の釈明に対して　Responding to the student's apology

1. Okay.
2. That's okay.
3. No problem.
4. Forget it.
5. That's (quite) all right.
6. Don't worry about it.
7. Please don't worry.

8. Never mind. You're not so late.
9. Don't mention it.
10. That's perfectly all right.

〈発展的表現〉

11. It's not your fault.
12. You couldn't help it.
13. You don't need to apologize.
14. There's nothing to apologize for [about].
15. There's no reason to apologize.
16. Do you have a written excuse?
17. Don't let that happen again.

**Notes:** 1～4 はやや informal. 5 で quite を省略するとやや informal に近くなる．9, 10 はやや formal. 11～15 は正当な理由を聞いたあとで使える．16 の written excuse は遅刻理由を証明する文書．

> **Student Response**
>
> 教師が遅刻　That's all right with me [us]. / Are you all right now?
> 本人が遅刻　I'm sorry I'm late. / Please forgive me for being late again.
> ついてない　Whew! A flat tire again. / This isn't my day.
> 遅刻した友人に　What happened? / Are you okay? / The bus is always late.

> **Interaction**
>
> S：遅れてすみません．　　　　I'm sorry I'm late.
> T：どうしたの．　　　　　　　Why are you late?
> S：自転車がパンクして駅まで　I got a flat tire, and I walked my bike
> 　　歩いたんです．そうしたら　to the station. Then I missed the
> 　　急行に乗り遅れてしまって．express.
> T：おやまあ．ま，いいから座り　That's too bad. Anyway, please take
> 　　なさい．今 24 ページをやっ　your seat. We're on page 24. Here's
> 　　ています．ハイ，プリント．today's handout.
> S：すみません．　　　　　　　Thank you.

## C. 自習にして　In the teacher's absence

### ア．自習の予告　Announcement of the teacher being absent
1. No class tomorrow.
2. We have no class tomorrow.
3. There's no lesson tomorrow.
4. I won't come tomorrow.
5. I'm not coming to school tomorrow.

〈発展的表現〉
6. I need to tell you that we'll have no class tomorrow.
7. I'm sorry I can't see you tomorrow.
8. I'm sorry I won't come to school tomorrow.
9. I'm sorry I'm not coming to school tomorrow.
10. I'd like to tell you that I won't be here tomorrow.
11. There's no lesson tomorrow. But you will be expected to come to class and work quietly by yourselves.

**Notes:** 1, 2は休講のお知らせの最も一般的な表現．英語では「自習」という短い語句がないため，中学・高校での自習の意味を正確に伝えるためには，11が最も適切である．

### イ．理由の説明　Explanation
1. I'll be out of town.
2. I have to make [go on] an official trip. / I have to attend a meeting in Tokyo.
3. I'm going on a business trip.
4. I'm visiting a school in Tokyo tomorrow.
5. I'm scheduled to go on a business trip.
6. I have to attend a teachers' conference [meeting].
7. We'll have practice for Sports Day tomorrow.

〈発展的表現〉
8. We need to get everything prepared for the School Festival.

9. We have a teachers' meeting tomorrow, and all the teachers are supposed to be there.
10. My father is going to be hospitalized tomorrow, and he needs my help.

**Notes:** 「出張」に相当する便利な英語はないので，生徒にその用務の内容まで言う必要がないときには1のような言い方で十分であろう．

ウ．**予告なしの自習のあとで**　After sudden cancellation of the class
1. I'm sorry I cancelled the class yesterday. I had a fever [cold].
2. I'm sorry I didn't come last week. My mother-in-law passed away.
3. I'm really sorry I couldn't see you last week. I had to attend a funeral of one of my relatives.
4. I'm very sorry we had no class yesterday. My husband was very sick and was taken to the hospital by ambulance.

〈発展的表現〉
5. Have you finished your assignment?
6. Have you finished what I told you to do?
7. Did you work quietly [study well] while I was away?
8. Were you good students while I was away?
9. Have you finished the assignments that I gave you the day before yesterday?

**Notes:** 4の to the hospital の部分はイギリス英語では，to hospital となることが多い．また5はアメリカでは「宿題」の意味では homework（不可算）よりも assignment（可算）が使われることが多い．提出物を受け取るとき日本人教師は無言のことも多いが，英語圏では生徒に対しても Thank you. と言うのが普通．

---
**Interaction**

T：昨日は休講にしてすみませんでしたね．家内が入院して，付き添っていっ　　I'm sorry I was absent yesterday. My wife was hospitalized, and she needed my help. Have you finished

|  |  |  |
|---|---|---|
|  | たもので．出しておいた課題は済みましたか． | the assignment I gave you? |
| Ss: | はい．／まだです．／まだやっている最中です．／あとちょっとです． | Yes, I have. / No, not yet. / Still working on it. / I'm finishing it now. |
| T: | 今，出せる人は出してください． | Please hand in your work sheets now if you can. |

## d. 宿題が多すぎて　Too much homework

1. Did [Does] it annoy you?
2. Was [Is] it too much [unbearable]?
3. Did I give you a lot of homework [assignments]?
4. Did I give you too much homework [too many assignments]?
5. Didn't you sleep at all last night?

〈発展的表現〉

6. Hmm . . . you have a point. Let me think about it.
7. All right. I understand. Leave out Assignment 4, then.
8. All right. Let's put off the deadline. Let's see . . . next Monday. How about that?
9. Do some group study. And get your work done.
10. Do some brainstorming with your classmates. Then you may find a good topic for an essay.

> **Notes:** 1, 2 で現在形の表現は宿題を出した当日，過去は提出日の発話．6.日本語の「考えておきましょう」とは意味が正反対であることに注意．英語ではほとんど yes に近く，相手の頼みごとなどに対して積極的に実現に向けて努力することを示唆する．10 の brainstorming は自由に思いつきなどを出しあうこと．

### e. 勘違いして　Misunderstanding

1. Oops!
2. Excuse me.
3. I'm sorry.
4. Sorry.
5. Oh, that's a [my] mistake.
6. Wait a bit [minute].

〈発展的表現〉

7. Please excuse my spelling mistakes.
8. Excuse my typo [typographical error]. Please correct it like this.
9. Oops! Yes, you're right. I'll give you five points.
10. Oh, I'm sorry. We finished this page last week. So we should be on page 21 today.
11. Excuse me. This is not today's topic. Here it is.
12. Oh, I'm sorry. We're reading the wrong page.
13. We're talking about the wrong item. Look at the bottom of the page. This is the one.

**Notes:**　1, 4, 6 は informal. 6 の wait は「おっと」という感じで，他人に命令しているのではない．7 で Even Homer sometimes nods.（弘法も筆の誤り）を引用したくなるが，この格言はそれほど popular ではない．8 の typo とはプリントなどの誤植の口語表現．11 で Here it is. と言いながら該当するところを指さす．

### f. 急用で授業を中座して　Leaving the classroom for urgent business

#### ア. 教師　Teacher

1. Excuse me.
2. Excuse me for a second [few minutes].
3. You must excuse me for a moment.
4. I'll be back soon.

5. I have to leave the room for a couple of minutes.

〈発展的表現〉

6. I just remembered. I have [am supposed] to go to the Dean's office.
7. I just remembered something I have to do right now.
8. I have to be away for a few minutes, but you should go on with your work.

---
**Student Response**

いいです　That's okay. / Don't worry about us.
ごゆっくり　Take your time. / There's no hurry. / Don't hurry.

---

イ．**生徒の発言**　Students

1. Excuse me.
2. May [Can] I be excused?
3. May I go to the rest room?
4. Excuse me. I have to go to see the nurse.
5. I have to leave the class around eleven o'clock.

〈発展的表現〉

6. I don't feel well. Can I leave for the nurse's room?
7. I've got a message from home. I have [need] to leave the class around ten o'clock.

　**Notes:**　生徒の発言としては，4が最も一般的．きわめて応用の広い表現であるからふだんから慣らしておくといい．

# 9. 感 謝
## Saying Thanks

### a. 一般的な「ありがとう」 "Thank you"

1. Thank you (very much).
2. Thank you so much.
3. Thanks a lot [awfully].
4. Many thanks.
5. A thousand thanks.
6. Thanks for your help.
7. It's very kind [nice] of you.
8. I appreciate your kindness.
9. I'm very thankful.
10. I'm very grateful.
11. I'm very much obliged.
12. How kind of you!
13. I'd like to say, "Thank you."

〈発展的表現〉

14. That's just what we wanted.
15. That's just the thing I have needed.
16. I'll definitely accept your help.
17. I'd love to accept your offer of help.
18. Your help will certainly be welcomed.
19. That would really be a valuable help.
20. We won't be able to do it without your help.

**Notes:** 1〜7が最も一般的でどのような状況でも使える感謝の言葉．3の awfully はイギリス英語的．9〜12 はかなり formal で時として冷たく響く．13

も同様にやや冷静な響きがある．14〜20 は直接感謝の言葉を用いずに，その意を伝えるもの．

## b. 手伝いに対して　For help

### ア．手伝いを頼む　Asking for help
1. Please.
2. Help me, please.
3. Can [Will] you help me?
4. Would you help me?
5. Lend me a hand (please).
6. Would you mind helping me?

〈発展的表現〉

7. Bring me a tape recorder, please.
8. Take this OHP to the teachers' room, please.
9. Put the DVD [CD] player on that desk.
10. Take this VTR [VCR] to your classroom and set it on the teacher's desk.
11. Take these handouts to your classroom and hand them out to the students.
12. Bring the wall-map here and hang it on this wall.

> **Notes:**　6 の would you mind の形は生徒に対しては普通丁寧すぎるが，特に生徒のやっている仕事などを中断させて依頼するような場面では可能である．なお肯定の応答は Not at all. のような否定になるから気をつける．9 の put が普通の言い方．10 の set はやや改まった言い方．VCR = video cassette recorder.

### イ．生徒が手伝いを申し出る　Students' offering help
1. I'll help you.
2. Can I help you?
3. Shall [Could] I help you?
4. We'll carry the books for you.

5. O.K. I'll do it (for you).
6. Wait. I'll take care of it.
7. May [Can] I lend you a hand?
8. Let me help you.

〈発展的表現〉
9. Where shall I put this vase?
10. When shall we come to help you?
11. When do you want us to come and carry these boxes?
12. Shall I open the windows [door] for you?

**Notes:** 1〜7はきわめて頻繁に用いられる句であり，普段から簡単に口から出るようにしておきたい．3のShall I〜はややかたい響きがある．

## ウ. 手伝いに感謝する　Gratitude for help given
1. It's very kind of you to do that.
2. I really do appreciate your help.
3. Oh, thank you very much. You are so kind.
4. You were really helpful. Thank you very much.
5. That will be of a great help (to me).
6. That will save me lots of time and trouble.

〈発展的表現〉
7. You are so kind to have brought me this book.
8. Thank you for moving the OHP. I couldn't have managed it by myself.

**Notes:** 6〜8は状況に合わせて，さまざまな言い方が可能であることの例である．なお感謝に対してNever mind. と言うがDon't mind. とは言わない．

---
**Student Response**

引き受ける　O.K. / Sure. / Yes, I can. / Yes, I will.
断る　Sorry. / I'm sorry. I'm busy now. / I'm sorry. I can't now.
どういたしまして　You are welcome. / Not at all. / Don't mention it.

## Interaction

| | |
|---|---|
| T： 誰か，OHPを持って来てくれませんか． | Would someone bring the OHP here? |
| S： 私がします．OHPはどこにありますか． | O.K., I will. Where is the OHP? |
| T： 私の部屋にあります．<br>（生徒がOHPを持って来る） | In my office. |
| S： えーと，どこに置きますか． | Here it is. Where shall I put it? |
| T： そこの机の上に置いて下さい．どうもありがとう． | Oh, put it on that desk. Thank you very much. |
| S： どういたしまして． | Not at all. |

## c. 黒板などの掃除　Cleaning the blackboard

### ア. 掃除を頼む　Directions for cleaning

1. Clean it (please).
2. Bring me that eraser.
3. Please wipe the blackboard.
4. Put the chalk and the erasers in order.
5. Sweep up the chalk dust.
6. Put the eraser on the (eraser) cleaner.
7. Don't scribble on the blackboard.
8. Please clean the teacher's desk.
9. This desk is too messy. Will you put the things in order?

〈発展的表現〉

10. Wipe the white board with a wet cloth.
11. Don't wipe the blackboard with a wet cloth.
12. Please go to the teachers' room and bring me a new eraser.
13. Don't put a pin in the blackboard. Use a magnet.
14. There's chalk dust on the desk. Will you dust it off?

**Notes:** 9や14の前半の文だけで命令や依頼になることがあるのは，日本語と同

じで，前半の文を言う話者の意図が次の文の内容になる．

イ．**掃除に感謝**　Gratitude for cleaning
1. This is really clean.
2. How clean! Thank you very much.
3. Thank you for cleaning the blackboard.
4. You did a good [thorough] job. Everything is so clean.
5. I'm very happy to see such a clean blackboard.
6. It's very good of you to have put everything in good order before I came.

> **Student Response**
> 黒板を消す　Hey! Wipe the blackboard. The teacher is coming.
> 僕じゃない　It's not me who drew [wrote] that.

d.　**花などに対して**　For flowers, etc.

1. Beautiful! Thank you.
2. Thank you for the flowers.
3. I appreciate the flowers you brought.
4. What pretty flowers!
5. They look really beautiful, don't they?
6. I'll put them in a flower pot.
7. Let me arrange the flowers in a vase.
8. I wish I knew flower arrangement.
9. The roses are blooming now.
10. The cherry trees are in full bloom now.
11. The sweet peas are at their best.

〈発展的表現〉
12. We have to water the flowers with a watering can every day.
13. Who has decorated the bulletin board? I like it.
14. Thank you for the new poster. It's really nice.

15. Kenji is very kind to have brought lots of pretty picture postcards.

**Notes:** 生徒が持ってくる花には英語ではあまり馴染みのないものもある．花の名前については pp. 326–9 を参照．8 はあまり見事な花なのでただ花瓶に投げ入れるのはもったいないという感じ．

---
**Student Response**

花の世話をする　I'll take care of those flowers. / I'll change the water in the vases once a day.

花で飾る　I'll put them in the vase. / Let's hang this flower pot on that hook over there.

---

### e. プレゼントに対して　For the gift

1. Oh, what a surprise! Thank you.
2. Thank you for the present [gift].
3. You are very kind [nice].
4. I'll take good care of it.
5. This is a splendid present.
6. This is just beautiful [wonderful / gorgeous].
7. I'm very surprised but also very happy.
8. I didn't know she was so kind.
9. I didn't expect such a wonderful gift (from you).

〈発展的表現〉

10. I'll keep it as the best memory of my happy days with you.

**Notes:** 教師の離任・結婚・出産・退職などに際してのプレゼントに対する言葉である．このあとその品物についてのコメントが続くのが普通．10 は退職・離任などでの言葉．

# 10. 生徒発言への対応
### Dealing with Students' Responses

### a. 誤りの訂正　Correction of mistakes

**ア．誤りを指摘する**　Pointing out errors
1. That's not correct.
2. That's incorrect. Try again.
3. That's wrong. Take your time and try again.
4. You can't say that. Give me another answer.
5. I'm afraid [I'm sorry] that's wrong. Can anyone else answer?
6. Are you sure about your answer?
7. Can you give me another answer?
8. I'll give you some time. Think about it.
9. Can someone else give me another answer?

〈発展的表現〉
10. That's not quite right. What other answers can you think of?
11. Is there anyone who has a different answer?
12. I'm afraid your answer is wrong. Come and see me after class, and I'll tell you why it's wrong.
13. Let's see. Can you think of any other answer?
14. Well, I wonder if that [your answer] is right. Why don't we ask someone else what his [her] answer is?
15. Your answer isn't very clear. Can you say it again (in another way)?

**Notes:**　1〜5, 10, 12 ははっきりと誤りを指摘．6〜9, 11, 13〜15 は誤りを間接的に指摘．9, 11, 14 は第3者に正解を求める．12 は教室外の個別指導を含む．15 の say it again は必ずしも repeat と同意ではなく，in another way は「別な言い方で」．

> **Student Response**
> 勘違いする　I'm sorry I was confused. / I think I was mixed up.
> 間違いがわからない　I don't understand why my answer is wrong. / I don't know what's wrong with my answer. Please explain it to me.
> よくわからない　I'm not sure. / I'm not sure if I have another answer.

## イ．小さな[大きな]誤り　Slight [Serious] errors

1. Just a slight error. Say it again.
2. It's only a small mistake. Try again.
3. Don't worry. It's a very small mistake.
4. This is a serious mistake. Correct it.

〈発展的表現〉

5. It's a trivial mistake, but it's important for you to correct it. Can you try again?
6. There are a couple of minor mistakes in your answer. What do you think they are?
7. Can you find the small mistake you made?
8. It's not a hundred percent correct. Is there anyone who can point out the minor error [mistake]?
9. You've made a very serious mistake in your answer. Can you tell me what it is?
10. It's absolutely impossible to understand what you are saying. You must say it [do it (over)] again.
11. I see a very serious mistake in this answer. I want someone to explain what's wrong and why it's wrong.

**Notes:**　1～3, 5～8は小さな誤りの訂正．4, 9～11は大きな誤りの訂正．10の do it (over) again は書く作業について用いられることが多い．over を入れるのは主として米語．

> **Student Response**
> ヒントを求める　Give me a hint. / Tell me what kind of mistake I've made. / Is it a grammatical mistake or spelling mistake?

| | |
|---|---|
| 考える | Let me think. / Let me see. / Give me a little time to think. |
| 問題がわからない | I couldn't understand the question. |

## b. 場面ごとの誤りの訂正　Correction in specific skill areas

### ア．音声　Sound

1. That doesn't sound right. Try again.
2. Wait. Look at my mouth and try again. Don't be shy.
3. Please watch how my lips move and repeat after me.
4. Look at my upper teeth. They're touching my lower lip. Say it once more 'vase'.
5. Your /th/ sound isn't correct. Look at my mouth. Say /θ/.
6. No, you didn't pronounce 's' after 'like'. Say it again "Tom likes pop music."

〈発展的表現〉

7. Your /v/ sound is wrong. Put your upper teeth on your lower lip and say /v/. You must feel the lower lip vibrate.
8. You must correct your /l/ sound. The tip of your tongue didn't touch the back of your upper teeth. Say 'a long line' again.
9. Stop. Your /r/ needs correction. Curl the tip of your tongue and don't let it touch any place. Say after me 'a red ribbon'.
10. I didn't hear your /th/ sounds. Did you push your tongue between your front teeth? Say once again "They thought that way."
11. No, you didn't stress the right word. In a sentence, the verb is usually stressed, not the subject. Say once again "I love you."
12. Oh, you accentuated the wrong syllable. The word 'pocket' has the accent on the first syllable. Try again.
13. It isn't a WH-question. So you must raise your voice at the end of the sentence, O.K.? Try again.

   Notes:　基本的指示は説明より口の動きに注目させるもの．(☞ p. 209)

> **Student Response**
> ゆっくり言う　A little more slowly, please. / Could you speak more slowly, please?
> 正しさを確認する　Is this all right? / Is this better? / Am I right?

## イ. 文 法　Grammar

1. No, there's a mistake in your sentence. 'I go, you go, he goes. I swim, you swim,' then what?
2. You forgot something after the word flower. One flower, two flowers and three what?
3. There's one mistake in your sentence. You usually get up at seven in the morning, but ... You eat, you ate, ... You get up, you what?
4. Don't say 'a orange'. It's 'an orange'. Say 'an apple, a banana and an ...'

〈発展的表現〉

5. You forgot about the subject-verb agreement. Add 's' at the end of the verb since the subject is the-third-person singular.
6. Your tense is wrong. 'A while ago' is past. Use the past tense.
7. No, you can't use a perfect tense with adverbs showing a definite time. You must say "He came back two weeks ago."
8. There're two mistakes in the use of prepositions. Open your grammar books to page 36 and read the explanation.
9. Oh, you seem to be repeating the same grammatical mistakes in the subjunctive past. Let's have a quick review of it.

**Notes:**　1〜4 では比較によって誤りに気づかせる．5〜9 は文法用語を用いての訂正．8, 9 は確認のための復習指導を伴う．

> **Student Response**
> わかる　I see. / I understand. / I've got it.
> 用語がわからない　I don't understand what the word subjunctive means. / What does the word subjunctive mean?
> 'it' がわからない　What does this 'it' stand for?

## ウ. 綴り字・句読法　Spelling / Punctuation

1. This is *b*. Don't take *d* for *b*.
2. How about a question mark [period / comma]?
3. Change the first letter of your sentence into a capital letter. You must always start a sentence with a capital letter.
4. Don't start the name of a person or a place with a small letter.
5. I see two spelling mistakes in your sentence. Correct them.
6. The word 'cutting' has two *t*'s. Yours has only one *t*.
7. Your sentence has no period or full stop at the end. Add one.

〈発展的表現〉

8. You've left out [omitted] the apostrophe between *o* and *c* in the word 'o'clock'. Add one [Put it in].
9. You spelled 'headache' and 'lying' incorrectly. Check their spellings in the dictionary.
10. When you begin a paragraph, you must indent the first line. But you didn't.
11. Who can point out a basic punctuation mistake in the first sentence on the board?

**Notes:**　1. Don't take *d* for *b*. は「d を b と間違わないように」. 9 は辞書指導を含む.

---
**Student Response**

辞書がない　I don't have a dictionary today. / I left my dictionary at home. / My dictionary is in the locker. May I go and get it?

書き直す　Let me rewrite the whole sentence. / I'll write it once more.

---

## C.　理解の確認　Checking students' understanding

1. Okay?
2. Right?
3. You see?
4. Do you understand?

5. Do you understand my English?
6. Am I speaking too fast?
7. Do you understand the sentence on the board?
8. Is this clear to you?
9. Oh, you don't understand?

〈発展的表現〉

10. Do you understand what I've said? Are you sure?
11. Well, do you want me to repeat it?
12. Are you following me? Is there anyone who needs my assistance?
13. Are you with me? Anyone who has problems, just let me know.
14. Do you understand what's written on the board?
15. Is there anyone who doesn't understand what's written here?

**Notes:** 5, 6, 10〜13 は話されたことに対する理解の確認．12, 13 は援助も申し出ている．7, 14, 15 は書かれた内容の理解の確認．9 は理解できないことが前提になる．語尾を上げ過ぎると驚きの表現になるので注意すること．

## d. 任意参加を求める　Eliciting students' responses

1. Anyone?
2. Any volunteers?
3. Does anyone want to try?
4. Who wants to try?
5. Now who wants to answer this question?
6. Can anyone come to the board and write the answer?
7. Who can draw a picture of it on the board?
8. I need two volunteers. Does anyone want to try?

〈発展的表現〉

9. I want you to volunteer and give the class a model answer. Is there anyone who wants to try?
10. Now what do you think? Any comments?
11. Who has an opinion about this? Any volunteers?

12. Instead of choosing someone, I want some volunteers. Now who wants to try?
13. Now please practice your skits. I want some of you to volunteer to show them to the rest of class later, O.K.?
14. I want five volunteers to come up to the board and translate the five sentences into English.
15. Is there anyone who wants to read the passage aloud to the class?
16. No one wants to try? Come on. Someone must try.

**Notes:** 1〜4, 12 はどの状況にも用いられる. 9 はモデルとなる答を求める. 6, 7, 14 は板書への, 13 はスキットへの, 15 は音読へのボランティアを促す. 11 は任意に意見を述べることを促す. 16 は任意参加を強く促す.

---
**Student Response**

自信がない　I'm not very confident. / I'm not sure if I can. / I'm afraid I can't do it well.

---

## e. 指名して反応を喚起　Eliciting responses from specific students

### ア. 指名　Naming students

1. Toshio, you try.
2. How about you, Hanako?
3. Will you try, Keiko?
4. Number seven, read page thirty-one aloud, please.
5. All the students in the first row, please come to the front.
6. Toshio, come to the blackboard and write your answer.
7. Keiko, you're going to be Fiona and Kazuo, you'll be Robert. Now, read the dialog together, O.K.?
8. This time everyone on this side of the class, in chorus.

〈発展的表現〉

9. Now let me ask a couple of students to share their answers with the class. Junko first and then Kazuo. Will you try?
10. What do you think? Let's see, Toshio, would you like to say some-

thing [a word]?
11. I want someone to read the paragraph aloud to the class. Well, Satoshi, please.
12. I'm sure all of you have brought your homework. May I ask some of you to show the class what you have done? How about you, Akio?
13. All the students in this row, stand up and read the paragraph in chorus.
14. Since there're no volunteers, I must pick some of you. Yumiko and Haruo, will you two try, please?

**Notes:** 14 は任意の参加者がいないため指名したもの。

**Student Response**
できない　I'm sorry but I can't. / I'm afraid I can't.
忘れる　I'm sorry but I forgot to practice at home. / I forgot to prepare at home. I'm sorry.

## イ．反応を促す　Encouragement
1. Pardon?
2. Excuse me?
3. Once more, please.
4. Will you say it once again?
5. Would you repeat that? More clearly this time, please?
6. Sorry? Try again and a little louder.

〈発展的表現〉
7. Pardon? You speak so softly that I can't hear you. Could you say that again?
8. Sorry? I can hardly hear you. Try again.
9. Excuse me. I couldn't catch that.
10. What did you say? Your voice is hard to hear. Will you try again louder, please?
11. Sorry, we couldn't hear the beginning. Please try again and a little louder this time.

**Notes:** いずれの場合も自信不足で発表の声が小さかったり，誤って答えたとき，聞き返して再度の発表を促す．必ずしも誤答が正答になるとは限らないが，繰り返すことで自己修正できる場合もある．

### ウ．助け舟を出して　Giving help

1. (Student: Tom is er...) Tom is what?
2. (Student: I go home er...) You go home at what time?
3. (Student: I couldn't do the homework, beca...) You couldn't do the homework because of what?
4. (Student: Yesterday I went to...) Well, where did you go yesterday? You went where?

〈発展的表現〉

5. (Student: I think er... I think... er) Yes, you think what? Do you think it's a good idea or a rather poor idea?
6. (Student: People sometimes er... er) People sometimes do what?
7. (Student: The reason is um... er) Why are people against the idea? The reason is that...

**Notes:** 1〜7はすべて発表の途中で詰まっているところにヒントを与え，発言を続けることを促している．生徒の力にあわせてヒントの量を増すとよい．

---
**Student Response**

繰り返して　Please repeat it. / Please say it again. / Excuse me? / I beg your pardon? / Pardon me?

---

### f．無反応の状況で　Dealing with silence

1. Don't be so quiet.
2. Well, say something. Anyone?
3. Why are you so quiet? Speak out.
4. Don't be shy. Raise your hand and say something.
5. Any answer is all right. Just try.
6. Don't be afraid of making mistakes. Go ahead and try.

7. Do you understand what I'm saying? Yes or no?
8. You understand? No? All right. I'll repeat it, more slowly this time.

〈発展的表現〉

9. What's happened? You're so quiet. Do you want me to repeat the question? Yes?
10. Why are you keeping so quiet? Just relax and say freely what you think about it.
11. Well, why do you remain silent? If you don't understand what I'm saying, raise your hands and let me know.
12. Well, is this such a difficult question? You don't have to make a perfect answer, so just try.
13. Do you understand what's written here? If you do, the answer shouldn't be that difficult.
14. Well, you should say something. Let's not [Don't] waste time. Now someone really must try.

**Notes:** 7, 9, 11〜13 は理解の確認をして反応を促す．8 は理解促進のために説明を繰り返す．14 はかなり強い調子で発言を促す．

---
**Student Response**

試みる　All right. I'll try. / Let me try, then.

難しすぎる　It's too difficult for me to try. / I'm sorry but it's a little too difficult for me.

## 11. 学習活動への指示
Directions for Activities

### a. グループワーク  Group work

1. Form groups of four.
2. Practice the conversation in groups of three line by line.
3. Introduce each other using your names.
4. Change roles so that you can practice all the parts.
5. Stand up and say good-bye to your neighbors.
6. Do the exercise on page 21 in groups of three to four.

### b. ペアワーク  Pair work

1. Taking turns, pick up an object and ask its name.
2. In pairs, ask and answer questions about the objects.
3. Try to ask two questions about a picture on page 45 when possible.
4. In pairs, take turns asking and answering questions about your favorite sports.
5. Change partners and ask your questions again.

### c. 聞くこと  Listening

1. Listen twice to the CD, and then circle the correct answer in your handout.
2. I'll play the CD again so that you can check your answers.
3. Listen to the recipe and instructions for making strawberry ice cream.

4. Listen to the CD again and complete the ice cream card.
5. You'll hear a story about Mars, and then you'll get an answer sheet. Fill in the missing information.

## d. 読むこと　Reading

1. Look at the OHP screen. Read the sentences and say T for true and F for false.
2. I'll show you five sentences by an OHP. Tell me which is true or false.
3. I'll set a time limit for your reading task. Complete the task within ten minutes.
4. Work with a partner and find the three keywords of Section One.
5. I want some of you to read the story aloud. Try to read so that you can express your feeling about the story.

**Notes:** OHP は，英語では OHT (Overhead transparency)〈T は TP シートのこと〉というが，使用頻度は高くない．projector のことを簡単に overhead というからである．

## e. 文法　Grammar

1. I'll show you five sentences by an OHP. If you find any mistakes, raise your hand.
2. If you find mistakes in sentences, mark an X next to the sentence.
3. Complete the exercise individually, and then exchange your answers with a partner to check.
4. Fill in the following dialog with WH-questions, and then practice with your partner.
5. There are three descriptions of the picture. Which is correct and which is wrong?

## f. 語 彙　Vocabulary

1. Identify items of clothing you're wearing.
2. Work with a partner, and say the names of the 12 months by turns.
3. You'll see an illustration of a human body. Fill in the blanks in your handout.
4. Tell me the names of the seven days of the week. You can start either from Sunday or from Monday.
5. Look at the pictures, and then match the pictures with the jobs.

## g. 子どもたちの活動　Activities for children.

1. Color these animal drawings with crayons.
2. Color the numbers 1, 3, 5, 7 and 9 green, and the numbers 2, 4, 6, 8 and 10 yellow.
3. I'll say the names of ten animals. Circle the numbers of the animals that I say.
4. Count the children in the picture with me from left to right. Are you ready?
5. Come to the front and point to the pictures that I talk about.

# 授業展開
# Teaching Procedure

第Ⅱ部

# 1. ウォームアップ
Warm-up

## ① 挨拶 Greetings

**a. 挨拶** Greetings

**ア. 普段の挨拶** Informal greetings
1. Good morning, class [everybody / everyone / boys and girls / students].
2. Good afternoon.
3. Hello.
4. Hi there!
5. How are you?
6. How are you doing?
7. How is it going?
8. How are you getting on?
9. How are things (with you)?
10. How are you feeling today?
11. How's everything?
12. How's everyone today?
13. What's new?
14. What's up?
15. Beautiful morning, isn't it?
16. What a lovely morning!
17. Nice day, isn't it?
　〈発展的表現〉
18. I hope you are all okay today.

19. Please ask the student next to you how he or she is doing.
20. How was your lunch?
21. Did you enjoy today's school lunch?

**Notes:** 挨拶はコミュニケーションを始める第一歩である．言葉自体にそれほど意味がなくても，繰り返し毎時間行うことで英語に慣れてくる．How are you? の問いかけに対して，いつも I'm fine. でなく，その時の状況によって "A bit tired." とか "Very sleepy." などの言い方を覚えさせよう．4は教師と生徒が慣れてリラックスした雰囲気のとき．7はくだけた言い方．19は生徒同士の挨拶を促す．20, 21は午後の授業に．

---

**Student Response**

おはようございます　Good morning [Hello], Mr. Suzuki.

元気です，等　I'm fine [all right / so-so / okay / not too bad / not well / not so good / better than yesterday], thanks.

　I feel very well [great / excellent / good / terrific / fantastic / awful / terrible / not so good / better than yesterday].

別に　Nothing much. / Nothing special.（What's new? などの質問に）

先生は？　How are you? / How about you?

---

イ．**休み明けの挨拶**　Greetings after the vacation

1. Hello again, class.
2. Welcome back, everyone!
3. Happy New Year!
4. Nice to see you again.
5. How have you been (doing)?
6. I haven't seen you for a while.
7. Long time no see!
8. How was your vacation?

〈発展的表現〉

9. Are you rested?
10. Does anyone have anything special to say?
11. Ready to get back to work?

12. Well, it's back to studying English again.
13. Let's work hard this term!
14. Are you ready to start the new term?

**Notes:** 3は3学期の初日に．7は親しみやすい［くだけた］言い方（かなり長期にわたって会わなかった場合）．9はイギリス英語．11〜14．さてまた勉強に戻って頑張ろう．同じ休みでも holiday は祝祭日，vacation はある程度まとまった休暇，単なる日曜日は weekend という具合に異なる．

┌─ **Student Response** ─────────────────────
久しぶりです　Nice to see you again.
楽しかった　I had a great holiday [vacation].
もっと休みを　I wish we had more holidays.
└─────────────────────────────────────

## b. 生徒の反応に続けて　Respond to students' greetings

1. I'm fine, too. Thank you.
2. I'm glad to hear that.
3. That's very nice.
4. What's wrong?
5. Sorry to hear that.
6. That's too bad.
7. What a shame [pity]!
8. Anything wrong with you?
9. My goodness!
10. What's the matter with you?
11. Really?
12. Are you?
13. Why is that?
14. What happened?
15. (Did) anything happen?

〈発展的表現〉
16. Don't say that! It's only the beginning of the day. Come on!

17. Can you tell me more about it?
18. Could you explain more?
19. I'm interested. Tell me more.

**Notes:** 1は生徒のHow are you? に対しての返事．2, 3はfine, greatなどに対するコメント．生徒の反応がnegativeのときは4〜9のように同情をもって問い直す．風邪などにはThat's too bad. でよいが，交通事故など重大な事件には7のWhat a shame! などを用いることが多い．9は驚きの気持ちを表すが，よいことについてはあまり使わない．16は朝から眠いと言う生徒を叱咤激励．もっと話を聞きたいときには17〜19のように言う．

---

**Student Response**

誕生日　Today is my birthday.
いいことがあった　Something good happened to me, but it's a secret.
風邪　I have a cold. / I've caught (a) cold. / I've got a cold.
寝不足　I didn't sleep well last night.
宿題をしていない　I didn't do my homework. / I forgot my homework.
勉強のしすぎ　I had to study too much last night.

---

**Interaction**

T: おはよう． Good morning, class.
S: おはようございます，先生． Good morning, Mr. Suzuki.
T: みんな，今日も元気かな．静子，元気か？ I hope you're all okay today. Shizuko, how are you?
S: だめです． Not so good.
T: どうしたんだ． What's the matter?
S: 風邪を引いているんです． I have a cold.
T: 風邪か．それは大変だ．早く直しなさい． Oh, you have a cold. That's too bad. Take good care (of yourself).

## C. 時間　Time

1. What time is it now?
2. What time do you have?

3. Look at the clock!
4. Kenji, will you tell me the time?
5. What time did you get up this morning?
6. What time do you usually leave for school?
7. How long do you usually study [watch TV] at home?
8. How long does it take from your house to school?
9. How much sleep do you get each night?

〈発展的表現〉

10. I left home at 7:50 and got to school at 8:15. How long did it take?
11. Inoue, what time is it by your watch? Oh, my watch is three minutes slow.
12. I'll give you some math problems in English: How many minutes are there in an hour? How many hours in a day?
13. You must've heard the expression 'Time is Money'. What does it mean?
14. A history quiz in English: When [What year] did World War II end? Nineteen what?
15. How long does it take from here to Tokyo by car? If we drive at 80-kilometers an hour and it is 240-kilometers from here to Tokyo..., what's the answer? How many hours does it take?
16. Now it is 3:00 p.m. here. What time is it in London? England is 9 hours behind.

**Notes:** 数字が英語ですらすら出てくるには練習が必要．時間を聞いたりクイズをしたりして数字になじませる普段の努力を．2は生徒が自分の時計を見る．イギリス英語では Have you got the time? となる．3は授業が始まっても着席しない生徒などへ．11の slow は時計が遅れている，進んでいるのは fast. 時間の答え方として，英では「～分前」は to,「～分過ぎ」は past で表す．It is five minutes to [past] six. 米では「～前」は同じく to,「～過ぎ」は after が用いられる．It is five minutes to [after] six.

**Student Response**

答え　It is 10:45 [ten forty-five / a quarter to eleven]. /

> I went to bed at 12:30 [twelve-thirty / half past twelve]. /
> It takes thirty minutes by bus.
> 数字に弱い　I'm not good at using numbers.

### d.　曜日・月日　Days of the week [month]

1. What day of the week [month] is it today?
2. What day was it yesterday? And tomorrow?
3. What day do you like best? And why?
4. Then what day don't you like? Give me your reasons.
5. At last it's Friday.
6. What's today's date?
7. Today is July (the) seventeenth, two thousand four.
8. Is today the end of June or the first of July?
9. What are your most interesting TV programs [What TV programs do you like most]? And when are they on?

〈発展的表現〉

10. Can you spell the days of the week?
11. Can you write the days of the week on the blackboard?
12. This week seemed very long. What are you doing tomorrow? Any plans?
13. Today is Monday. There is an expression 'Blue Monday'. Do you know why it is 'blue'?
14. Friday's supper is 'fried chicken'. That makes it easier to remember Friday, doesn't it?
15. It is already the first of March! You have only twelve more days to stay in this school.

　Notes:　2で単に what day と言えば普通曜日のことを指す．日付なら date を使う普通．13 の blue は「憂うつな」という意味．14. 食べ物のフライに引っ掛けて．

> **Student Response**
> 土曜が好き　Saturday, of course! I can watch TV all night.
> 嫌いな曜日　I don't like Wednesdays. We have all the difficult subjects then. / Why does Thursday have seven classes? / I'm never happy on Monday.

## e.　自己紹介　Self-introduction

### ア.　教師から　Teacher
1. My name is Ms. [Mrs.] Takano and I'm your new English teacher.
2. Nice to meet you all.
3. I'm glad to meet you, class.
4. How do you do, class?
5. I'll be teaching you English this year.
6. I'll [Let me] introduce myself now.
7. I'll tell you a bit about myself.
8. I've got five lessons a week with you.

〈発展的表現〉
9. I'm happy that I'll be teaching you this year.
10. My name is Matsuki. Matsu is 'pine' in English and ki is 'tree'. So I'm Mr. Pine Tree.
11. My name is Aoki. Please call me Ms. Aoki, not Miss or Mrs.
12. Any questions are welcome. You can ask me anything except my age.

> **Notes:** 相手に自分を知ってもらいたい．この気持ちがないと，ただ言えばいいというような形式的な自己紹介になってしまう．まず教師が自分をアピールして手本を示す．親しみやすく印象に残る教師像で，生徒は英語授業への期待が高まる．2. 初めて会ったときは Nice to meet you. だが，2回目以降会ったときは meet は使わず Nice to see you. がよい．3 の class は「みなさん」で，生徒たちに呼びかけて students と言うことはない．4 の How do you do? は formal (ないしは old-fashioned)で，それだけだと冷たい感じを与える．Nice to meet you. のほうがより自然．

イ． **生徒に自己紹介を促す**　Asking students to introduce themselves
1. Your name, please.
2. May I have your name?
3. What is your name, please?
4. Can you tell us something about yourself?
5. Please tell your name, the name of your school and your hobby.
6. Will you introduce yourself to your neighbor?
7. Please introduce yourself to all of us in one minute.

〈発展的表現〉

8. Let's do it like this, "Hello, my name is Ken. Nice to meet you." And then shake hands. Repeat this with [Please meet] five different classmates.
9. Write down your introduction. Remember these five things.
10. Let's ask him ten questions. Each of you, please think of a question.
11. Ask your neighbor some questions and get the information you need. Later, I want you to introduce your partner [neighbor / him / her] to all of us [the class].
12. When you introduce yourself, don't look down. Look up, smile and be confident.

> **Notes:**　生徒の紹介も先生や全員に向かって話すだけでなく、ゲーム形式や列を移動してパターンを繰り返すなどいろいろな方法が考えられる．9. 質問項目が書かれた紙を見ながら．11 は友人紹介．12 は態度の注意．Student Response で「私の家族は4人です」は four of us が普通の表現で、four people や four members などとあまり言わない．

---

**Student Response**

紹介例　Hello. My name is Akiko Kato. My family and friends call me Aki [My nickname is Aki]. So please call me Aki. I'm from Daiichi Junior High School. There are four of us in my family, father, mother, sister and me. My hobby is reading books. Nice to meet you all.

---
**Interaction**

| | |
|---|---|
| T: さてみなさん。今日は1回目の授業だから自己紹介をしてもらいます。私の名は江口恵美子だから、エクセレント・エミコ。名前の前に姓と同じ文字から始まる語を入れて下さい。 | Listen to me, everybody. This is the first lesson, so I want you to introduce yourselves. Let's do it this way. Choose a word which starts with the same letter as your last name and put it before your first name. My name is Emiko Eguchi, so I am Excellent Emiko. Do you understand? |
| S₁: 私はヤング・ユキコです。よろしく。 | Uh ... I am Young Yukiko. Nice to meet you. |
| T: まあ，ヤング・ユキコね。こちらこそよろしく。 | Great! Young Yukiko! Nice to meet you, too. |
| S₂: ぼくはトール・タツヒコです。 | I am Tall Tatsuhiko. |

---

## ② 出欠・遅刻　Roll Call

### a. 出席の確認　Checking attendance

1. (I'll do the) roll-call.
2. I'll call the roll
3. I'm going to call your names.
4. Let me take the register [roll].
5. When I call your name, please say 'here'.
6. Is everybody here?
7. Anybody absent?
8. No one is absent?
9. Who is absent [missing / not here] today?
10. I'm glad that everyone is here.

11. Let's see if everyone's here.

〈発展的表現〉

12. Have you seen Akira today?
13. What's the matter with Reiko?
14. Where is Sachiko?
15. Does anyone know why she is absent?
16. Was she in the last class? Where is she now?
17. If I say your name incorrectly, please let me know [tell me].

**Notes:** 出席の生徒の返事は Here が一般的，Present はやや formal．英語の授業はそれぞれの生徒が自分の好きな English name をつけて，それで通すのも1つの方法である．

---
**Student Response**

はい　　Here. / Present.
名前が違う　No. My name is Ojima, not Kojima.
保健室　　She went to (see) the nurse.
早退　　　He went back home.

---

## b. 欠席[遅刻]の理由　Reasons for being late [absent]

### ア．欠席の理由　Reasons for being absent

1. Did you have a cold?
2. Have you been ill?
3. Were you sick?
4. Are you okay [all right] now?
5. What was wrong [the matter] with you?
6. I'm glad to see you today.
7. Are you feeling better now?
8. Why were you absent last week?

〈発展的表現〉

9. What happened? You were never absent before.
10. You still look pale. Go to the nurse if you feel sick.

11. I hear you were absent because of your club match. How was it? Did you win?

   **Notes:** 11. 公欠で休んだ生徒に試合結果を聞く.「公欠」という英語はないから,このようにその具体的状況を述べることになる.

   ┌─ **Student Response** ─────────────────────────────
   病気　I had a cold. / I had a stomachache. / I was sick in bed.
   忌引　It was my grandmother's funeral.
   公欠　Our basketball team had a game. / I took the entrance exam.
   └──────────────────────────────────────────

**イ．遅刻の理由**　Reasons for being late
1. Where have you been?
2. Why so late?
3. Why are you late?
4. How come you were so late today?
5. Tell me why you are late.
6. What happened to you?
7. What's the matter?
8. What made you come so late?
9. Have you just arrived?
10. Is your watch correct [okay]?

〈発展的表現〉
11. Did you oversleep [miss the bus]?
12. Is anything wrong (with you)?
13. Is anything the matter with you?
14. We started fifteen minutes ago. What have you been doing?

   **Notes:**　教師のほうから遅刻理由を追及するより,生徒が I'm sorry to be late. のあとに簡単な英語で理由をつけるという約束を新学期の段階で確認しておいたほうが,両者にとって気持ちがよい.

   ┌─ **Student Response** ─────────────────────────────
   ベルが聞こえなかった　I'm sorry I didn't hear the bell. / I forgot the time.

> 寝坊　I got up late this morning. / I got up at eight.
> バスに乗り遅れ　I missed the bus.
> 先生に呼ばれて　I had to see my homeroom teacher.

## ウ．注 意　Admonishing

1. Never again.
2. Don't be late (ever) again.
3. Be here on time. Okay?
4. Hurry up and sit down. We've already started.
5. Don't let it happen again.
6. This is your last chance.
7. Oh, that's too bad. Are you all right now?
8. That's all right. You couldn't help it.
9. Never mind. It can happen to anyone.

〈発展的表現〉

10. Don't sit down without apologizing.
11. Class starts at 8:50. Not 9:00!
12. Please apologize before you go to your seat.
13. Make sure it won't happen again.
14. You again! This is the second time this week. Come (and) see me after class.

> **Notes:**　1は例えば生徒が I promise, never again. などと言ったことに対する言葉で，しばしば人差し指を立てて前に振るなどの動作がつくことを想定している．6．おどしをきかせて．7〜9は生徒が仕方なく遅刻したとき．10はかなりきつい叱責になる．14．怒りを爆発させて．

> **Student Response**
> すみません　I'm sorry. / I'll never be late again. / I promise.
> 僕のせいじゃない　It's not my fault.

## C. 健康チェック　Showing concern about students' well-being

1. How's everyone (today)?
2. Many people have colds. Take care.
3. Take care. There's a cold going around.
4. Are you all well this morning?
5. Takeo is still absent today. Does he have a cold?
6. You look pale. Are you all right?
7. Oh, you're back. That's good. Are you feeling better now?
8. You were absent yesterday. Have you been ill? [Was anything wrong?]
9. You look flushed [You're sweating]. Did you have PE (class)?

〈発展的表現〉

10. You all look sleepy. It's not bed time. Wake up, class!
11. You had better go to the nurse. Susumu, will you go with him?
12. The flu is going around. Be careful.
13. What's the matter? Why (do you have) that bandage? Did you get hurt?
14. Keep yourself warm. That's the best thing to do when you have a cold.
15. What time did you go to bed? Oh, so late. No wonder you're sleepy. You should have [get] at least seven hours of sleep a night.

**Notes:**　米では I am sick. が一般的であり，I am ill. は少し formal に聞こえる．英では ill の方が一般的で，sick というと「吐きそうな」というニュアンスがある．I don't feel well. は気分が悪いときに．7, 8 は欠席後に出てきた生徒に．9. PE = Physical Education. 12. インフルエンザがはやっている．14 は風邪をひいている生徒に．

---
**Student Response**

大丈夫　I'm all right. / No problem. / Never mind. / That's okay.
だいたいよい　I don't feel very well, but it's okay.

## ③ 天 候  Weather

### a. 晴 れ  Fine

1. Nice day, isn't it?
2. It's [The weather is] fine today, isn't it?
3. It's such a beautiful day!
4. What a sunny day!
5. It's a great day!
6. Look at that blue sky. No clouds at all!
7. Isn't it a beautiful season? I really love spring.
8. I'm glad to see the sun at last.

〈発展的表現〉

9. It's nicer today than yesterday. I hope it stays this way.
10. The weather changes very quickly. What was it like yesterday?
11. We can see Mt. Fuji clearly today.
12. Is it too bright? Should we draw the curtains?
13. I don't feel like staying inside. How about you?
14. Such a fine day! It seems a shame to stay inside and study, doesn't it?

**Notes:** 天気について話すことは自然な日常生活の一部である．天候や季節の移り変わりを話題にしよう．8 は長く続いた雨のあとで．12 窓側の席に座っている生徒に．13, 14. こんないい天気の日に部屋の中にいるのは惜しい．

**Student Response**

外へ出よう　Let's go outside. / Let's not study today. / We want to play softball. / Let's take a walk.

まぶしくて　I can't see the blackboard. It's too bright.

## b. 曇り  Cloudy

1. It's cloudy today.
2. I'm afraid it will rain soon.
3. What a gloomy [gray] day!
4. Look at the sky. What a big black cloud!
5. It's getting darker. Will you turn on the lights?
6. Look at that mountain. The top is covered with snow.

〈発展的表現〉

7. Did you bring your umbrellas? What does [did] the weather forecast say?
8. The weather forecast says 'cloudy, fine later'. I guess that's not so bad.
9. This week has been very cloudy. We [I] haven't seen the sun for some time [for ages].
10. November is always just like this. Gray, gray every day.
11. The clouds are moving fast, aren't they? The wind must be strong today.
12. Have you seen clouds from an airplane? They're pretty. And it's also fun to go through clouds.

**Notes:** 3. なんとうっとうしい日だろう. 7. 天気予報が新聞なら does であろうし, テレビやラジオの報道なら did になる. 10. 11月は毎日が灰色の天気. 12. 天候に関連して簡単な英語で話題を提供する.

## c. 雨  Rainy

1. It's raining.
2. It's rainy today.
3. It looks like rain.
4. It has started to rain.
5. It's pouring rain [pouring down].

6. It's raining again today. I'm so tired of rain.
7. Another wet day! How long will it last?
8. Did you know that we had a heavy rain last night?

〈発展的表現〉

9. It's raining very hard. In English we [they] say [there's an expression] "It's raining cats and dogs."
10. The rainy season has finally set in.
11. I love the sound of rain. It makes me feel calm [relaxed]. How about you?
12. The weather is so boring with all this rain.
13. I'm afraid the baseball games will be canceled because of the rain.
14. Tomorrow is our hiking day. Let's hope the rain will stop soon.
15. What a terrible typhoon last night! I couldn't sleep at all.
16. Rain? It is just a shower [sprinkle]. It will be fine [clear up] soon.
17. Have you heard of 'Acid Rain'? It is a big problem now, because it destroys the trees.

**Notes:** 5, 9 は共に激しく降っているときに．ただ rain cats and dogs という表現は日本語の「土砂降り」というほどには使われていないから注意．7. また雨か，とうんざりしたように．10. 梅雨の季節に入った．12. うっとうしい天気．16. 天気雨だからすぐ晴れる．17. 酸性雨についてふれる．環境問題など世界で起こっていることに関心を持たせる．(☞ p. 318)

―― **Interaction** ――

| | |
|---|---|
| S: わっ，虹！ | *Wa! Niji!* |
| T: ほんと？ すごくきれいだね．英語で虹ってどう言うか知っていますか． | Is it? Wow! How beautiful! It's so clear. Do you know the English word for 'Niji'? |
| S: レー… | Re... |
| T: そう，レインボウですね．虹の色全部を英語で言える？ | Yes, rainbow. Can you say all its colors? |
| S: 青, 赤, 緑, 黄色, オレンジ…？ | Blue, red, green, yellow, orange...? |

## d. 暖かい  Warm

1. It's warm today.
2. It's getting warmer.
3. It's nice weather, isn't it?
4. It's much warmer than yesterday.
5. Spring has come. I really like spring.
6. Today it's warm and comfortable. I'm afraid you'll get sleepy [fall asleep].

〈発展的表現〉

7. It's warm today. But the weather changes quickly. Be careful not to catch cold.
8. I'm glad that this winter is mild.
9. Look outside. The cherry blossoms are beginning to bloom [in full bloom].
10. The classroom is nice and warm [comfortable]. It's great to have a heater finally.
11. Have you been to view cherry blossoms or 'Hanami'? Maybe this Sunday will be the last chance.
12. It's too warm in this room. Let's turn the heater off [down].
13. If those of you around the stove are too warm, why don't you move back a little?
14. The warm and comfortable seasons are always really short. Soon it will be very hot.

**Notes:** 7. 季節の変わり目は天気も不安定. 13. ストーブのそばの席の生徒に.

---
**Student Response**

眠くなる  I'm getting sleepy.
気持ちがよすぎる  The weather is too comfortable.

## e. 暑い Hot

1. It's very [a little / terribly / awfully / boiling] hot today.
2. It's really hot!
3. Why is it so hot every day?
4. Another hot day, isn't it?
5. It's getting hotter every day.
6. Your face is red. Are you too hot?

〈発展的表現〉

7. Wow! You are all sweaty [sweating all over]. Was your last lesson PE?
8. It's hot in here. Would you draw the curtains [let the blinds down / open the windows], please?
9. Won't you open the window? Nice breeze! It feels good.
10. Maybe your writing pad is a good fan. But please don't use it as one in class.
11. This summer was terribly hot, wasn't it? Did you go swimming a lot?
12. Is the heat really bothering you? I don't mind the heat.

**Notes:** 1. boiling は焼けつくような暑さ. 3, 4. 毎日暑くてうんざりだ. 7 は体育の授業のあと, もしそうでなければ What's the matter? と聞く. 10 は下敷きをうちわ代わりに使っている生徒に向かって. 12. そんなに暑いの？

---
**Student Response**

勉強できない　I can't study. / It's too hot (to study).
夏バテです　I can't cope with the summer heat.
体育の授業だったんです　We had PE. / The last class was PE.

---
**Interaction**

T: 今日も暑いね.　　　　　　Another hot day, isn't it?
S: ほんと, 勉強できないよ.　Yes! I don't want to study. It's too
　　この暑さじゃ.　　　　　　hot.

| | |
|---|---|
| T: わかってる，わかってる．でも，もうすぐ夏休みが始まるじゃないか． | I know, I know. But the summer vacation is coming soon. |
| S: だけどその前に期末テストがある． | But the term exams are before that! |
| T: そりゃそうだ．嫌でもやらなくちゃいけない．だってそれが生徒の本分だもの． | Of course. You can't help it. Don't forget. Studying is your job! |

## f. 蒸し暑い　Humid

1. It's very warm [sticky].
2. What a muggy day!
3. It's hot and humid.
4. Why is it so muggy today?
5. You all look so hot and sweaty.

〈発展的表現〉

6. It's very hot [stuffy] in this room. Won't you open the windows?
7. It's rainy and humid every day. I don't like the rainy season. How about you?
8. I don't mind the heat itself. But the humidity is too much for me.
9. I know it's hot and humid, but we must continue the lesson.
10. It's no use complaining about the heat. Let's get started.

**Notes:**　8. 蒸し蒸しするのは我慢できない．10. 天候に文句を言ってもしょうがない．

---
**Student Response**

もうだめ　I have no energy to study. / Give me [us] a break. / I can't study.
---

## g. 寒い　Cold

1. It's cold today.
2. It's freezing cold.
3. It sure is cold this morning.
4. It's cool and crisp.
5. It's getting colder every day.
6. It's sunny outside, but it's chilly.
7. It's so cold you can see your breath.

〈発展的表現〉

8. What is the temperature? Look at the thermometer.
9. You look pale. Are you cold? Wear your jacket and keep warm.
10. Don't you think it's cold in here? Would you mind turning up that heater?
11. I wish we had a heater on now. It's too bad we can't use a heater [have to wait] until December.
12. It's very drafty in here. Would you close the windows tightly?
13. Do you know this morning's temperature? It was one degree Celsius [centigrade]. It's the lowest of the year.
14. I don't like cold weather. I'm looking forward to the spring. How about you?
15. Something is wrong with the heater. It's not getting warm.

> Notes:　2. 凍えるような寒さ．freezing は中学校では難であるが冷蔵庫の連想で理解できるであろう．4 は身が引き締まるようなさわやかさ．6. 戸外は晴れていてもまだ寒い．7. 英語では「吐く息が白い」と言わないので注意．中学生には breath は動作で示す．12 の drafty はすきま風が入って寒い．(☞ p. 323)

> **Student Response**
>
> 暖房はいつ？　When will we get a heater [stove]?
> 先生はいいな，暖房が入って　You have heaters on in the teachers' room. Why don't we have them on?

## h. 霜・氷　Frost / Ice

1. The season's first ice. (凍りついた窓外を指して)
2. Did you see the frost this morning?
3. There was a heavy frost last night.
4. Poor plants! It's because of the frost.
5. Look at the window. It's white with frost.
6. Did you notice the school pond is frozen?

〈発展的表現〉

7. Do you know the English word for 'tsurara'? It's 'icicle'.
8. It was very cold this morning. The temperature was two degrees below zero. No wonder we had frost.
9. This morning is very cold. But I think it will get warmer later.
10. The roads were [The ice made the road] very slippery. Did you fall down on the way to school?
11. Last night was very cold. This morning the pipes were frozen and we had no water. How about at your house?

　Notes:　1は初雪・初霜の決まり文句，isn't it? をつけて生徒の反応を見てもいい．4.霜枯れを起こした植物を見て．because of の表現が難しければ The frost killed it. とする．

## i. 雪　Snow

1. It's snowing fast [heavily / a little / lightly].
2. Look outside! Snow!
3. Look at the snow falling. How beautiful!
4. Snow, snow every day.
5. What a blizzard!
6. What a snowstorm!
7. How deep is the snow?
8. It has been snowing for three days [since Monday].

〈発展的表現〉
9. There was a heavy snowfall last night.
10. We've had much [a lot of] snow this year.
11. Have you ever skied before? It's the best way to enjoy the snow.
12. Which has more snow, here or in your town?
13. I'm worried about my car. Can I go (back) home safely?
14. It's no wonder the rain has turned into snow. It's so cold.
15. Do you help your parents (to) shovel [clear] away the snow?
16. Did you have a snowball fight after school [during lunch break]?
17. I spent all the day clearing snow from the roof of my house yesterday. How about you?

**Notes:** 5, 6は風まじりの激しい吹雪. 13は積雪で駐車中の自動車が大丈夫か，道路は車で通行可能かなどの状況. 15. 雪かき. 16は雪合戦. 17.「雪下ろし」に相当する単語はなく，道路も屋根も同じ「雪かき」の表現でいい．

## ④ 前日等の話題　Topics of the Preceding Day [Week]

### a. 普段の生活　Everyday life

**ア．家庭生活　Home**
1. What time do you usually go to bed [get up]?
2. What did you have for breakfast this morning?
3. Tell me what you did yesterday.
4. What is your hobby?
5. What do you usually do on Sundays?
6. Do you have a pet? What kind of animal is it?
7. Do you help your parents at home? What do you do?

〈発展的表現〉
8. I want you to ask your neighbor what TV program he or she likes.

9. Oh, you had your hair cut. It looks nice. I like it.
10. Did you see that movie last night, too? How did you like it?
11. Can you cook? What can you cook? Curry and rice?
12. What instrument can you play? Piano? I wish I could play it, too.
13. Some people like dogs and other people like cats better. I'm curious about who likes which. Those (of you) who like dogs more, please raise your hand(s).

**Notes:** 楽しい話題を選んでくつろいだ話が英語でできると,教師と生徒の間に信頼関係(rapport)が生まれる.教師が自分の個人的な話をわかりやすい英語で話すと生徒は興味をもって聞く.13. このように教師の英語をただ聞き流すのではなく,生徒の反応を求めるような場面を取り入れるようにしたい.

---
**Student Response**
趣味　My hobby is baseball [reading, etc.]. / I like sports [doing sports].
いつか〜したい　I wish to travel [climb mountains, etc.] someday.

---

### イ. 学校生活　School life

1. How do you come to school?
2. What subject do you like most [best]?
3. Then what subject don't you like? Why?
4. Who is your homeroom teacher?
5. What junior high school did you go to?
6. What club do you belong to? Do you enjoy it?

〈発展的表現〉

7. Do you have club activities on Sunday?
8. Where did you go for the game?
9. How many students are there in your club?
10. Do you make your own lunch?
11. How do you spend your lunch break?

**Notes:** 6〜9. クラブ活動についての話題.勉強が苦手でも,クラブで一生懸命やっていることを誇りにしている生徒は結構多い.生徒の好きな話題を出してコミュニケーションを図る.

> **Student Response**
>
> 好きな科目　I like Japanese [math, etc.].
> 不得意科目　I don't like math, because it's too difficult [complicated / boring / not interesting].

## ウ．社会生活　Social life

1. Do you read the newspaper every day?
2. Did you read today's newspaper?
3. I have a newspaper here. I'll read an interesting article to you.
4. What news [current events] are you interested in?

〈発展的表現〉

5. There was a car accident last night near my house. It was terrible.
6. Are you interested in today's horoscopes? I'll read them to you.
7. This is (a copy of) *TIME* magazine. Who is the person on the cover?
8. There's a very interesting movie playing. The title is . . . Has anyone seen it?
9. Did you watch the NHK documentary last night? It was a very interesting program.
10. I'm very happy this morning. The Giants won! I'm sorry, Kenji. You don't like the Giants, do you?

> **Notes:**　4. news は新聞やテレビでのニュースであり，current events と言うと社会で起こっている出来事など広い意味．6. 今日の星占いを読んであげる．7は雑誌 *TIME* を手にして．

> **Student Response**
>
> 新聞　I always [sometimes / never] read a newspaper.
> 私の運勢は？　I am a Leo. Is my fortune [horoscope] good today?
> 雑誌を見せて　Let me see the magazine. / Please pass the magazine.

---
**Interaction**

T: ここに写真が1枚あります．みんなに見てもらいたい．　　I have a picture here. I want you to look at it.

| | |
|---|---|
| S: ワー，ひどい，かわいそうに！ | Oh, that's terrible! Poor children! |
| T: そう．飢えている子どもたちです．Starving というのは食べ物がないことです．死んでしまう子も多いのです． | Yes. They are starving children. Starving means having no food. Many children starve to death. |
| S: この写真，アフリカですか． | Is it in Africa? |
| T: ええ．でも世界中に飢えた子どもがいるんです． | Yes. But there are many starving children in the rest of the world, too. |

## b. 週の始め・休暇明け　Earlier part of the week

1. How was your weekend [holiday]?
2. Did you have a good weekend [enjoy your weekend]?
3. How did you spend your vacation [holiday(s) / weekend]?
4. What did you do over the weekend?
5. Did you go out or stay at home yesterday?
6. Do you usually stay with your family or go out with friends?

〈発展的表現〉

7. Make a one-minute speech on [about] how you spent the 'Golden Week'.
8. Won't you tell us the most interesting thing about your vacation?
9. You look refreshed from your holiday(s).
10. You're all suntanned! You seem to have grown a little.
11. Did you go skiing or skating? Where did you go? Who did you go with?
12. You went to Australia this summer. How exciting! How was it? Tell us a little about it.

**Notes:** 7. the Golden Week はもちろん日本人にだけ通用する英語であるが，固有名詞としてかなり確立しているので，教室英語としてはいちいち a week of consecutive national holidays と言う必要はない．10. 2学期開始日，日

焼けして成長したように見える生徒を目の前にして．12．休暇中に海外体験をした生徒は，以前に比べてずっとオープンな態度を身につけていることが多い．そういった態度を授業で出せるように工夫したい．(☞ p.315)

---
**Student Response**

スピーチ例　During the vacation I came to school every day, because our brass band club had a contest. I didn't have time to swim. But during *Obon*, I went to a hot spring with my family. And I had a good time.

---

## c. 週の終わり頃　Latter part of the week

1. Tomorrow is a holiday.
2. This week was very long, wasn't it?
3. What will you do tomorrow?
4. How was this week for you?
5. What are you doing tonight?
6. Will you go out or rest at home all day tomorrow?
7. You've been waiting for Saturday, haven't you?　Me, too.

〈発展的表現〉

8. You must be tired (now), because this is the first week of school.
9. Oh, you'll have the club activities tomorrow. You sure practice a lot!
10. Tomorrow is Saturday. But you have a practice exam. I'm sorry about it. Good luck!
11. Today is the last class of the week. Let's relax and listen to an English song.
12. You've studied very hard this week. So today I want you to enjoy a game.

　　Notes:　10．明日は土曜だが模擬試験がある．日本人教師は Do your best. と言いたくなるところ．11, 12．週の最後の授業では，英語の歌を聞いたり英語のゲームをするなど，楽しみを用意するのも1週間の区切りとしてよい．Student Response の Thank God, it's Friday. は学生仲間でよく T.G.I.F. と略されることがある．

**Student Response**

疲れた　I'm tired [exhausted]. / I have no more energy (left).
やっと金曜　Friday at last! / Thank God, it's Friday!
宿題なんてやめてくれ　No homework, please.

## 2. 復　習
### Review

### ① 宿題の提出　Handing-in Homework

**a. 係が集める**　Students in charge of collecting

1. Now, homework.（係に集めるように身ぶりで示す）
2. All your homework to Emi-san. Hurry up.
3. Hand in your assignment to Sachiko-san.
4. Have all of you handed in your sheets to Motoru-kun?
5. Who collects homework? Start collecting right now.
6. Who is in charge of (collecting) homework [the assignment] today?
7. Those who are in charge of homework, gather everyone's papers.
8. Who's going to collect homework? Is it you, Yoko? Pass your papers to her, please.

〈発展的表現〉

9. Are you ready with your homework? Give it to the student who is to collect them.
10. Hand in your home tasks to the group in charge of them.
11. You didn't forget your assignment, did you? If you forgot it, say so to the student on assignment duty.
12. The persons who forgot homework, go to Noboru and tell him your registration numbers and your names.
13. Open your notebooks to [at] the pages on which you did your work. The students in charge of homework will collect them. Are you ready?

**Notes:** 2〜4 の名前は宿題係．英語には「〜係」に相当する単語がない．中学校レベルでは "homework" students と言うのもやむを得ないであろう．11, 12 は集配係に忘れたものをチェックさせるとき．13 で open . . . to は米語的で，open . . . at はイギリス英語的な表現．

> **Student Response**
> 係は誰？ Who is in charge? / Who takes charge of collecting homework?
> (係が教師に)いつ集めるの？ Should we collect homework now or later? / Tell us when we should bring homework to you.

## b. 列ごとに集める　Collecting by row

1. Pass them [it] in. (手の動きで指示)
2. Pass the papers forward.
3. Pass your homework up to the front.
4. The students in the front seats of each row, collect the [today's] homework.
5. Hand in your papers [work sheets] to the person in front of you.
6. Don't leave your seat. Just pass it to the person in front of you.
7. The students at the back will collect the assignment.
8. Those at the end of each row, will you please stand up and collect the notebooks?

〈発展的表現〉

9. Pass your sheets from back to front. But don't look at others' when you pass them in.
10. The first person in each row, please count the number of task papers. And check who handed in and who didn't.
11. Are you ready with your homework? Put it on the right side of your desk. Then pass it to the front.
12. Before you pass in the task sheets [pass your sheets forward], don't forget to write your names on them.

**Notes:** 1〜4が一般的な言い方．7, 8は最後尾の生徒が集める．10は最前列の生徒に数をチェックさせるとき．11は置き場所の指示．12は記名の確認．

> **Student Response**
> 欠席者の分は？ Can we skip Masao's? He is absent today. / Masashi is in the health room now. What shall we do about his homework?

## C. 教卓に出す　Bringing homework to the teacher's desk

1. (Put it) here on my desk.
2. Come and put your assignment on my desk.
3. Leave your work here.
4. Place your homework on that table.
5. Everyone, come and show your notebooks to me.
6. Come and put your notebooks here group by group.

〈発展的表現〉

7. Put your homework on this desk in the order of your registration numbers.
8. Bring your notebooks and place them on my desk neat and tidy.
9. Boys, bring your home tasks [notebooks] here. Girls, take them over there.
10. Everyone, come here with your notebooks and line up. I'll check all of them.
11. I want to look at what you did individually. Come and [to] see me with your homework sheet one by one.
12. Look. The notebooks are heaped [piled] up on that desk. You all put your assignment there, didn't you? But what a mess! Takashi, arrange them in some sort of order.

**Notes:** 1は宿題を集めているという明確な状況の中で．2が一般的な言い方．10, 11は1人1人点検したいとき．

## d. 授業後に提出　Handing in after the class is over

1. Give it to me after class.
2. Put your homework on that desk after class.
3. Hand in your assignment as you leave.
4. Leave your papers here as you go out of the room.
5. I'd like to collect your homework when the class is over.
6. Before you leave, you must hand in your papers to me.

〈発展的表現〉

7. Have you handed in your papers? If not, come with them [bring] to the office after class.
8. I don't want your homework now. I want it after class. Don't forget [Be sure] to write your name on it.
9. You are supposed to have finished your homework. I want you to pass it up to me after class.
10. All of you have done the assignment. I'm so glad. Will you turn it in at the end of the class?
11. At the end of the class, the student in charge of homework will collect your homework.

**Notes:** 3, 4 の as が中学生に難しければ，when, before などを用いる．11 は係を使って集めたいとき．

---
**Student Response**

忘れたんだけど　I forgot my paper. Can I hand it in tomorrow? / I have not done the homework yet. May I bring it later to your room?

---

## ② 宿題の発表　Presentation and Checking of Homework

### a.　口頭で　Orally

1. Tell me what you did.
2. Tell us your answers to the questions (for the homework), Masashi.
3. Stand up and say what you wrote for the assignment.
4. Come here and read aloud the answers (for the homework).
5. I want to hear you read what you've done, Hiroyuki.
6. Who will be the first person to read out the sentences?
7. Let's take turns to read aloud what you have written.

〈発展的表現〉

8. If there are any questions you could not answer on this sheet, tell me.
9. Did you read these five sentences ten times at home? Now, show me [Let me hear] the result of your practice, Kenji.
10. There are ten blanks on the homework (sheet). Did you all fill in the blanks? What word is the most suitable for blank 1, Mie?
11. We have ten short compositions in this worksheet. Could you [Were you able to] translate them orally into English?
12. You made as many sentences about your family as you could, didn't you? Now tell them to us.
13. You three practiced this drama very well. You did a good job. Now, come and act it (out) in front of everyone.

**Notes:**　7は次から次へと発表させたいとき．8は宿題について不明な箇所は質問するように促す．9は音読練習の発表．10は穴埋め問題の発表．11は英作文をまず口頭で発表させるとき．12は自由作文の発表．13は英語劇の発表．

**Student Response**

今ここで言うのですか？　Shall I read it right now? / When and where

should I tell my answer?
そこだけやってない　I could answer all the other questions, but this is the only one I could not answer. / Will you give me more time to answer the question?
発音は？　How do you say b-u-s-y in English? / Please tell me the pronunciation of this word.

## b. 板書で　On the (black)board

1. Write it here.
2. Write it next to [below] answer No. 1.
3. Take a piece of chalk and write the answer there.
4. Here's a piece of chalk. Write it up there [here].
5. Come and write what you prepared at home on the board.
6. I'll show you the answers [examples] on the board.

〈発展的表現〉

7. I'll write the correct answers to the homework here.
8. Tomoko and Yumiko showed us good examples. But are there any mistakes in them?
9. Let's look at the sentences they have written. Can you see anything wrong with them?
10. You made a fine composition. I want to show it to others [share it with others]. Will you write it up on the board?
11. Ken, your homework is done very well. You don't mind writing it on the board, do you?
12. Yuka and Yuta showed us good examples on the board. Now, compare Yuka's sentence with Yuta's. Both are O.K. in grammar, but Yuka's is more English-like [natural in English].

**Notes:**　6, 7 は教師が宿題の正答を板書で示す場合．8〜12 は生徒が宿題でやってきたものを板書を通して解説したいとき．（☞ p. 194）

> **Student Response**
>
> 見えません　I can't see those letters. / Please write in much larger letters. / How did you spell it? Write it more clearly.
>
> 間違ってますよ　There is a mistake in answer No. 3. / You'd better add 'e' at the end. / I am afraid there is something wrong with sentence No. 4.

### c. OHP で　By an overhead projector

1. Let's do it with the OHP.
2. Here's a felt-tip pen [marker]. Come and write down your answer.
3. Come here and write it on the transparency. Use this pen.
4. Will you show us what you did on [by using] the overhead projector?
5. Junko, look at the screen carefully. You left something out.
6. Thank you for showing your homework on the screen.
7. Look at the OHP screen again. There is something missing, isn't there?

〈発展的表現〉

8. Mayumi, Mie, Takeshi and Akira, come here. Write your answer to question No.1 on this transparency. You can use these felt-tip pens.
9. I'll give each of you a small transparency. The people [students] in this row, write the answers to question No.1. And this row, No. 2 ... Then pass it (back) to me.
10. There are five small pieces of transparency on the screen. Osamu, rearrange them into a meaningful sentence. You did this as homework.

> **Notes:**　9 は宿題の解答を各自に OHP シートの小片に書かせ，それを提示するとき．10 は宿題として出した整序問題を OHP シートの小片を使って解答するとき．(☞ p. 272)

> **Student Response**
> 見えません　I can't see the bottom of the screen. / Will you put the screen up a little higher? / Please draw the curtains.

## d. 隣の人と宿題チェック
Checking with neighbors each other's homework

1. Check the answers with your friend.
2. Exchange your homework sheets with your neighbors.
3. Check for errors in your neighbor's assignment(s).
4. Ask your neighbors to look [go] over your compositions.
5. Work in twos [pairs] and show your sheets to each other.
6. How about working in pairs? Let's check each other's compositions.

〈発展的表現〉

7. You prepared a skit, using 'have [has] + p.p.'? Now, try it with your neighbors.
8. As homework, you had to put ten Japanese sentences into English sentences. Make a comparison [Compare] between yours and your neighbors'.
9. Did all of you write a speech on air pollution? Now, make the speech to your neighbor. If you have some errors, check them with each other.
10. You made interesting speeches about the environment. First, try them with your partners. Then make corrections and comments for each other.

> **Notes:**　1. 普通はこれで隣席の friend と十分わかる．7 はスキットを隣とやってみる場合．p.p. = past perfect（過去分詞）．8 は英作文を隣と比較するとき．9, 10 はスピーチをまず隣とやらせるとき．Interaction の「3人で」は in threes が普通．

> ──────── **Interaction** ────────
> T: 宿題の答えを発表します．　Now, I'll show you the answers to

| | |
|---|---|
| 宿題の紙を隣の人と交換して．<br>S：チョット待ってください．隣が欠席なんです．<br>T：3人で交換して．さて1番の答えはこれです． | the homework. Exchange the papers with your neighbors.<br>Wait a moment, please. My partner is absent.<br>I see. Do it in threes [trios]. Are you ready? Now, No.1, the answer is this. |

## ③ 暗唱文の確認　Checking Memorized Key Sentences

### a.　口頭英作文として　As an oral composition

1. Say it in English.
2. Let's do some oral practice.
3. Let's practice it orally.
4. Change the sentence into English. Say it.
5. Ask your neighbor to read out the sentence.
6. Who will be the first to say the target sentence?
7. Let's change the key sentence slightly and say it.

〈発展的表現〉

8. Look at the board. This was the target sentence, you know. Now, change it and say 'to the garden' instead of 'to school'.
9. Listen to this sentence, "Have you ever eaten with your fingers?" Can you repeat it with your eyes closed?
10. Now, without looking at anything, say the key sentence of Page 10 to yourselves.
11. This is the target sentence of the previous class. I'm going to rub off [erase] some words. Can you still say the sentence?
12. Now, Review Time. Look at this table. You have to make English sentences for what I'll say in Japanese.

13. These are the sentences you have learned by heart at home. Now, turn around, Hiroko. Then, say them aloud.

    **Notes:** 9, 10 は目を閉じて，または教科書，ノート等を見ないで暗唱文を言わせるとき．11 は暗唱文の一部を消して．12 は代入の文型練習として行うとき．13 は後ろを向いて言わせる．

    ─ **Student Response** ─────────────
    出かかってます　Well..., let me see. / The word is on the tip of my tongue. Wait a moment, please.

## b. 対話形式で　In dialog

1. Talk with your friend.
2. Stand up and do the dialog, please.
3. Let's say [practice] it in a dialog.
4. You play Mary's role. I will play Jack's part.
5. Let's do the skit, using the key sentences you have learned.
6. Now, boys, ask the questions. Girls, answer them.

〈発展的表現〉

7. I'd like you to work in twos. One of you, make a question using Key Sentence 1. Others, answer it using Key Sentence 2.
8. In the dialog you made [In your dialog], you have made a good use of the key sentences. So come here and tell it to us.
9. Look at the pictures on the screen. Use the target sentences we learned last time and make some conversations about the pictures.
10. Here is a skit. In this skit, the target sentences you memorized at home are used again and again. Ryuta and Sayaka, try it first.
11. Let's stand up and do *janken*. The winners can order the losers to do the actions. The losers should say, "Okay, I will."

**Notes:** 1〜6 は暗唱文をそのまま対話形式で発表させるとき．7〜11 は暗唱文を発展させて，それをもとに対話練習をさせるとき．

> **Student Response**
> 教科書閉じますか　Textbooks closed? / Should we close our textbooks?
> 開いたままにしたい　I want to look at my textbook.

## c. 1人で　By oneself

1. Read the sentence, Sachiyo.
2. Can you read it by yourself?
3. This row, take turns and read it one by one.
4. Say it again. And try to say it a little faster.
5. What was the target sentence of the last lesson?
6. You have learned the key sentence by heart, haven't you?
7. You have memorized the target sentence. I want to hear you say it again.
8. Don't read it in chorus, class. One person at a time, please.
9. Your voice is too soft. Read it a little louder, please.

〈発展的表現〉

10. That's good. But you forgot the adverb at the end. Try it again.
11. You got 'since' and 'for' mixed up. Do you remember the rule for using 'since' and 'for'?
12. You said, "Do you know when will he come back?" But it is better to say, "Do you know when he will come back?"
13. It sounds nice. But you'd better place your lower lip against your upper teeth softly when you pronounce /f/.

**Notes:** 8は一斉に読もうとするのを遮って、1人ずつ読ませる。11, 12はやや細かい注意。「暗唱文だから正確に覚えさせたい」と思ったとき。(☞ p. 203) 13の it は生徒の発音。

> **Student Response**
> 自信ないけど...　There may be something wrong, but.../ I am not sure of my reading, but...

## d. 意味を考えて　Thinking of the meaning of the sentences

1. Read it and think of the meaning.
2. Read the target sentences, thinking of their meaning.
3. Think what the sentence means and read it aloud.
4. What does this mean? How do you pronounce it? Who will try it?
5. Start reading it after you are sure of its meaning.
6. First, think hard about the meaning. Then, start reading.
7. Do you understand the sentence? Okay. Then read it.

〈発展的表現〉

8. I hate to interrupt your reading, but don't read too fast. Make sure of the meaning.
9. I know you have memorized it. But did you understand the meaning of the words?
10. You did a good job on [with] the oral practice. But are you sure of its meaning?
11. Your reading was fine. But do you know the meaning of this sentence? In short it is something like 'he is a great fan of his teacher'.
12. All of you read very well. But is there anything I should explain further?
13. Is there anything that you want me to explain further [again]?

**Notes:** 1～7は意味を考えながら読むように指示するとき．8～13は一度読んだあとに意味を確かめて，もう一度読ませたいとき．(☞ p. 201)

---
**Student Response**

この単語の意味何でしたっけ？　I forgot the meaning of 'cruel'. / What does 'parent' mean?

---

## e. 気持ちを込めて　Expressing your feeling

1. More emotion, please.

2. Read it with emotion [feeling].
3. Read it much more slowly.
4. Make some gestures when you read it.
5. You should read this part more softly.
6. Express your feelings when you read.
7. With more emotion! Because this is an exclamatory sentence.
8. You'd better express your feelings more strongly. Intonation helps carry your emotions.

〈発展的表現〉

9. Listen to the tape again. The woman on the tape raises her voice at the end of the sentence. Try to do the same.
10. You must let your voice fall at the end of this target sentence. Do as I do.
11. Look at the board. When you read this sentence, you should put the first stress on this word. And the second stress here.
12. How is this sentence used in the text? In this context, it must be read slowly and distinctly.
13. You should think of the situation in which this key sentence is used. Listen to the way my voice goes up.
14. Don't read 'May I ask you a favour?' flat. We use this phrase when we ask someone to do something.

**Notes:** 3は内容を考えないで一気に読んでしまう生徒に．9～14はどのように気持ちを込めるのか，詳しく説明するとき．

---
**Interaction**

| | |
|---|---|
| S： 先生は感情込めろって言うたけど，どうやるの？ | You said we should read it with emotion. But I don't know how. |
| T： 暗唱文をもう一度見て．これは，長崎の原爆の話のなかで使われたよね．だとすると，どの単語が大切なのかな？ | Well, look at the sentence again. It is used in the context of the atomic bomb dropped on Nagasaki. So what words are important? |

| | |
|---|---|
| S：'killed' だと思う. | I think 'killed' is important. |
| T：'killed' だけかな？ | Only 'killed'? |
| S：'thousands' も大切だ. | 'Thousands' is important, too. |
| T：そうだね．それじゃ，この2つの単語を強調して，もう一度読んでみよう． | That's right. Now, try to put stress on these two words and read out the sentence again. |

## ④ 前時のテキスト　Last Lesson

### a. 要約　Summary

1. Tell me what page 23 says.
2. I'll read out the summary of the text in Japanese.
3. Listen to what I'll say in English about the text.
4. Let's look at the passage once again. What does it say?
5. Tell me in your own words what happened.
6. Explain the outline of the text in your own words.
7. Use your own words to describe what happened.
8. Give me a brief summary of it.
9. Can you summarize the text we learned in the last class?
10. Can you give me the main idea of the last lesson?

〈発展的表現〉

11. Let's draw some pictures and explain the outline of the text we read last time.
12. Write down a brief summary of the passage, first. Then give it a short title, within ten words.
13. Do you remember the two main points in the story? What are they?
14. Find the word 'gray'. I said it has a special meaning in this context. Tell me what it is.

15. I picked out three sentences from the passage which summarize the content. But I changed the order of them. Put them into the right order.
16. Look at the last line. You see 'that' there. What does it mean? Write down the answer. This activity will summarize the text.

**Notes:** 11は絵を描いて要約. 12は要約とタイトル. 14はキーワードの確認. 15は文の並べ換えによる要約. 16は代名詞からコンテクストを読み取る活動. (☞ p. 212)

> **Student Response**
> うまく言えません　I can't summarize it well. / Give me more time to summarize.

## b. 主人公の行動　What the characters in the story did

1. What did Lassie do in the last paragraph?
2. Tsu was a crane in fact. When Yohyo found it, what happened?
3. When Laura's Pa came back, what did he say to her?
4. Tom Sawyer didn't go to school that day. Then, where did he go?
5. The text says, "Tom had a good idea." What was it?
6. What did the prince ask the person for on page 45?
7. What was the drunkard ashamed of? Don't you think it's funny?
8. Turn back to page 83. What was Rev. King's main idea?
9. The text says, "No animals live in the Dead Sea." Do you remember why?

〈発展的表現〉

10. Turn back to the previous page. Tell's arrow cut the apple in two. If you were his son, how would you feel [have felt]?
11. Look back at the last paragraph of the previous page. It says "Blind people aren't helpless." This sounds great, doesn't it? Why do you think they aren't helpless?
12. Della sold her rich hair to buy a watch chain for Jim. Jim sold his

gold watch to buy combs for Della. Write in your notebook what you think true love is.

13. To understand Ann, Chin and Kan's feelings better, how about acting them out? Susumu, pretend that you are Kan. You be Chin, Yoko. Then who wants to be Ann?

**Notes:** 1～9は主人公の行動などを確認するとき．10～13は主人公の行動などをどう思うか尋ねるとき．(☞ p. 167)

┌─ **Student Response** ─────────────────────────
私には理解できない　I can't understand the feelings of this person. / Why did he do [say] such a stupid thing?
└──────────────────────────────────────

## C. 対話の理解　Understanding of the dialog

1. What does "What's up?" mean?
2. How do you say "I'm a stranger here" in Japanese?
3. When do you use the phrase "Let me see"?
4. What is another expression for 'by the way'?
5. Give me another phrase that means more or less the same thing.
6. Can you say the same thing as 'in short', using different words?
7. They said, "Go get 'em!" Explain the meaning of this expression.

〈発展的表現〉

8. In this skit, Steve said, "I feel blue." In what sense is the word 'blue' used here?
9. Look back at the conversation on the previous page. There the word 'good' has a special meaning. What's another word that means the same?
10. In this skit, Al answered "Yes, I am." If you were in his position [place], what would you say?
11. In the story Pete said to Anne: "Please laugh, Anne." But Anne said, "Why must I laugh?" Why did she ask such a question?
12. Do you remember that Jiro said, "I wonder what we can do to stop

stupid wars." Everyone agrees. Write down your opinions on "What can we do?"

**Notes:** 1～9 は対話の解釈の確認. 10～12 は対話の内容について生徒の意見を求める場合.

---
**Student Response**

これ口語表現？　Is this spoken English?/Is this used in conversation?

くだけた文に使ってもいいですか　Is it all right to use it in informal sentences?

---

## 3. 導 入
Introduction

### ① 重要構文 Important Constructions

**a. 意 味** Meaning

**ア. 日本語で意味をとらえさせる** Through Japanese
1. Meaning?
2. In Japanese?
3. Put the sentence into Japanese.
4. What does this sentence mean?
5. What is the meaning of this sentence?
6. What does this word stand for?

〈発展的表現〉

7. Can you guess what this sentence means?
8. Tell me in Japanese what this sentence means.
9. How do you say this phrase in Japanese?
10. Can you think of a similar expression in Japanese?
11. Please put this part into Japanese first, and then go on to the next part.

**Notes:** 1〜6は文を読ませたあとですぐにその日本語の意味を問う場合. 9〜11は生徒の発言を援助する場合.

---
**Student Response**

この単語どういう意味だっけ？　What does this word mean? / What is this word (in Japanese)? / What is the meaning of this word?
これが主語でしょ？　This is the subject, isn't it? / Is this the subject? /

I think this is the subject, right?
動詞はどれ？　Which (word) is the verb? / Where is the verb?

## イ．聞いてその文の内容を考えさせる　Listening for meaning

1. Look at this picture, and listen carefully.
2. Who is 'she'? What does she want to do?
3. Does this boy know her?
4. How long have they been good friends?
5. The little girl is crying. Tell me why she is crying.
6. Who is introducing the man to the class?
7. Eric wanted to be a baseball player. When was it?

〈発展的表現〉

8. I'll say two sentences, so listen carefully and tell me the differences between the two.
9. I'm going to say two sentences. There are some differences between them. Listen carefully and say what they are.
10. Listen to the two verbs carefully in the sentences. Tell me all the differences that you hear.
11. You say these sentences are in the past tense. What is a hint for you to say so?
12. This sentence says, "English is a very important language." Do you think so, too? If so, please find some reasons in the second paragraph, and tell me.

**Notes:** 1〜7は絵を提示して推測を助ける場合で，直接的に文の内容が理解される．8,9は既習事項と新出事項とを比較して聞かせ，その違いに気づかせたり，同じ点や相違点を挙げさせる場合．10,11では着目する部分を指示し，文法事項を生徒自身に発見させる．10は文のコンテクストによって動詞の強勢などが違う場合．12は注目させたい文を見つけさせる場合．

**Student Response**

2つ目の文，なんて言ったの　What was the second sentence, please?
日本語で説明してもいいですか　May I use Japanese? / Can I speak

Japanese? / May I explain it in Japanese?

## b. 表現形式　Forms

1. Look at this part carefully.
2. Do you see anything new in the sentence?
3. There must be something different between the two words.
4. Look at the two sentences and compare them carefully.
5. Is everything clear? It contains [There's] one thing I haven't taught you yet.
6. These words all have the same endings. What do they mean?

〈発展的表現〉

7. This *-ed* has something to do with *yesterday* in the sentence.
8. The *-er* adjectives or adverbs are often used together with *than*.
9. See? These two sentences are put together by this *which*.

   **Notes:** 4は2つの文を対比させ，異なる部分に注目させるとき．6は語尾変化に注目させたいとき．7～9は文法など特定のポイントに生徒を注目させるときの具体例である．

## c. 読み方　Oral reading

1. Please read, Junko.
2. Read it again.
3. Read this page, Haruo.
4. Read the fourth line from the top.
5. Read the second line from the bottom.
6. Read it together.
7. Quickly.
8. Quicker. / Louder.
9. Read the sentence quicker.
10. Try to memorize target sentences on this page.

11. Read the sentences to your partner [neighbor].
12. Will you read it louder so that everybody can hear you?
13. Think about their meanings when you read the sentences.
14. Please think about the situation and then read the dialog.
15. First read the sentence silently, then say it aloud from memory [without looking at it].

〈発展的表現〉

16. This dialog is very short, so you can finish reading it with your partner in 20 seconds.
17. You'd better put stress here. Then it'll sound more English-like.
18. Rhythm, stress, and intonation are very important when you read. Listen to the tape again and repeat.
19. Your English sounds like Japanese. Do you know why? You should be careful about using intonation when you read.
20. I'll clap my hands. So put the stress as you hear the claps.
21. Prepositions, pronouns, and conjunctions are usually pronounced quickly and softly.
22. Now practice reading sentence by sentence with your partner until you can say it without looking at the book.

**Notes:** 7〜9は生徒の読み方に注意を促す．quickやloudを副詞として使うのは口語ではきわめて普通である．13, 14は内容や状況を考えて読む．17〜20はリズム，強勢，イントネーションなどに注意させる．(☞ p. 201)

---
**Student Response**

この文が読みにくい　This sentence is rather difficult to read.
語尾がはっきり聞こえない　The last part of the sentence isn't clear.
英語って歌を歌っているみたい　English sounds like a song. / I feel as if I were singing when I read it.
1語1語強く読まないんだ　Usually they don't put stress on each word in English.

## d. 言い換え  Paraphrasing

1. You can also say it this way.
2. Or you can say this, too.
3. The same meaning is expressed in this way, too.
4. The meaning in these two sentences is more or less the same.
5. You can rewrite the sentence into another one with the use of . . . [by using . . . ]

〈発展的表現〉

6. The 'be going to' and 'will' in the two sentences are almost the same in meaning. You can say it either way.
7. These two sentences describe the same scene. But the subjects are different. The second is in 'passive voice'.
8. Yes. The 'must' in the first sentence is changed into 'have to'. Still the meaning is the same.
9. The meaning of the sentence is somewhat similar to 'You had better go'.

**Notes:** これらの構文では，その内容が意味するところをできるだけ既習のやさしい英語で説明してやり，理解させた上で構文を実際に使った表現に慣れさせていく．6〜9 はそうした具体的な例．

---
**Student Response**

will と be going to の違いは？　Is there any difference between 'will' and 'be going to'?

受身にはいつも be 動詞がくるの？　Is 'be verb' always used in the passive voice?

どっちの言い方が普通？　Which is more usual to say? / Which is more common?

意味はどちらも同じですか　Are they really the same in meaning?

**―― Interaction ――**

| | |
|---|---|
| S：昨夜は全然勉強できなかった. | I didn't study at all last night. |
| T：またテレビ？ | Did you watch TV again? |
| S：違う，違う. too sleepy ですよ. | No, no. I was too sleepy. |
| T：おっ！ too 〜 to がわかったね. もう一度言ってごらん. | I'm glad that you understood too 〜 to. Say it again, "You were . . ." |

## ② 演示による導入　Introduction by Demonstration

### a.　教師の動作　By the teacher

1. Listen and look at [watch] me carefully.
2. Do as I do.
3. Follow me like this.
4. What am I doing?
5. Where am I going?
6. What am I looking at?
7. See how my eyes and eyebrows move.
8. See how my arms and legs move.
9. Tell me what I'm [he's / she's / they're] doing.

〈発展的表現〉

10. I'll do [give / make] some gestures. Guess and tell me what I'm doing.
11. I'll tell you an action [what to do] and you'll act.
12. I'll give you directions [commands] and you'll follow them.
13. This time you say the actions and I'll act (them out).
14. Let's say a word and act it out at the same time together.

## 3. 導入

---
**Interaction**

| | |
|---|---|
| S: 先生，なかなかうまいよ． | You are very good at giving gestures. |
| T: ありがとう． | Thank you. |
| S: 進路間違ったんじゃない？ | I'm afraid you have taken the wrong job. |
| T: 俳優になるのは今からでも遅くないか． | Then do I have a chance to be an actress? |
| S: それは甘いね．でもやってみたら． | Well, I think it's pretty hard. But you'd better try. |

---

### b. 生徒の動作　By the student

1. Make a gesture of approval.
2. Give a bigger gesture.
3. Listen to my words and make a gesture quickly.
4. Read the words and act quickly.
5. Hiromi will make an action. Say what she is doing.
6. Say loudly and give big gestures.

〈発展的表現〉

7. Takao will say [give] some actions and all of you must act (them out).

**Notes:** 一般的に「ジェスチャーをする」は give [make] gesture でいいが，修飾語句を伴うときは a gesture of approval（賛同を示すジェスチャー）や a big gesture というように可算名詞として用いることが多い．

### c. 動作の指示　Directing students' actions

1. Please do as I do.
2. Give the same gestures as I do.
3. Touch your head [forehead, etc.].
4. Lift your thumb(s) [forefinger(s), etc.].

5. Look up.
6. Look up at the ceiling.
7. Look at the sky.
8. Look out of the window.
9. Listen and give gestures.
10. Turn your desk and chair around.
11. Tap your partner's right [left] shoulder.
12. Tap your desk.
13. Clap your hands.
14. Pat your partner on the right shoulder.
15. Hold your neighbor's hand.
16. Close [Open] your eyes.

〈発展的表現〉
17. Act like [as if] you are opening [closing] the door softly.
18. Act like [as if] you are cooking in the kitchen.
19. Act like [as if] you are driving a car.
20. Give the gesture of playing tennis [baseball, soccer, etc.].
21. Give the gesture of swimming [skating, golfing, etc.].
22. Say the word and act accordingly.
23. Walk to the chalkboard and face your classmates.
24. Walk with your partner hand in hand until you come to a chair.
25. Walk slowly to the door like an old man.
26. Raise your right [left] hand.
27. Draw a circle [square, triangle, rectangle, star] in the air.
28. Smile and shake hands with your neighbor.
29. These are some examples of American gestures. You are going to communicate with your partner only with gestures. Don't talk, but try to understand each other.
30. Watch your partner's gestures and say in a loud voice what he [she] means.

**Notes:** 17〜19 の like は接続詞の用法であるが，アメリカの口語で頻繁に用いられる表現である．22 は動詞が書かれているカードを受け取って，その動作をする活動．29 はアメリカで使われるしぐさの例を単語とともに学習したあと，生徒同士でジェスチャーだけで対話させる．

## d. 2つの動作の相違
By showing difference(s) between the two patterns [behaviors]

1. Look at me carefully. Do you see any difference?
2. There is something different in these gestures, isn't there?
3. Look at them. What is Masako doing and what is Hiroko doing?
4. Is my arm up or down?
5. Are you sitting or standing?
6. Are you writing English or speaking English?

〈発展的表現〉

7. Is this little boy eating an apple or an orange? How do you know?
8. How can you say that the man is cutting a tree, not a branch?
9. Look at this picture. Is Ken running or walking? Is he running in the park or in the playground? How do you know that?
10. These two persons are raising their hands, but when they move them, their hands are saying different things. What does each of want to say?

**Notes:** 1〜6 は動作を見てクラス全員で違いを指摘し，全員で答えることができる．7〜10 は動作の違いがどこからくるのかを複数の英文で説明することを要求する場合．

---
**Student Response**

何やっているかわからない　I don't know what you are doing. / I have no idea about your gestures.

もっとはっきり　Please give a bigger gesture. / We can't see you well. Please stand closer to us.

えっ，英語で言うの？　Do I have to use English? / Must I explain it in English? / In English?

役者になれる　She acts really well. / Maybe she can become a TV star.

## e.　役割指定　By role plays

### ア．状況設定を教師が指定　Roles to be assigned by the teacher
1. You should be the teacher.
2. You are to play the teacher.
3. You are going to play the role of Mr. Sato.
4. You will play the part of Mr. Sato.
5. Boys, take the role of Mike, and girls, Nancy.
6. Someone must play Mr. Sato's part. Does anyone want to?
7. We need a handsome young man and a pretty girl. Who do you recommend?
8. Are there any volunteers that want to be Mr. Sato? He is a sportsman.

〈発展的表現〉
9. A girl and her father are riding a horse to a mountain. They look happy. Tomoko, you will be the girl. Kenta, you will be her father.
10. Suppose two of you are a (married) couple. The husband is watching TV, and his wife is ironing shirts. Fuyuki, you are the husband. Chikako, you are the wife.
11. Five of you are passengers on the ship, and you are the young lady, Mika. The lady must be gentle and courageous.

### イ．グループ内で生徒同士が役割決定　Roles to be assigned by students
1. Talk among yourselves and decide on the parts.
2. You should decide who is going to take whose part.
3. You can choose the roles after talking in your groups.
4. Each group should have four players and a narrator.
5. When you've decided, I'd like you to think hard about each character.

〈発展的表現〉

6. There are four characters in the story. Please decide in each group who will take the role of the grandfather, the father, the mother, and the son.
7. You need five people to act, but there are six members in each group. Please discuss and make a good decision. You can create a new role for the sixth member if you want [like].

**Notes:** 7は6人の班で5人のdialogからなる活動をさせるとき.

--- **Student Response** ---

春男がいいと思う  I think Haruo is good [suitable] for this character.
状況がよくわからないといけない  We need to know well about the situation. / What is the situation?
老人はどんなふうにすればいい？  How should the old man move and act? Show me.
アドバイスして  Please give me some advice. / Tell me what to do.

## ③ 新出語  New Words

### a. 発音  Pronunciation

1. Listen carefully and repeat.
2. I'll pronounce the word three times. Listen and repeat.
3. Please listen to the tape and repeat after it.
4. First listen very carefully. Don't try to repeat.

〈発展的表現〉

5. Can you say this after me: *ri li ri li ri li ri li, read lead.*
6. Please say this first: *ra ri ru re ro, la li lu le lo, rye lie.*
7. /f/ and /v/ are easy. Look at my mouth and say, 'friend, voice'.
8. /ɑ/ sounds like Japanese /あ/. Open your mouth wide. Say /ɑ/.

9. /i:/ sounds very hard. Your teeth can be seen when you pronounce /i:/ like this.
10. We don't have /æ/ sound in Japanese, but it's easy. Make your mouth for /え/, and say /あ/.
11. Touch your throat. Does it vibrate when you say /d/? Your pronunciation is correct if it vibrates. Say /d/, /d/, /d/.
12. Touch your throat. Does it vibrate hard when you say /t/? No? That's right. You don't feel your throat vibrate when you say /t/.
13. Now look at the lower column of the page. Repeat after the tape. And then look at the phonetic sign and say it.
14. Can you hear the difference between boat and bought? Yes, it is difficult.

Notes: 5〜12は一音ごとに日本語と異なる音を指導. 13. lower columnは教科書の下の欄.

## b. 意 味　Meaning

ア．実物で　By actual objects
1. What's this?
2. You know this.
3. What's the English word for this?
4. Do you know what this is called in English?
5. Listen to what I say in English about this.

〈発展的表現〉
6. What's this? (生徒: メロン.) Yes. This is a melon, melon, melon. Say melon. Good.
7. What's this? (生徒: ケシゴム.) Yes. 'ケシゴム' is an eraser, an eraser, an eraser.
8. You know this? This is a ball not 'ボール'. Tennis ball, golf ball, baseball, basketball . . .
8. What do I have? (生徒: カメラ.) Yes. I have a camera, camera,

camera. Say "You have a camera."
9. Do you like hamburgers? Hamburgers, hamburgers, hamburgers. Say "I like hamburgers."

**Notes:** 低学年ではさまざまな実物をクラスに持ち込むことができる．また，プラスチック製の実物模型を使うことも，生徒の興味を引き付ける．

### イ．絵で　By pictures
1. The girl in the picture is ～ing.
2. The picture shows the boy is ～ing.
3. What is the scene in this picture? Yes. It is...
4. Can you tell what they are doing? They are ～ing.

〈発展的表現〉
5. Look at the picture. What is Jenny playing?（絵では頭と上腕の部分まで示し生徒からいろいろ引き出す）（生徒: ピアノ, エレクトーン...）She's playing the guitar, the guitar, the guitar. Now repeat.
6. （テレビ番組表を見させて）This is a list of TV programs. Which programs do you watch every Monday? What kind of programs do you like, music programs or sports programs, dramas or news?
7. （裏返しの絵を示して）Is this a cat or a tiger? Guess.（生徒: It's a tiger.）Yes. It's a tiger.
8. Look. What is this girl doing? Is she singing or dancing?... Yes. She is dancing.
9. （線グラフを示して）The number of students playing soccer is increasing. Say, increase, increase, increasing...

### ウ．英語で　Through English
1. Listen carefully. I will explain the word in English.
2. Please guess the meaning of the word. I will say it in English.
3. No dictionaries. Guess what it means. I will explain in English.

〈発展的表現〉
4. When you had your birthday party, did you invite your friends to

your house? Did you send invitations? No? Well in the U.S., I received an invitation. This is it. Invitation, invitation …
5. Yesterday there was a rock concert. Did anybody go there? We say 'コンサート' in Japanese, but in English they say 'concert.' Repeat.
6. In the science class you were using a gas burner, a flask, and a test tube. Were you doing some chemical experiments? Yes? You were doing an experiment. Say, "We were making an experiment."
7. You must decide which high school to go to soon. Have you decided yet? Oh, you haven't decided yet. 'Decided' or 'have not decided'. Anyway good luck [do your best].

**Notes:** 4の invitation は招待状の意. birthday card, Christmas card などでは card が必要であるが，invitation card と言わなくともよい. 4〜7は具体的な例. 新語を既知の文型に入れ，繰り返し提示している.

**Student Response**

絵が見えない　I can't see the picture. / Put the picture up higher.
日本語だと言えるんだけど　I know that in Japanese, but I don't know it in English. / I wish I could use Japanese. / May I say it in Japanese?

**Interaction**

| | |
|---|---|
| S: 先生, いろんな国へ行った？ | Have you been to many foreign countries? |
| T: アメリカとヨーロッパの国のいくつかね. | Not many, but I visited the U.S. and some European countries. |
| S: 危険じゃなかった？ | Wasn't it dangerous? |
| T: 危険そうな所へは行かないから. | I didn't go to such dangerous places. |
| S: 食べ物に困らなかった？ | Did you have any food problems? |
| T: ぜんぜん. | None at all. |
| S: 先生, 何でも食べるからね. | Oh, lucky you! You eat anything, don't you? |

## c. フラッシュカード  By flashcards

1. Look at the cards.
2. Read the words all together.
3. Can you read the words?
4. Please pronounce each word correctly.
5. Pronounce each word quickly.
6. Now read the words more quickly.
7. Only this row. Read quickly.
8. Spell them.

〈発展的表現〉

9. I'll hide some letters of the words. Can you still spell them?
10. You can see only the first letter. Guess and say the word.
11. Now you see the Japanese on this side of the card. What is the English word for it?

**Notes:** 9 はフラッシュカードの単語の文字をいくつか隠して．

## d. 連 語  Collocations

1. Remember all the three words together.
2. The phrase always occurs with . . .
3. 'At [With / For]' usually comes after this phrase.
4. Once combined, these words mean very different things.
5. You should remember those words in combination.

〈発展的表現〉

6. 'be good at'（スポーツと主人公の絵を組み合わせて）
   Paul is a good baseball player. He is a good basketball player, too. He is a good swimmer and a fast swimmer. He is very good at sports. Who is good at sports in this class?
7. 'get to 〜'（黒板に絵を描きながら）
   I went to the station yesterday. I left home at 11:00 and got to the

station at 11:15. How long did it take from my house to the station? ... Yes. I got there in 15 minutes.
8. 'more than'（クイズ形式で）
    T: Do you know how old Mr. Kimura is? Guess.
    S: Is he 31?
    T: More than 31.（31＜— と板書）
    S: Is he 40?
    T: No, less than 40.（— ＜40 と板書）
    S: He is 35?
    T: More than 35.（35＜— と板書）
9. 'look for'（ジェスチャーで）
    I'm looking for my eraser. Please look for it with me. I dropped it somewhere around here.
10. 'all the way'（生徒の行動を取り上げて）
    Sadao and Yutaka were singing all the way from the music room to their classroom. Have you learned the song by heart, Sadao and Yutaka? Our music festival is coming soon. I hope you will sing all the way home, too.

**Notes:** 6〜10 のように中学2年以上ではできるだけ文の中での使い方を示し, 理解させる.

--- **Interaction** ---

(look like 〜 指導の例)

| | |
|---|---|
| T: 君はお父さん似, それともお母さん似? | Do you look like your father or mother? |
| S: お母さん似だって言われるけど, 僕はそう思わない. | They say I look like my mother, but I don't think so. |
| T: じゃ誰に似てるのかな? | Then who do you look like? |
| S: おじいさん. | I think I look more like my grandfather. |

## e. 同音異義語　Homonyms

1. These words sound the same, but are different in spelling and meaning.
2. Though they are read the same, they are spelled differently.
3. They have the same pronunciation, but different meanings and spellings.
4. The two are entirely different words, but they happen to have the same pronunciation.

〈発展的表現〉

5. Listen. "The strong wind blew over the blue sea." You heard the same word twice. But actually they are different words. Look at their spellings.
6. There are two /eit/s in "The little boy ate eight strawberries." The first is the past of 'eat' and the second is the number of eight.
7. *buy / by*
   Let's buy the doll sitting by the window.
8. *eye / I*
   I use eye-glasses when I see things.
9. *hear / here*
   We can hear his voice clearly here in front of the chalkboard.
10. *our / hour*
    Our teacher kept us in class an hour after school.
11. *right / write*
    Many of us write with our right hands.
12. *sea / see*
    Can you see a white sail on the sea today?
13. *new / knew*
    He knew a lot of new songs in his high school days.
14. *road / rode*
    I rode my bicycle on a nice road with lots of green trees on both

sides.

**Notes:** 語呂合わせのように聞こえるが，語彙の導入に有効な場合がある．この場合も2語を並べるのではなく，5以下のように文の中で示す．7以下は例文のみを示してある．

## ④ 本文・対話　Main Text and Dialog

### a. 要点　Summarizing

1. In short the paragraph says that . . .
2. Tell me in your own words what happened.
3. Give me a brief summary of the contents.
4. Use your own words to tell me about Mary.
5. I'll tell you about the passage in simple English.
6. The paragraph can be summarized as follows.
7. Simply put, the idea of the passage is like this.
8. The gist of the story is something like this.
9. What is Mike trying to say? Tell me [it] in a few words.
10. In short, what is the main point of the text?

〈発展的表現〉

11. In a word what is this passage about? . . . Right. It's about a dream. Then what dream is it about? . . . Right. It's about a bad dream.

**Notes:** 要点を把握させる場合，できるだけやさしい英語で，例えば3年の内容なら2年次の既習言語材料を多用することが考えられる．（☞ p. 212）

---
**Student Response**

よく聞き取れなかった　I couldn't hear well. / I didn't hear that.
もっと簡単に言って　Please say it in easier English. / Please say it more simply.
ゆっくり読んで　Please read more slowly. / Slow down, please.

もっとゆっくり言って　Please speak more slowly.

---- **Interaction** ----

T: 彼女は何が欲しかったのかな？　What did she want after all?
S: 洋服とか，指輪とか．　Well, she wanted a ring, a dress ...
T: でも，どれも満足しなかったでしょ．　But she was not happy about those things.
S: 結局，愛情かな．　She wanted his love, didn't she?
T: そうですね，多分．　I agree. Probably she didn't want anything else.

## b. 質 問　Asking questions

1. Now questions.
2. Answer the questions.
3. Let's see if you've understood.
4. Let's ask some questions about [on] the passage.
5. You have to prepare five questions about the passage.
6. I'll ask some questions about the passage (you have just read).
7. Who is going to ask us the questions about [on] page 120?
8. There are five questions. Answer them according to the text.
9. There are five questions you have to answer. Remember the text.

〈発展的表現〉

10. Let's make sure you understood the text. I'll ask some questions.
11. Now I'll ask some questions to check your understanding of the text.

## c. 登場人物の相互関係　Relation between the characters

1. How many people are in the story?
2. Who is the hero [heroine] of the story?

3. Who are in the same family?
4. What's the relationship between John and Mary?
5. Who is the bad guy?
6. Who wins in the end?
7. How did John and Mary know each other at school?

〈発展的表現〉
8. Is Keiko Emi's friend?
9. How long have Emi and Keiko been friends?
10. How old were Emi and Keiko when they first met?
11. Do Emi and Keiko still write to each other?
12. Is Mr. Young one of Mike's teachers?
13. What subject does Mr. Young teach to Mike's class?
14. Why is Mr. Green in Mike's class?
15. Are Mike, Paul, Kathy, and Emi in the same class when they study science?
16. Is Kazuo Emi's classmate or Keiko's classmate?
17. Who teaches English in Kazuo's class?
18. Who is Kazuo staying with when he goes to Minnesota?
19. Who is Kazuo's American mother?
20. Did Mr. Sato study at Keiko's school?
21. Why is Ms. May talking with Mr. Sato?
22. Is Mr. Hill an English teacher or a history teacher?
23. Who is in Mr. Hill's class?
24. Where does Mike's aunt live?
25. Does Mike's aunt have any sons?
26. Are her sons Mike's uncles or his cousins?

---- **Interaction** ----

T: アメリカで和夫はどこに滞在しているの？　　Where does kazuo stay in the U.S.?
S: ホストファミリーのところ　　He's staying with his host family.

|  |  |
|---|---|
| です. | |
| T：何州に住んでいるのかな？ | What state (in the U.S.) is he in? |
| S：テキサス州です. | He's in Texas. |

## 4. 練 習
## Practice

### ① 語と文  Words and Sentences

**a. 強 勢  Stress / Accent**

1. Please say 'récord', 'récord.'
2. Say 'récord', not 'recórd'.
3. Say once again, 'récord'.
4. Please say 'interesting' after me.
5. Please repeat 'interesting' three times after Miss Ford.

〈発展的表現〉

6. Please stress the first syllable.
7. Stress the second syllable, not the first.
8. You must stress the second syllable of the word.
9. The stress [accent] of this word falls on the last syllable. Please repeat the word.
10. This word is accented on the third syllable, not the second.
11. The second syllable is stressed [accented] in this word. Say 'record' once.
12. The word 'transportation' has the primary stress on the third syllable and the secondary stress on the first syllable. Everybody, pronounce the word once again, please.

**Notes:** アクセントは語のレベルにとどめた．1~5ではアクセントに注意して教師のモデルをまねることを中心に指示している．12では第1アクセント，第2アクセントに注意を向けさせている．（☞ p. 208）

## Interaction

| | |
|---|---|
| T: 吉田さん，最初の例文を読んで下さい． | Miss Yoshida, read the first example, please. |
| S: はい．（教科書を読む） | Yes. |
| T: はい，結構．ただし，'ecólogy' をもう一度． | Good, but will you pronounce 'ecólogy' again? |
| S: イコロジー． | Écology. |
| T: 注意して聞いて．Ecólogy. はい，もう一度． | Listen carefully. Ecólogy. Try once again. |

b. **イントネーション**　Intonation

1. Please raise your voice at the end.
2. Raise your voice at the end a little higher.
3. Please lower your voice at the end.
4. Repeat after me, "Is Tom a student?"
5. This is an A-or-B question. Listen to me again.
6. Say once again, "Is Mr. Smith an American or a Canadian?"
7. It's a Wh-question. Don't raise your voice at the end.
8. Repeat after me, "My favorite subjects are English, Japanese, music and PE."

〈発展的表現〉

9. The end of a Wh-question requires a falling intonation. Try it again, "What's up there?"
10. Mind the intonation. It's an A-or-B question.
12. If you raise your voice too high at the end, the meaning of the sentence changes. Be careful.
13. In conversation, you can express doubt by applying a rising intonation to a declarative sentence. Everybody, repeat after me, "You go to St. John's High?"
14. Mind the question mark after 'Yes'. Here, the speaker is expecting

a positive response. So you must say "Yes?" Say it again.

**Notes:** イントネーション練習は口頭に加えて，板書や手による指示を与えることでよりはっきり理解させることができる．8ではA,B,CとDのように3つ以上の語を例示するときのイントネーションに注意させている．12では極端な上昇調を用いることで「驚き」を表すことを暗に指摘しているが，It expresses surprise. とつけ加えてもよい．13, 14ではダイアローグ練習を想定したもの．(☞ p. 207)

### c. 例文　Example sentences

1. Please read the model sentence, Toshio.
2. Please read the model sentence in chorus.
3. Give me another example, Keiko.
4. Write one more sentence, please.
5. Say the model sentence three times all together.
6. I'll give you an example. Repeat after me.
7. Here is an example. Listen and repeat after me.
8. I'll give you a few minutes. Please memorize the model sentence.

〈発展的表現〉

9. Look at the model sentence. Change it into a question form. Yoko, will you try it?
10. Have you finished writing another example? Now, let me hear yours, Akiko.
11. Please write a short paragraph (by) using the model sentence on the board.

**Notes:** 11は例文を書き出しに用いてさらにいくつかの文を加え，コンテクストのある文を作文させる．

### d. ルックアップ・アンド・セイ　Look up and say

1. Everybody, look up and say the sentence.

2. Please read the sentence aloud once, then look up and say it.
3. Please don't look down. Look up and say the words.
4. Don't read from your (note)book. Look up and say it, please.
5. When you forget, you may look down. But don't read from the textbook. Just look up and say it.
6. You may use your memo, but don't read it. Just look at your notes quickly, then look up and say it.
7. Look into the eyes of your partner when you speak. Don't read from the textbook.

〈発展的表現〉

8. I'll give you a few minutes for memorization. Then you look up and say the sentences.
9. Eye contact is important in speaking English. When you do the skit with your partners, don't read from the paper.
10. (Yoko), you shouldn't read your memo. Please look down and see what you are supposed to say, then look up and say the sentences.

**Notes:** Look up and say というのは，まず例文・語句などを理解・暗唱し，そのあとは顔を上げて話し相手を見ながら話すように言うことである．

―――― **Interaction** ――――

| | |
|---|---|
| T: 山田君，小川さん，そのダイアローグを実際に演じてみて下さい． | Yamada-kun and Ogawa-san, please act out the dialog. |
| Y: ジェーン，あなたは何のスポーツが好きですか． | Jane, what sports do you like? |
| O: (メモを読みながら)野球と水泳です．ええと… | I like baseball and swimming. Er ... |
| T: 小川さん，メモは見てもよいのですが，見ながら話さないように． | Ogawa-san, you may look at your memo, but you must look up and say the words. |
| O: でも，セリフが長くて覚えられないのですが． | The words are too long to learn by heart. |

## e. 綴り　Spelling

1. Please spell out the word.
2. Spell it out, will you? Kajiki-san.
3. Read the spelling of the words, please.
4. Give me the spelling of the phrase, will you?
5. Please check the spelling of the word with your dictionary.
6. Class, is Ken's spelling correct?
7. Write the spelling of the word five times and memorize it.
8. Start a sentence with a capital letter.
9. How do you say 'nesshinna' in English? Spell out the word, please.

〈発展的表現〉

10. I'll say three words for you to spell out. Are you ready?
11. Kazuo's sentence on the board seems to have three spelling mistakes. Is there anyone who wants to help him?
12. Check the spellings before you turn in your papers, O.K.?
13. Now, exchange your papers and check the spellings.

**Notes:** 5は作文等を板書させたあとで綴り字を辞書でクラス全体にチェックさせる．6は板書またはノートの綴り字の正誤を確認させている．12は提出前に綴り字の点検を指示している．13は隣と交換して綴り字をチェックさせる．

---
**Interaction**

T：さあ，みなさん．時間です．書くのをやめてパートナーとテスト用紙を交換して下さい．採点します．1問目．「正式な」は英語で何と言いますか．啓子さん．
All right. Class. Time is up. Stop writing and now exchange your paper with your partner. You are going to mark the paper. First question. What's the word for 'seishikina' in English, Keiko?

S：オフィシャルです．
Official.

T：綴り字は．
How do you spell it?

S：O-f-f-c-i-a-l です．
It's o-f-i-c-i-a-l.

T：啓子さんの答は正解ですか．
Is Keiko's answer correct, Junji?

純二君.
S：ええと．o-f-f-i-c-i-a-l だと　　Well, I think it's o-f-f-i-c-i-a-l.
　　思います．

## ② 文型練習　Pattern Practice

### a. 代入　Substitution drill

1. Substitution drill.
2. Change the words with the cues.
3. Replace the verb [noun / pronoun] with the cue.
4. Replace the verb with the one I'm going to say.
5. Change the time expression(s) with the words I provide.
6. Substitute the singular nouns for the plural nouns I'm going to say.
7. "I am a teacher." "You are a student." Everybody together. "Toshio . . . a student."
8. "I teach English." "You learn English." "Yoko . . . ," "They . . . " Very good.
9. Say altogether 'swim-swam'. Now let's make a sentence. "You swim today." Right? "We swim today." How about yesterday?

〈発展的表現〉

10. You tend to drop the 's' after plural nouns. In this room, we have one window, two windows, three, four, five, yes, six what? We have six . . . in this room. Everybody together. Good.
11. Let's quickly review the subject-verb agreement. I'll say a sentence. Then a new subject. You complete the sentence with the new subject, O.K.?

　　Notes:　文型練習の実際では，2〜6のような指示をしなければならないことはなく，7〜9で示したように教師の問いかけで自然に生徒が了解していくのがい

い．いずれの場合もなるべく実際の状況を利用し，現実感のある例文で練習するよう配慮したい．10, 11 は文法用語を用いた．

## b. 語順転換　Inversion drill

1. Question, please.
2. Into the question form.
3. Change the sentence into the interrogative sentence.
4. Form a question sentence from what I am going to say.
5. "You like English." Into the question. Ask Keiko, Akio.
6. "Jane likes to read." Keiko, ask Toshio about Mary.

〈発展的表現〉

7. I'll write two sentences on the board. Change them into question forms, O.K.?
8. The sentences on the board are affirmative. Change them into negative sentences.

**Notes:** 素早く文型練習を進めるには，1 すら必要でなく，教師の手の動きや顔の表情で十分なときもある．

## c. 文転換　Conversion drill

1. Conversion.
2. Change the sentences.
3. Put the sentences into a proper form with the cues.
4. Listen to the cue and change the whole sentence to fit with it.
5. Put the sentences into the passive [direct speech / correct tense].
6. Make passive all the sentences I'm going to say.

〈発展的表現〉

7. Let's practice the past tense. I'll give several sentences in the present tense. You change them into the past tense.
8. "Americans speak English." Then what do you say in the passive

voice? "English . . ."

9. Look at the sentences on the board. Some are in the active voice and others in the passive voice. Change the voice. Let's do it orally.

**Notes:** （☞ p. 218, 223）

## d. 拡大　Expansion

1. Add the cue.
2. Make the sentences longer.
3. Insert the word I say into the sentences.
4. Put the word I('ll) say at the end of the sentences.
5. Let's make the sentences more specific with the cue words.
6. Complete the sentences with time and place expressions.
7. Now please repeat after me. "John comes to school." Add yesterday at the end, everyone. . . . Right. You've changed the tense.
8. "Mrs. Yoshida ate steak last night." Add every day at the end and change the tense.
9. Repeat after me. "There is a dictionary." Add on the table. . . . Good. "There is a dictionary on the table." Now I'll move the dictionary to different places. Under that table.

〈発展的表現〉

10. Let's expand the sentences by adding adverbs and adverbial phrases showing time and place. The first sentence is "Tom plays tennis," so you can say it like this: "Tom always plays tennis at a nearby park." O.K.? Let's go.
11. Add an adverb of time to each sentence, for example, today, five days ago, for two weeks, etc, etc. Remember [Be careful with] the tense.

**Notes:** 例文は場所・時の副詞を加えて拡大することにとどめた．9では教師が辞書を実際に手で移動し，目で確認させながら練習させている．

### e. 短　縮　Contraction

1. In a short form.
2. Make the sentence shorter.
3. Say the sentence using a contraction.
4. What's the most important part for the question?
5. Don't repeat every word. Say only the answering part.
6. Long answers are not needed. Answer me in a short form.
7. Your mother has a full time job, doesn't she, Kumi? How about your mother, Ken? Answer in a short form. . . . Right. Your mother doesn't.

〈発展的表現〉

8. In speaking you use contractions very often. Say these sentences by using contractions. Are you ready?
9. In answering a question, you don't have to repeat the whole sentence. Use a contracted form instead. Let's practice. I'll ask you several questions. Now, Toshio, do you ski? . . . O.K., you don't.

**Notes:** 7では "My mother doesn't." と答えられたと仮定している．いずれの場合も，意図した通りの答が得られるとは限らないので，リアルでしかもできるだけ意図した答が生じるようなターゲット・センテンスの利用が必要となる．

### f.　結合・完成　Combination and completion

1. Into one sentence.
2. Complete the sentence.
3. Put the two sentences together.
4. Combine the sentences using relative pronouns.
5. Complete the sentences, using the words I give.
6. Fill in the gaps (by) using the cue words I'm going to say.
7. You were late for class this morning. Why? . . . I see. Say the whole sentence again.

8. After school is over today, what will you do, Yoko? . . . Okay. Say the whole sentence starting with 'After'.

〈発展的表現〉

9. Use a relative pronoun and combine the two sentences.
10. Well, I'm sure all of you have different ideas. Say whether you agree or not. Then explain why you think so. Answer in one sentence. Any volunteers?

**Notes:** 7, 8 は実際の状況を利用した拡大・完成練習とした. (☞ p. 223)

### ③ 動作を伴う練習　Practice Using Actions

a. **CLL** (Community Language Learning)

1. You can talk about anything in this class.
2. Please say it in Japanese.
3. What do you want to say? Use Japanese.
4. Let's decide what to talk about.
5. I'll translate your words into English.
6. Let's record the dialog.
7. Replay the tape again.
8. Let's write it down.
9. Make up more sentences using the key expression.
10. What do you think of this type of lesson?
11. Feel free to express yourself.

〈発展的表現〉

12. Say in Japanese what you want to say, and I will tell [give] it to you in English.
13. Listen to how your message is restated in English.
14. Record only your English on the tape.

15. Shall we transcribe our tape-recorded conversation?
16. Let's study the transcription of our English sentences.
17. I'll give you a few more minutes to compose a few more sentences.
18. Think about [Reflect on] your feelings.
19. How did you feel about the lesson?
20. Tell me frankly your feelings about what you have learned.
21. Tell me exactly what you think about what we learned and how we learned it.

**Notes:** CLLでは教師と学習者が1つの"小社会"を形作り，そこではお互いに打ち解けて，何でも自由に話せる雰囲気になっていることが重要である．1, 3, 4, 12は生徒に会話の口火を切らせたいときの表現．6～8, 14, 15は本時で学んだ表現を口頭で繰り返し，テープに録音し，文字で書き表すまでの作業の指示．9と17は本時に学習した表現を応用して英文を作らせる場合．10, 11, 18～21は生徒に授業の感想を述べさせるときの基本表現．13の message は学習者が，今，表現したいと思っていること（what you want to say）を日本語で発表させ，それを教師が英訳する場合に使う．

## b. TPR　(Total Physical Response)

1. Look back [right / left / up / down].
2. Raise your right [left] hand.
3. Close your eyes.
4. Kneel down.
5. Cross your legs.
6. Listen and look.
7. Bend your knees.
8. Shrug your shoulders.
9. Fold your arms.
10. Stand on one foot.
11. Touch your nose with one hand.
12. Point to the loudspeaker.
13. Take two steps forward.

14. Stretch your arms out wide.
15. Open your hands.
16. Make a fist.
17. Rest your head on your arms.
18. Shake hands with your partner.

〈発展的表現〉

19. Rub your stomach and pat your head at the same time.
20. Listen to me and look at [watch] my actions first.
21. I'll give a command and demonstrate the action.
22. Listen carefully and respond physically to my commands.
23. Please perform the action together with me.
24. Now (you) give us some commands.
25. I'll give you a command, so please write it down.
26. Group One, stand up and shake hands with Group Two.
27. Only boys [girls], please turn around.
28. Read the commands to your partner to perform the actions.
29. Now make pairs. One from each pair will read a command, and the other will act it out.
30. Look at the cues and say the commands so that your partner can carry out the actions.
31. I'll call a student number. If yours is called, please perform the action immediately.
32. Now it's your turn. As long as you use English, I'll follow any command you give. Who wants to begin?

**Notes:** Total Physical Response では，学習者に「指示」,「命令」などを与え，学習者に身体で反応させることによって基本的な表現を理解させようとする．10は片足で立て，13は前に2歩進み出よ，19は片手でお腹をさすり同時に片手で頭を軽くたたけの意味．20～22はTPRを開始する前に一般的諸注意として与える．26, 27はある特定の生徒またはグループに対しての命令．28～30はペアワークでTPRを行わせる場合．32は教師に対してTPRの命令を生徒に出させるように指示する場合．

## c. サジェストペディア　Suggestopedia

1. Relax.
2. Now you can relax.
3. I want you to relax during this lesson.
4. Please make yourselves comfortable.
5. Don't worry about anything.
6. I have some music for you.
7. How about listening to some music?
8. Let's listen to some Classical [Romantic / Baroque] music.
9. Relax in your chairs and listen to the music.

〈発展的表現〉

10. Sit comfortably in your chairs, relax the muscles in your shoulders, neck, etc.
11. Lean back in your chairs and breathe deeply and regularly.
12. Close your eyes. Let's do some meditation.
13. Are you ready? If yes, open your eyes. Welcome to English.

**Notes:** サジェストペディアでは学習者を緊張や心理的束縛，不安から開放して，幼児期に見られるような素直さと柔軟性をもたせることに注意が払われる．1〜5と10, 11は緊張をほぐし，楽な気持ちで授業を受けさせたいときに．6〜9はリラックスさせるために音楽を聴かせる前に．12, 13は授業前に瞑想をさせ精神統一を図りたい場合．13でWelcome to English. と言うのは，精神統一のあとで初めて学習をスタートさせるからである．

## d. コミュニカティブ・アプローチ　Communicative approach

1. Act it out.
2. Let's act out this conversation.
3. Please act out the scene for us.
4. Use your own words.
5. Can you express this sentence by using simpler words?

6. Can you say the same thing in another way?
7. Explain what it means in this context.
8. Use your own words to describe what you did last night.
9. Write sentences about things which you used to enjoy.
10. Have you been in a similar situation? If yes, tell us about it.

〈発展的表現〉
11. Let's suppose that we can fly. Where would you want to go first?
12. Now I'll ask you a couple of questions about your personal experiences related to the dialog.
13. Offer your own response and show us what new things you can say about yourself.
14. On the blackboard, I have written down a model sentence. Use it for (your) in-class work and make up your own answer.

**Notes:** 1〜3 は学んだ対話で生徒に演技を交えた寸劇をさせる場合．4〜7 は表現力に幅を持たせることをねらいとした活動の指示．8〜14 は自分自身のことを英語で表現させる練習の指示．

## e. ジャズ・チャンツ　Jazz chants

1. Listen to the chant.
2. Pay attention to the rhythm.
3. Listen to this rhythmic pattern.
4. Let's practice this rhythm and intonation pattern.
5. Keep a steady beat and rhythm, please.
6. That's a good rhythm.
7. Keep up the rhythm.
8. Slow down [Step up] the tempo.
9. Now, let's try it at normal speed.

〈発展的表現〉
10. Let's set the dialog to a beat.
11. I'll clap my hands [snap my fingers], so please set [establish] a

steady beat.
12. Listen to the beat of the metronome.
13. The first group, please repeat the first line. And the second group, please repeat the next line. Let's continue this pattern for each line. Ready?

**Notes:** 1〜3 はモデルを聞かせる前に．5,6 はよいリズムを保つことであり，その調子を続けてほしい場合の表現．8 はテンポを上げたり下げたりしてほしい場合．10 は会話を拍子に合わせて行わせたい場合．11 は生徒を教師の拍子に合わせるようにさせる場合．13 は会話形式になっている Jazz chant を 2 つのグループでコーラスさせる場合．

## ④ 練習の指示　Directions to Practice

### a. 個人，班ごとの切り替え　Individuals vs. Groups

1. Work by yourselves [individually].
2. Work on your own.
3. Work in pairs [threes / fours].
4. Work with your neighbor.
5. Now let's do some group work.
6. Please form groups. Six students in each group.
7. This is an exercise to work on in groups.
8. Let's form small circles, shall we?
9. Move the chairs and make straight rows.
10. Let's change partners.

〈発展的表現〉

11. Why don't we work in pairs, and ask and answer the list of questions?
12. Please exchange answer sheets with your neighbors and mark

them.
13. Let's divide the class into two groups. This group will read Diana's line and the other group will read Tim's line.
14. I'll divide the whole class into two groups, A and B. Group A, please stand up and read aloud the first paragraph in chorus. Group B, just listen.
15. Each person, please find a new partner. Now exchange the information that you have received from your last partner.

**Notes:** 1, 2 は個人で作業をさせる際の指示. 2〜7 はペアとかグループで作業をさせる際の指示. 12 は小テスト等を生徒同士で採点させる場合. 13 はクラスを二分して対話形式で音読練習を行う場合. 15 は 1 人 1 人が教室内を回り生徒同士で情報を交換するコミュニケーション活動の指示.

## b. ノートの取り方・板書の写し方　Note-taking / Copying

1. Write [Copy / Take / Jot] them down.
2. Copy this down into your notebooks.
3. Write this in the empty space at the top.
4. These idioms are the most important part of today's lesson. So copy them into your notebook.
5. Rewrite the sentences in(to) your notebook as shown on the blackboard.

〈発展的表現〉
6. Don't be lazy. Write them down in your notebooks.
7. Don't put down only the answers. Write the questions, too.
8. Open your notebooks and write down what I say in Japanese. Then translate it into English.
9. Copy these English sentences into your notebooks, and put the Japanese translations below them.
10. When you look up a word in the dictionary, write down its pronunciation, and part of speech, as well as its meaning.

Notes: 3は何かを余白に書かせるとき．6は怠惰でノートを取らない生徒へ．7は練習問題等で答えしか書かない生徒へ．10は単語を辞書で調べる場合の指示．

## c. 図・絵などの説明　Explanation of charts, pictures, etc.

1. Look at the chart.
2. Can you all see this picture?
3. Look at the picture on page 15.
4. Look at the chart on the foldout of your textbook.
5. This picture is of an American shopping center.
6. This is a photograph of a German castle.
7. This picture shows part of a Greek myth.
8. Here is a picture of a railway station in Europe.
9. In this picture you can see two boys playing a computer game.

〈発展的表現〉

10. This is a simplified map of one small village. Find the place your partner wishes to visit.
11. These pictures show a small town with many shops. Choose the one that you wish to shop in.
12. The pictures tell John's activities on Sunday. Study the sequence of events.
13. This picture shows what the inside of a typical American house is like. List the major differences between it and your house.
14. You and your partner have been given the same set of three pictures. Choose one of them and describe what it is like to your partner. Can your partner find [identify] it by listening to your description?
15. You're going to spend the summer vacation with your pen pal, Steve, in Canada. Read the letter from him and identify the places he talks about on the attached map.

**Notes:** 4は教科書の折り込みになったページに載せてあるチャートを見るように指示する場合．10～15はすべて絵を使ってコミュニケーション主体の活動をさせたい場合．10, 14はペアワークが可能．(☞ p. 35)

## ⑤ 書く作業　Writing Activities

### a. プリントの配布　Distributing handouts

1. Pass these (to the) back.
2. Please pass out the exercises.
3. Please take one and pass them back [on].
4. Let me hand out these copies.
5. Here are some handouts for an extra exercise.
6. I'll give you these handouts.
7. Please hand them to those behind you.
8. Is there anybody without a copy?
9. Did anyone get an extra copy?
10. Have you all got a copy of the exercise?

〈発展的表現〉

11. Does your row need any more copies?
12. Write your name at the top of the handout.
13. Once you get it, start the exercise.
14. Take one but don't turn it over until I tell you to do so.

**Notes:** 9はプリントを余分に取った生徒がいないかどうか尋ねる場合．13はプリントをもらったらすぐ練習問題を始めよという指示．14は試験の問題用紙を受け取って「始め」の合図があるまで裏返しにしておくようにという指示．

──── **Interaction** ────

T：これから，演習用プリントを配布します．一番前に座っ　　Now I will give you a handout for the exercises. The first student of each

|   |   |
|---|---|
| ている生徒，何人分か言いなさい．この列は？ | row, please tell me how many copies your row needs. |
| S₁: 6枚です． | Six, please. |
| T: はい．じゃ，この列は． | Here you are.  How about this row? |
| S₂: 休んだ生徒の分はどうすればいいですか． | What should we do with the copy for the student who is absent today? |
| T: 欠席している生徒の分はこちらでとっておくのでいいです． | Oh!  I have one for him, so don't worry about it. |
| S₂: じゃあ，5枚です． | Well, then five, please. |

## b. ワークブック　Workbooks

1. Now, open your workbooks, please.
2. Take out your workbooks.
3. We shall do some drills.
4. Open to page 12 and do the exercise.
5. Write an appropriate word in each blank.
6. Put the proper [correct] word in the blank.
7. Choose a verb from the list to complete each sentence.
8. Make the necessary changes in word order.
9. Complete each sentence with a phrase from the list below.
10. Put [Translate] the following into English.

〈発展的表現〉

11. Fill in the blanks with the correct forms of the verbs.
12. Complete the conversations using the questions in parentheses.
13. Complete these sentences with a verb using its proper tense.
14. When [While] you do the exercise, don't open your textbook, and don't use your dictionary.

**Notes:**　5〜13は書く作業の具体的な指示．そのまま試験の設問として使用可能．
14は練習問題を解いているときは教科書や辞書は見ないでという指示．

## c. （OHP用）TPシートを使った練習　Exercises on transparencies

1. Here is a transparency.
2. Write (out) your answers on the transparency [OHT].
3. Copy the projected sentences into your notebooks.
4. I'll write down the answers to the exercises on the transparency.
5. I'll project the answers on the screen with the OHP.

〈発展的表現〉

6. Is the picture in focus?
7. Can everyone see the picture?
8. Am I blocking your view?
9. Student C, could you come over and write down your answer on this transparency?
10. I'll pass out a transparency to each group. Please identify the grammatical error in each sentence on the transparency.

**Notes:**　2. OHT = overhead transparency. 6はOHPのピントがあっているかという質問. 8は生徒がOHPのスクリーンを見るとき教師が邪魔になっていないかという質問. 9は生徒にOHPの所まで来させ自分の答えを書かせる場合. 10はTPシートに予め文法的な間違いを含む英文を載せておいて生徒たちに直させる場合. (☞ p. 272)

## d. 筆記体・活字体　Handwritten [Script] and block letter style

1. Print it.
2. Write it in longhand [cursive / script form].
3. You may print or write by hand in [longhand / script form]
4. Print clearly with a pen.
5. You should learn to print by the end of this term.

〈発展的表現〉

6. Write it in capital letters.
7. You should learn to read handwriting.

8. When (you use) handwriting, your 'f' sometimes looks like a 'b'.
9. You don't have to master writing in cursive, but you must learn to read it.

   **Notes:** 1は活字体で書けという意味の基本的な指示．2は筆記体で書けという指示．6は活字体の大文字で書かせたい場合．8は筆記体で書く場合，小文字のfとbがまぎらわしくならないようにという注意．

### e. なぐり書き・丁寧に書く　　Jotting and writing carefully

1. Write it neatly.
2. I want you to write neatly.
3. Take your time and write neatly.
4. I won't accept messy writing.
5. I won't read any scribbled homework.
6. What messy writing!

〈発展的表現〉

7. Neatness counts.
8. No chicken scratches, please.
9. Your handwriting is difficult to read [is not easy to read].
10. Most markers [graders] prefer neat writing to scribbling.
11. I am sure that neat handwriting gives the marker [grader] a better impression.

   **Notes:** 4〜6はなぐり書きをする生徒への戒めの表現．7は小テスト等で丁寧に書かない生徒への注意．8は非常に読みにくい字を書く生徒へのユーモアを交えた注意．10, 11は丁寧に書かれた答案はなぐり書きの答案より採点者によい印象を与えるという旨の表現．

### f. ペン・鉛筆　　Pens and pencils

1. Write it in ink.
2. Write with a pencil [mechanical pencil / fountain pen / ball-point

pen].
3. Too light. Press harder.
4. Use an HB pencil [a Number 2 pencil].
5. Mark your answers with a red pen.

〈発展的表現〉
6. Has anyone got a pencil sharpener?
7. Has anyone got an extra pencil?
8. This is an application form for admission, so you must use a pen.
9. You are not supposed to write on the answer sheet with a ball-point pen.

**Notes:** 3は字が薄いのでもっと強く書くようにという指示．4のNumber 2はHB (= hard black) と同様に鉛筆の芯の硬さを表している．8は入学願書なのでペンで書けという指示．9は解答用紙に書く場合はボールペンを使ってはいけないという指示．

## g. 色を塗る　Coloring

1. Let's do some coloring [painting].
2. Color [Paint] the picture.
3. Take out your colored pencils [crayons / pastels].
4. Color the train blue.
5. Draw a plane, and then paint it gray.
6. Color the map yellow, green, brown and blue.

〈発展的表現〉
7. Paint the triangle below the horizontal line green.
8. Paint the picture whatever color you like.
9. Which color do you want to choose for the roof of this house?
10. You might as well use red here because it stands out.

**Notes:** 4はすでに描かれているものに色を塗らせる場合．5はあるものを描かせたあとで色を塗らせる場合．7は聞き取りの練習としても有効な指示．図形と線と色のところは適当に変えることができる．8と9は生徒に塗る色を選ば

せたい場合.

---

**Interaction**

T: A さん，何か赤のペンはありませんか.
S: ボールペンならありますけど.
T: ああ，それでいいです.
S: はい，どうぞ.

Student A, do you have any kind of red pen?
Yes. I have a ball-point pen. Would you like to use it?
Sure. Let me use it.
Here you are.

---

## h. 図を描く　Drawing

1. Let's do some drawing.
2. Shall we draw some pictures?
3. Draw the picture as you're told. / Draw the picture as I describe it to you.
4. Draw a vertical [horizontal / diagonal / curved] line.
5. Draw a square [circle / rectangle / triangle / diamond].
6. Your partner will choose a picture from this page and will tell you what to draw.

〈発展的表現〉

7. Draw an upside-down cat.
8. Draw a house. There's a big tree next to it.
9. Draw a happy [sad / cheerful / questioning] face with a beard [mustache].
10. Draw something that you see at a department store.
11. I want you to draw a picture to illustrate the following: Draw a big rectangle. Now everything else you draw must be put inside the rectangle. In the center, draw an angry face, in the upper righthand corner, draw an airplane, and in the lower left corner, draw a flower.

**Notes:** 4 はいろいろな線を描かせる場合．5 はいろいろな図形を描かせる場合．6 はペアになった生徒の 1 人が指示を出し，相手の生徒がその指示に従って絵を描く活動．7〜11 はすべて具体的なものを描かせる場合．

## ⑥ 黒板での作業　At the Board

### a. チョークの指示　Using chalk [colored markers]

1. Use white chalk [a black marker].
2. Use yellow chalk, not the red one. It's easier to see.
3. Use colored chalk [markers] for correcting.
4. Are there enough pieces of chalk for everyone?
5. Use a longer piece of chalk, Kazuo. It's easier to write with.
6. Press heavier with your chalk.
7. Draw your picture with different colored chalk [markers].

〈発展的表現〉

8. You can't write well with such a tiny piece of chalk. Isn't there a longer one?
9. Don't erase what you have written. Use colored chalk [markers] for editing.
10. Oh, there is no chalk here. Why don't [Can] you go to the teacher's office and get some?
11. Pay attention to the phrases written in red. You will be tested on them in the ten-minute quiz next class.

**Notes:** 黒板ではなく白板の場合は colored markers を使う．4 は複数の生徒に同時に板書させるときにチョークについて確認している．5, 8 はもっと長いチョークを使用するよう指示している．6 は筆圧を問題にしている．10 はチョークがなくて教員室へ生徒が取りに行くところを示す．11 は赤で示したところを次の時間にテストするという指示．

## b. 板書　What and where to write

1. Write here (not there).
2. Don't use the lower part of the blackboard.
3. Write in the middle of the board.
4. Use the left side of the board.
5. You may use the board at the back of the room, too.
6. Write your answers neatly in each block.
7. Toshio, you are tall, so use the higher part of the board.
8. Write your sentences in order from top to bottom.

〈発展的表現〉

9. Before you write, divide the space into eight sections [parts] and number them. Write your answer(s) in your section(s), O.K.?
10. Let me divide the space by drawing the lines so that you can write neatly.
11. If you like, you can use the board in the back.
12. Save what is written on the board. Make use of the space you have.

**Notes:** 5, 11 は後ろの黒板の使用についての指示. 6 は教師が複数の生徒が板書できるよう予め仕切っておいた場所に書くよう指示している. 9 では生徒が仕切り, そこへ番号をつけてそれぞれの番号のところへ板書するよう指示を与えている. 10 は複数の生徒がきれいに書けるよう教師が線を引いて仕切ろうとしている. 12 は書いてあるものを消さずに, 空いたスペースを利用するように指示. (☞ p. 137)

---
**Interaction**

| | |
|---|---|
| T：俊雄さん, 和雄さん, 裕子さん, 里美さん, 啓子さん, 答を板書して下さい. | Toshio, Kazuo, Yuko, Satomi and Keiko, write your answers on the board. |
| $S_1$：これを消していいですか. | May I erase this? |
| T：左半面だけ消して結構. | You may erase the left half. |
| $S_2$：どこへ書いてもいいですか. | May we write in any space? |
| T：5人だけですからどこへ書 | You may write in any space you find |

| | |
|---|---|
| いても結構です． | since there are only five of you. |

## c. 下線を引く  Underlining

1. Please underline the word [sentence].
2. Look at the underlined word. There is a mistake in it.
3. I've underlined two important words. Read them aloud.
4. Taro's answer on the board has two mistakes. I'll underline them. Please think why they are not correct.
5. You must learn the two phrases in this sentence. I'll underline them.
6. Draw a double line under the most important word.

〈発展的表現〉

7. Underline the subject [verb] of the sentence.
8. Point out all the nouns by underlining them.
9. Underline the words which include mistakes and write correct answers beneath them.
10. Underline the expressions which were difficult for you to translate into English.
11. I'll underline the places where you've made mistakes.
12. Do you understand why I underlined those words?

**Notes:** 1, 6～10 は生徒に下線を引かせる場合．他は教師が下線を引き，生徒に注目させる場合．

## d. 消す  Cleaning the board

1. Clean the board, Toshio.
2. Will you clean the board, Kayo?
3. Who is in charge of cleaning the board today?
4. You must wipe the board before class begins.
5. May I erase these?

6. Is it all right to erase this side of the board?
7. May I erase it now? I want to write a little more.
8. Now copy it quickly. I want to erase the first part.

〈発展的表現〉

9. Clean the board before class begins, or I won't use the board at all.
10. Don't erase the whole sentence. Just cross out the wrong word and write the correct one below (it).
11. Erase the board quickly so that the next group can write their answers on it.
12. I'll erase the model sentence on the board. Now you write your own (sentence), please.

**Notes:** 1〜4, 9, 11 は生徒に黒板を消させる場面であるが、特に 4, 9 は休み時間のうちに黒板を消しておくよう指導している。12 は教師が例示した文を消して、生徒に作文させている。

# 5. 教科書本文
Main Text

## ① 読み方 Reading

### a. 範読 Model reading

1. Now we'll listen to a tape [CD].
2. Now we'll do a tape-listening exercise.
3. First [Now] let's listen to the tape [CD].
4. Listen to the tape for new words [today's lesson].
5. Listen to a model reading on the tape [by the teacher].
6. We'll listen to the tape for new words [today's lesson].
7. I'll show you how to read the new words.
8. Let's see how to pronounce the new words.
9. We'll listen to the tape to see how to read the text.
10. First [Now] I'll read the text for you.
11. I'll give you a model reading.
12. I'd like Susan to read the text for the class.

〈発展的表現〉

13. When you listen to the tape [me], listen to a group of words, not just a word at a time [individual words].
14. When you hear a pause, put a slash [ / ] where you hear it in your textbook.
15. While (you are) listening to the tape [CD], put a slash [ / ] where you hear a short pause, and put a double slash [ // ] where you hear a long pause.

16. When more than two words are read together, some sound changes often occur.
17. When we read "Did you?" (/did juː/) quickly, it becomes /dɪdʒúː/. Let's listen to the tape to see how the phrase "Did you?" actually sounds.
18. Let's listen carefully to the sound of the phrase "Did you?"
19. The sound /æ/ in 'an' becomes a weak sound /ə/ in 'an apple' when it is read fast. So /æn ǽpl/ becomes /ənǽpl/. Listen to the tape for that change.
20. The sound /t/ in 'sit' drops out [disappears], when it is read in 'sit down' (/sit daun/), like this: /sít daun/, /sídàun/.

**Notes:** 12はALTか音読の上手な生徒に範読してもらう場合．13はセンス・グループで聞くことに注意を促す場合で，14, 15はさらにポーズの聞き取り．16以降は連音等の音変化を指導する聞き取り．

## b. 教師のあとについて読む　Reading after the teacher

1. Repeat [Read] after me.
2. Listen to me carefully and repeat [read] after me.
3. I'll read first; then you read.
4. First I'll read for you. Then you'll read the same part.
5. Now let's read the text aloud. You'll follow along as I read it.
6. Watch my mouth and move your mouth as I do.

〈発展的表現〉

7. Now let's start [begin] reading aloud. While I'm reading the text, please look at it. But when you repeat after me, look up and try not to look at the text.
8. Close your textbooks and look at me. I'll read the text for you. You repeat what I read.
9. Let's practice [reading] some new words. I'll read every word twice. Please repeat each word twice after me.

10. Now for a pronunciation drill. I'll show you how to pronounce the new words. Please read each of them after me.
11. Now I'll read it bit by bit [sentence by sentence]. Listen to me carefully and repeat after me.
12. I'll read the whole paragraph for you. I'd like you to listen to me carefully and get ready to read it after my reading.

---- **Student Response** ----

よく聞こえません　Not clear. / Clearer, please. / Please read more clearly. / I'm sorry. / Excuse me, I cannot hear you well. / In a big [loud] voice, please. / Read more loudly, please.

読み方を教えて下さい　Show me how to read it, please. / Could you give me the sound of the word? / I don't know how to pronounce it. / How do you pronounce this word?

速すぎます　(You read) too fast. / (Please read) more slowly.

---- **Interaction** ----

T: 今度はもっと速く，自然な速さで読んでみよう。やってみせるからね。
This time we'll try to read faster, at natural speed. First I'll show [give] you an example.

S: 先生速すぎます。そんなに速くなんて読めませよ。
You read so fast. I can't read that fast.

T: 読めるよ。
Yes, you can.

S: どうやってですか。
How can I?

T: 1語1語じゃなくて，まとめて読む練習をすればいいんだよ。あとについて繰り返してごらん。．．．ほら，ずっと速くなっただろ。
You'll practice reading a group of words, not just word by word. Listen and repeat after me. ... So you see, you can read much faster.

## c. テープ [CD] のあとについて読む　Reading after the tape [CD]

1. Repeat [Read] after the tape [CD].

2. (Please) listen and repeat after the tape [CD].
3. Listen to the tape [CD] first. Then we'll read the text.
4. Are you ready to read? O.K. I'll start the tape.
5. This is to give you practice in reading after the tape [CD].

〈発展的表現〉

6. Let's have a word pronunciation drill. I'll turn on the tape. You'll repeat each word (twice) just after the tape.
7. Read the phrase [sentence] in the same way that you hear it on the tape [CD]. Listen to the tape [CD] and repeat after the tape [CD].
8. We'll listen to the tape [CD] sentence by sentence, reading each sentence aloud just after the tape.
9. Let's listen to the whole paragraph on the tape [CD]. Then a couple of students will take turns reading the same paragraph aloud.
10. Put on your headphones. You are to repeat the sounds which you hear on the tape [CD].

**Notes:** 10 は教科書を見ないで音声を再生する方法.

--- **Student Response** ---

音量を上[下]げて下さい　Volume up, please. / Turn up the volume. / (Excuse me, / I'm sorry,) could you turn up the volume? / The tape [CD] is too loud. / Turn down the volume.

テープ[CD]を止めて[繰り返して/回して]下さい　Stop [Repeat / Play] the tape [CD]. / Play the tape [CD] again. / I'd like to hear it once more. / I'd like to hear it from the beginning (again).

もっとポーズを入れて下さい　Stop (the tape / the CD) more often. / Give me more pauses. / Play the tape [CD] little by little [bit by bit].

--- **Interaction** ---

T: 何してるんだ，宏樹と真二は．聞いてないじゃないか．質問でもあるのか．　Hiroki and Shinji, what are you doing? You are not listening to the CD. Do you have any questions?

| | |
|---|---|
| S：いいえ，ありません。<br>T：じゃあ，話をしないで CD を聞きなさい。それとも代わりに音読してもらおうか。<br>S：すみません。CD をちゃんと聞きます。 | No. No questions.<br>Then don't talk. Listen to the CD carefully. Or would you like to read the text for us?<br>No, thank you. We will listen to the CD very carefully. |

## d. 音読　Oral reading

1. Now let's start oral reading [reading aloud].
2. Let's read (the text) aloud.
3. Now let's try (some) oral reading [an oral reading exercise].
4. Now it's time to read the text aloud.
5. Now let's try reading the text aloud.
6. This time you will repeat the text orally.
7. Read the text aloud with feeling.
8. Let me hear you read the text aloud. Are you ready? Please begin [Here we go].
9. I cannot hear you well. Read in a big [loud] voice.
10. Your reading is not clear enough. Read more clearly.
11. I'd like you to read in a clear and loud voice. Open your mouth wide.
12. Let's see how naturally we can read the text aloud.

〈発展的表現〉

13. Read the text aloud, giving special attention to the correct pronunciation of each word.
14. Read the text aloud by sense groups. You should not read it just word by word.
15. When you read, put the words into sense groups. Do not read just by pronouncing one word after the other [a line of words].
16. When you read the text aloud, pay attention to the rhythm, accent,

intonation, pauses and so forth.
17. Now I'd like to hear you read the text aloud. Make your reading (sound) as natural as possible
18. When you read your part, read dramatically, as if you were really the person in the conversation [story].

**Notes:** 音読の指導は,正確さから自然さ(題材に応じての normal speed)へと徐々に移行するようにしたい.12は文章の意味がわかり,その内容に合った読み方ができるかどうかを確認する場合.18はいわゆる oral interpretation とか dramatic reading と呼ばれるものである.物語風の内容で,表情豊かな範読が提示できるのであれば是非とも指導したい.(☞ p. 143, 151)

## e. 黙 読　Silent reading

1. Now, let's try silent reading.
2. And now it's time for silent reading.
3. Please read the text silently.
4. Let's read the text with our mouths closed.
5. First we'll read the text silently and then we'll read it aloud.
6. We will read the text again. But this time we'll do silent reading.
7. No more oral reading. This time we will read the same part silently.
8. Listening to and following the tape, we'll read the text silently.

〈発展的表現〉

9. When you read silently, don't try to translate into Japanese.
10. Read the text silently and get the message [catch the meaning] as you read it.
11. Now move your eyes much faster to speed up your reading.
12. Try to read silently as fast as you can. I'll time your (silent) reading. [I'll keep track of the time.]
13. Let's try rapid reading. In rapid reading (try hard to) look at as many words as you can at a glance.

14. Now try to look at whole [entire] groups of words [sense groups] at once. In this way you can read very fast.
15. When you read silently and rapidly, don't stop even if you cannot understand (the meanings of) a couple of words or phrases. Just go on reading and get the general idea [gist] of the text.

   **Notes:** 4は「黙読」のときに生徒がついうっかり音読をした場合にジョークで言う.「口を開けて読む」という表現は自然だが,「口を閉じて読む」とは普通言わないので一種のジョークとなる. 8はテープのスピードに合わせての黙読. 9以降は黙読の具体的な方法を指示している. 10は直読直解を促しており, regressという言葉を生徒に説明したあとなら, Don't regress. という指示にしてもよい. 12では, 2, 3回続けて時間を計測し, いわゆるwpm (= words per minute, 1分間の読語数)を算出させるとよい. 15の指示のように, 黙読が精読だけでなく, 速読になる必要のあることを生徒に指導したい.

## f. 個人読み  Individual reading

### ア. 個人の生徒が読む場合  Reading for the class

1. Ikeda, will you read (the text) aloud (for the class)?
2. Any volunteers to read the text?
3. Would anyone like to volunteer to read the text?
4. Who would like to read (aloud) for us (this time)?
5. I'd like someone to read for the class. How about you, Tashiro?
6. Now Morita and Sakai will read this paragraph to the class.
7. Morita, you'll read the first three sentences, and Sakai the last four sentences.

   〈発展的表現〉
8. Daisuke, read the text for us sentence by sentence [one sentence at a time]. We'll repeat each sentence after you.
9. Yoshiko will read the text for us. Everyone else, close your textbooks.
10. Miyuki will start reading (this paragraph). The rest of you will listen to her with your textbooks closed.

11. When I say "Stop," Miyuki will stop reading. Then I'll ask someone else [another student] to read.
12. Yuka-chan, would you read the text (, please)? You can read anywhere in this lesson.
13. Emiko, will you help me to read this paragraph? After I read a sentence, you read the next sentence. Then I read the third sentence and you read the next [fourth] sentence.
14. Let's have a reading relay. Each student will read just one sentence. The first student will read the first sentence, the second student the second sentence ...

> **Notes:** 8は生徒の音読が機械的にならないようにする一工夫．10は The rest of you, please close your eyes. と言ってもよい．11は復習のときに多く用いられるが，他の生徒がいつ同じ箇所や次の箇所を読まされるかわからないので，注意して音読を聞くことになる．13は生徒と教師が掛け合いで行なう音読で，生徒を教師の音読のペースに引き込むことができる．14はクラス全体だけでなく，グループごとに行うことができる．時間を制限するという手もある．
> (☞ p. 142)

### イ．生徒が各自で読む場合　Buzz reading

1. Now, (let's try) individual reading.
2. Start your individual reading.
3. Please read by yourselves.
4. Please read individually.
5. Everyone, read at your own pace.
6. You don't have to read in chorus.
7. You may read slowly or you may read fast.

〈発展的表現〉

8. When you find it difficult to read some words or sentences, ask me or your friends for help.
9. I want you to do individual reading. You may read slowly but read clearly and accurately.

10. This time try to read as fast as you can. So you don't have to read each word in a big [loud] voice.
11. You'll read the same part three times. Each time I'll time you.

   **Notes:** 机間巡視で生徒がよく読んでいるかを確認し，個々の生徒の音読の問題点を指導するようにしたい．8〜10 は黙読の場合同様，正確さから速さへ移行する音読指導．11 では生徒に wpm を算出させてみる．

## g. ペア読み　Pair reading

1. Let's do pair reading.
2. Let's practice reading in pairs.
3. Now we'll do pair reading.
4. One of you will read aloud and the other will listen (to him or her).

〈発展的表現〉

5. One of you will read as the other listens and writes whatever he or she hears.
6. In this pair reading, (the) two of you will take turns reading one (sentence) after another.
7. Let's practice the conversation in pairs. One person will read A's part and the other will read B's part. Then change parts.
8. First Masato and Toshiko will read the text for the class. Then another pair will read the same part [the following part].

   **Notes:** 5 はペアでの書き取りである．7 はあとでいくつかのペアにロールプレイをさせてもよい．

## h. 斉読　Choral reading

1. Let's read the text all together.
2. Let's begin choral reading.
3. Let's read in chorus.
4. Read [Repeat] all together.

5. Now all of you will read after me [the tape / the CD].

〈発展的表現〉

6. Tsutomu, you're not reading. Read together with your friends [the class]. Again, all together.
7. Stop reading, class. A few students are not participating. Hisashi, Shizuka and Toru. You must join the class. Now, let's read again from the beginning.
8. Let's practice the dialog between you and me. You're Kate and I'm Tom . . . This time you're Tom, and I'm Kate.
9. You (have) read the paragraph sentence by sentence [one sentence at a time] after the tape [CD]. Now read the whole paragraph after me.
10. Let's read the text sentence by sentence between you and me. After I read, it's your turn. After you read, it's my turn.
11. We'll read paragraph by paragraph in groups. The first paragraph by Ayako's group, the second by Nobuo's group, the third by Shigeru's group . . .

**Notes:** 6, 7 は斉読に加わっていない生徒がいた場合．9 は文単位からパラグラフ単位への移行．10 は生徒と教師の掛け合いによる斉読で，音読のスピード化がはかれる．11 はグループ単位での斉読．

## i. 読む箇所の指定　Directions about where to read

1. Page 31, line 5.
2. We will begin at Lesson 7, Section 2.
3. We will practice reading the new words at the bottom of pages 22 and 23.
4. Let's read the second sentence of the first paragraph [sentence 2 of paragraph 1].
5. Let's read paragraph 1, sentence 2.
6. Will you read from the first line [line 1] on page 58 (to line 5 on the

same page)?

〈発展的表現〉

7. We will read from page 18, line 15 to page 19, line 10.
8. I'd like you to read paragraph 2 on page 77.
9. Do you know where we are? We are on page 15, line 4.
10. Stop reading. You're reading the wrong part. Will you begin on page 38, line 4?
11. Let's return [go] back to page 42. We'll read again from line 3 [beginning at line 3] on this page.
12. Open your textbook to page 102. Start reading from the second paragraph [beginning at paragraph 2].

---
**Student Response**

どこですか What page (and what line)? / Where (are we [you]) in the text? / Where are we [you] reading? / I don't know where we are reading. / Where should I start and where should I stop?

---

**Interaction**

| | |
|---|---|
| T: レッスン5のセクション2から始めます．教科書の56ページを開いて… | We will begin at Lesson 5, Section 2. So open your textbooks to page 56… |
| S: 56ページ？ もう終わったよ． | Page 56? We've done it already. |
| T: あっ，そう．この前，どこまでやったかな．覚えてるかい． | Oh, really? Where did we stop last time? Do you remember? |
| S: 確か57ページの3行目だったかしら． | I'm not sure, but I think we stopped at page 57, line 3. |
| T: ありがとう．思い出したよ． | Thank you. Now I remember. |

## j. イントネーション　Intonation

1. With good [better / natural] intonation.

2. Be careful about the intonation.
3. Read the sentence with more attention to the intonation.
4. End the sentence with a rising intonation. Like this.
5. Read the sentence with a falling intonation at the end of the sentence.

〈発展的表現〉

6. "You'll be late (if you don't hurry up)." This statement is a warning. So read 'late' with a falling and rising intonation.
7. The tape [CD] has a slightly different intonation. So read just like you hear it [it is read] on the tape [CD].
8. Now I'll show you the standard intonation of these three sentences. Listen to me carefully and imitate my intonation.
9. Look at the board. The standard intonation is shown with the intonation pattern. Write it down in your textbooks.
10. Thank you for reading the text aloud. But your intonation of the sentence '∼' is not correct. The correct intonation is like this. Will you repeat just that part?

## k. 強 勢　Stress / Accent

1. The (strong) stress is on ∼.
2. Read the word with the correct stress.
3. Please listen to me [the tape] carefully.
4. Be careful about the stress of this word.
5. I'll give you the correct stress of the word.
6. You put a stress on the wrong syllable.

〈発展的表現〉

7. The strongest stress of this sentence [the sentence stress] is on the word ∼.
8. The strongest stress of this sentence is on the word ∼, and the second strongest stress is on the word ∼.

9. This word 'package' has a primary stress on the first syllable, like this: /pǽkidʒ/. Now repeat after me.
10. The stress of 'calendar' is on 'ca', not on 'len'. Say /kǽləndə(r)/. Don't say /kalénda/. Repeat, everyone, 'cálendar'.
11. The primary [strongest] accent of 'extraordinary' is on the 'or' (/ɔː/) sound, and the secondary [the second strongest] accent is on the 'nar' (/ne/) sound. So you have to read it /ikstrɔ́ːd(ə) nèri/.
12. In a sentence the stress comes on the most important word [words]. For example, we don't say just 'I mean it'. We say 'I **mean** it'.

   **Notes:** 9 以降では単語や表現の具体的な例を挙げての指導を示している．12 の例のように，文レベルでのアクセント指導も欲しい．ここでは mean が強く発音される．(☞ p. 170)

## I. 発音の訂正　Correcting mistakes in pronunciation

1. That's not good.
2. That's not a good pronunciation [accent / intonation].
3. There were a few [a couple of] mistakes in your reading.
4. Oh, you made a little mistake in your reading.
5. You read it in the wrong way.
6. Let me correct your reading.
7. You should try to read it more like the tape [CD].
8. I'm sure you can read much better.
9. Just a moment, Yosuke. That should be 〜, not . . .
10. Your pronunciation of the word 〜 is not correct. The correct one is . . .

   〈発展的表現〉
11. You have to read it with an /ai/ sound, not with an /i/ sound. Not /fínəli/, but /fáinəli/.
12. That's not a good pronunciation. Look at the phonetic alphabet. Now try again. . . . Yes, that's much better.

13. Wait a minute. That's not the right way to read the word [sentence]. Listen and repeat after me [the tape / CD].
14. You've made a little mistake in pronouncing the word [sentence] 〜. Now listen to the tape [CD] for the correct pronunciation.
15. I'm afraid you pronounced the phrase in the wrong way. You have to read it like this. Will you pronounce it again? . . . Good.
16. Don't read the phrase word by word [one word at a time]. You have to read the sentence [phrase] as a whole.
17. You shouldn't put a pause between A and B. Instead pause between C and D. Read the sentence with a pause in the right place.
18. Your reading is not bad. But it'll become much better if you read with a correct accent and a natural intonation. Listen to me [the tape / CD] very carefully, then read it once again.
19. Thank you for reading aloud. It was good. But your reading will be far better if you read some parts more carefully. So let's practice those parts now, together with your friends.

**Notes:** 5 は I'm afraid で始めれば響きが柔らかくなる。(☞ p. 91)

---
**Student Response**

どこが悪いのですか　What's wrong? / Anything wrong? / Correct my reading, please. / How can I read it better? / How can I improve my reading? / Is there anything wrong with my reading? / Tell me what's wrong with my reading.

---

## ② 内容把握　Comprehension

### a. 語[句・節・文]の意味
Meaning of words [phrases / clauses / sentences]

1. What does this word mean?

2. Tell me the meaning of this word [phrase] in Japanese.
3. What is the meaning of this word?
4. Will you give its meaning in Japanese?
5. What is the Japanese meaning of this word?
6. What does your dictionary say?
7. Look up this word in your dictionaries.
8. What does this phrase mean? Tell me in your own Japanese words, not (directly) from your dictionaries.
9. Tell me what this sentence means in Japanese. But don't just translate into Japanese. Use your own Japanese words.

〈発展的表現〉

10. Does this 'hard' mean 'kibishii' or 'katai'?
11. Which do you think is more correct as the meaning of (this word) 'happy'? Is it 'ureshii' or 'tanoshii'?
12. Which is the correct meaning of the word 'since' in this phrase, 'dakara' or 'irai'?
13. Does this phrase [clause] show a result or a purpose or something else?
14. What Japanese word comes to your mind for this word? Yuji? Masami? Midori? Anyone? ... O.K., then let's look it up in the dictionary.
15. Before you look up this word in your dictionaries, think about its meaning and discuss it with your friends.
16. Now let's think of the meaning of this word [phrase] from its context. After you guess the meaning, check it in your dictionaries.
17. Guess the meaning of this word [phrase] according to the context. Then look it up in your dictionaries to see if your guess was right or not.
18. What words tell you that the master of the dog was very sad when he lost it?
19. Was the master of the dog sad when he lost it? How do you know?

What words [phrases / sentences / expressions] tell you so?

20. I think there are a couple of words [phrases / expressions] that tell us how sad the master of the dog was when he lost it. Find those words [phrases / expressions].

**Notes:** 16, 17は語句の意味推測に取り組ませるもの。18〜20はより深い内容理解へと導くもの。

## b. パラグラフの大意　Gist of paragraph

### ア. 大意把握の指示　Summarizing

1. Now [Let's] summarize the paragraph.
2. Give me a summary of the second paragraph.
3. What's a summary of this paragraph?
4. What does this paragraph say in short?
5. How would you summarize [sum up] this paragraph?
6. Tell me just briefly what is written in this paragraph.
7. What's the message of this paragraph?
8. Can you restate that in your own words?
9. Say the gist of this paragraph in one sentence, either in English or in Japanese.
10. Give me the gist of the paragraph in your own Japanese [English] words.

〈発展的表現〉

11. Well, Toshio, don't try to translate but tell us only the gist of the paragraph.
12. What do you think the writer wants to say in this paragraph? Say it briefly in your own words, either in Japanese or in English.
13. Can anyone sum up the paragraph in a few words? I'd like you to sum it up in English. But if you cannot, you may do it in Japanese.
14. What are your summaries of this paragraph? Make your own summaries in Japanese [English] in three minutes.

15. What do you think is the main [general] idea of the 3rd paragraph? Read the whole paragraph again and talk about the main [general] idea with your partner [group members].

イ．大意把握の具体的方法　Skimming and scanning
1. What title can you think of for this paragraph (if you summarize it)?
2. What word or words are the most important in this paragraph?
3. Take out the key word [words] in this paragraph.
4. Make a short summary of the paragraph, using the key word [words].
5. What sentence summarizes the paragraph best?
6. Which is the topic sentence of this paragraph?
7. This paragraph seems to have no topic sentence.
〈発展的表現〉
8. Tell me the sentence number of the topic sentence of this paragraph. Is it sentence No.1 or sentence No.2?
9. What is the outline of this paragraph? Let's make it with the 5 WH's and 1 H question words. Who did what? When and where? Why or how?
10. What is the function of this paragraph in the whole passage? Is it to give some examples (of the main idea in the previous paragraph)?
11. How does this paragraph develop the central idea of the previous paragraph? Is it to give a different viewpoint [opinion]?
12. What are the relationships between these three paragraphs? Which paragraph is the most important to summarize the whole story?
13. Which paragraph talks about the main idea of this passage?
14. Which paragraph tells most about the kindness of the hero? And what paragraph tells about his hard experiences more than any other paragraph?

**Notes:** スキミングは文章の概要を素早くとらえる読み方，スキャニングは特定の情報を拾い読みすること．1～4は単語を中心に要約させるもの．5, 6, 8は主題文で要約させようとするもの．10以降はパラグラフのつながりや関係を見たり，パラグラフ単位で文章全体を要約しようとするもの．(☞ p. 145, 166)

---
**Interaction**

| | |
|---|---|
| T：この段落で一番重要な文はどれかな．1分間考えてごらん．(1分後) さあ，答えがわかる人． | Which sentence is the most important in this paragraph? I'll give you one minute to think. (One minute later) Anyone? |
| S：最後の文がそうだと思うのですが． | I think the last sentence is the most important. |
| T：最後の文ね．君はどう思う． | The last sentence? How about you? |
| S：最初の文です． | The first sentence. |
| T：最初の文か．じゃあ，最初の文と最後の文ではどっちがこの段落の内容全体をカバーしているだろね． | The first sentence? Well class, which sentence tells more about this paragraph, the first sentence or the last sentence? |

---

## c. 指示語の把握　Understanding determiners

1. Is this 'it' A or B?
2. What is this 'them'?
3. Tell me what 'these' refers to.
4. Who does this 'he' refer to? Find and tell me who he is from the text.
5. What does this 'they' (on line 7) stand for in the text?

〈発展的表現〉

6. The content of this 'it' has already been mentioned in the text. Find out where it is and underline the part.
7. Tell me in detail from the text what this 'that' describes. Read aloud exactly the words [phrase / sentence] in the text.
8. What does this 'they' actually mean? Are they people, living things or just things?

9. Do the 'it' on the 5th line and the 'it' on the 8th line mean the same thing? (If they are the same thing, what is it? If different, tell me what each 'it' means in the text.)

---
**Interaction**

| | |
|---|---|
| T：この文を訳す前に，it が何を指すか考えてみよう．わかるかな． | Before we put this sentence into Japanese, let's think what this 'it' refers to. Do you have any idea? |
| S：英語で答えるんですか． | Do we have to answer in English? |
| T：そうだよ．質問をくり返すよ．この it は何を指すかな，保君． | Yes. I'll repeat my question. "What does this 'it' refer to?" Tamotsu? |
| S：えーと，わかりません． | I...I...I don't know. |
| T：わからないわけはないんだがな．すぐ前のところにあるよ． | You should know. The answer can be found in the preceding sentence. |

---

## d. 和訳 Translation

### ア．和訳の指示 Directions
1. In Japanese, please.
2. Put it into Japanese.
3. Put this sentence into Japanese.
4. Will you translate this sentence into Japanese?
5. Give me your Japanese translation of this sentence.
6. What is your Japanese translation of this part?
7. Now class, let's see if we can translate it into Japanese.

〈発展的表現〉
8. First find a good Japanese word for the word A. Then it will become much easier to translate the whole sentence.
9. When you translate this sentence into Japanese, pay attention to the sentence structure. It'll be very difficult to translate without

understanding the whole structure.
10. This sentence is too long to put into one Japanese sentence. You may translate it into more than one Japanese sentence.
11. I'd like you to put this difficult sentence into Japanese. You don't have to make a perfect Japanese translation. Just make a translation that is understandable.

**Notes:** 8以降は和訳のコツを指摘しての表現。

## イ．和訳をよくしようとする場合　　Improving students' translation

1. You can make your translation better. Try it again.
2. You can improve your translation by changing the subject.
3. When you put this sentence into Japanese, try to make your Japanese translation (sound) as natural as possible.
4. Thank you for putting the sentence into Japanese. But it sounds a little like a word-for-word translation. Can't you make your translation (sound) more natural in Japanese?
5. It's better to translate the meaning of English sentences into natural Japanese than to translate each word exactly.
6. Can't you think of a more colloquial translation? This time use everyday Japanese.
7. If you use easier [simpler] Japanese words, you can get a better translation.
8. Your translation sounds strange, though it is understandable. Think about how you can improve it [make it better].

〈発展的表現〉

9. I'm afraid your translation has a problem. Let me ask another student to show us how he [she] has translated the same part.
10. What's wrong with her translation? Let's talk about it to make a better translation.
11. Now compare your translations with your neighbors'. Then tell me the differences and how you have improved your translations.

12. I'll give you my Japanese translation of this sentence. Listen to me carefully and compare it with your own translations. Check the difference between your translations and my translation.
13. Kazuya translated this sentence like this [in this way]; ～. Yukari's translation is like this; ～. Which translation do you like better and why?

**Notes:** 1～8は和訳した生徒によりよい和文を求める表現．9～13はグループまたはクラス全体で和訳文の検討を指示する表現．中学，高校の段階では日英語のニュアンスの差にあまりこだわらず，表現の意図を和訳する気持ちが大切である．

┌─ **Student Response** ─────────────────
│ 辞書を引いてもいいですか　Can I use the dictionary? / May I look it up in the dictionary? / Is it okay if I use a dictionary?
└─────────────────────────────────────

## e. パラフレーズ　Paraphrasing

1. Paraphrase this expression [sentence].
2. Will you paraphrase this part in easy English?
3. Tell me the meaning of this phrase in different but easy English.
4. Find a word [phrase] in the text which has almost the same meaning as this word [phrase].
5. What idea does this word really express? Tell me in your own words, either in Japanese or in English.

〈発展的表現〉

6. Will you explain the meanings of these sentences in Japanese? Don't give me just a Japanese translation of them. I want you to explain the situation behind the sentences.
7. What do you think the writer wants to say here? Please explain it in a few words of your own, either in Japanese or in English.
8. I don't think you can find a good Japanese translation for this word [phrase / sentence]. Instead explain the real meaning of it in your

own words.

9. I want you to say the exact meaning [idea] of this expression in other words. Talk about it with your partner [group members]. Then tell me what you've talked about.

## ③ 文法練習　Grammar Drills

### a. 書き換え　Rewriting

1. How do you rewrite it?
2. Rewrite the following sentence(s).
3. Rewrite all the sentences as in the example.
4. Rewrite each sentence, using the past participle.
5. Write the same idea in a different way.
6. Change the sentence form by starting with 〜.
7. Change all the adverbial clauses into adverbial phrases.
8. Turn the underlined phrases into clauses.
9. Use a different sentence structure to express the same meaning.

〈発展的表現〉

10. Rewrite each sentence (below) following the instructions.
11. Write a new sentence which emphasizes the underlined part of each sentence.
12. Rewrite the following sentences by starting new sentences with the underlined parts.
13. Rewrite the sentences (below) by changing the phrases into clauses.
14. Rewrite the following sentences by changing the comparative into the superlative, or the other way round.
15. What do we call a person who plays tennis? ... Yes, we call him a tennis player.  Now rewrite the sentence 'He plays tennis very well'

using the words 'a tennis player'.

**Notes:** 10 の following the instruction とは，例えば using the words given in the parentheses など．11 は強調構文への書き換えを指示している．14 は比較級の書き換えであるが，文法用語は日本語を用いてもよいであろう．15 は具体的にステップを踏んでの書き換えであり，派生語に注意を向ける．(☞ p.176)

---
**Student Response**
ヒントを下さい (Give me) a hint, please? / (Do you have) any hints? / Will you give me a clue?

---

## b. 和文英訳　Putting Japanese into English

### ア．和文英訳の指示　Directions
1. Now (let's try) English translation.
2. Let's try translating it into English.
3. Put this sentence [these words] into English.
4. Put the Japanese sentence(s) into English.
5. Translate the following Japanese into English.
6. Let's say in English the meaning of each Japanese sentence.
7. Let me see how you translate the following Japanese sentences.
8. Make the English counterparts of these Japanese sentences.

〈発展的表現〉

9. Put these sentences into English using the word(s) [phrase(s)] given (in each parenthesis).
10. Look at the words on the blackboard. Put these words below into the right order to make a sentence that expresses the meaning of each Japanese sentence.
11. Add one word to the group of words below. Then put all the words into the right order to produce an English sentence which has the same meaning as the Japanese sentence.
12. I'd like you to put into English the underlined part(s) of the following Japanese passage.

13. Complete each English sentence so that it expresses the idea of each Japanese sentence given in brackets.
14. Don't translate the Japanese sentence into English word for word. Try to put into English the idea expressed in Japanese.
15. It's no good just to change Japanese words into English words and put them together. Understand what the Japanese sentence really means as a whole. Then you can put it into good English.
16. Before you translate into English, first put the Japanese sentence into easy [everyday] Japanese. Then you can translate that Japanese into English.

**Notes:** 14〜16は意訳を心掛けることを指示している.

## イ. 誤りを訂正する場合　Correcting mistakes

1. No errors [mistakes]?
2. (Have you found) any mistakes?
3. Is this translation perfect?
4. Are there any mistakes [errors]?
5. (Have you found) any careless [spelling] mistakes?
6. (Doesn't this translation need) any correction?
7. (Does this translation have) any problems?
8. (Is there) anything wrong with this translation?
9. (Can you find) anything strange in this translation?

〈発展的表現〉

10. Look at the translation on the board. Are there any mistakes [errors]? Tell me if you've found any.
11. I'm afraid there are a couple of (small / spelling) mistakes in this translation. Look at it carefully and find them.
12. There is something wrong with the underlined parts. What's wrong? Let's see if we can correct it.
13. The underlined parts have some errors [mistakes]. Do you have any idea how to correct them?

14. If you have noticed any errors [mistakes] in this translation, tell me how you can improve them.

   **Notes:** 英訳の訂正は教師が一方的に行うのでなく，生徒に間違いに気づかせ，できれば訂正させるように指導したい．

### ウ．別訳を検討する場合　Alternative translation
1. Is there a different translation?
2. Isn't there a better translation?
3. Is there another way to translate this?
4. (Do you have) another way of translating this?
5. Did you use a different expression?
6. Raise your hand if you translated it differently.
7. Do you have a different version of this translation?

〈発展的表現〉

8. I wonder if you used a different expression [sentence structure] for this translation.
9. Doesn't anyone's translation start with 〜? / Did anyone use the expression 〜?
10. Yasuko translated it in a different way. Now, Yasuko, will you read your translation for us?
11. Two students will write their English translations of the same Japanese sentence on the board. Then we'll compare their translations, O.K.?

   **Notes:** 8は最初から異なる訳を検討することを意図している．あらかじめグループで検討して，グループごとの訳を検討することもできる．9は「〜を使って訳した人は？」の意．

### C．穴埋め　Completion

1. What word comes here?
2. What word should go here?

3. Fill in the blanks [gaps].
4. Put the right words into the blanks.
5. What word should we put into this blank?
6. Say which words may be used to fill the spaces.
7. Fill in each blank with the right word from below.
8. Write in the blanks the most suitable [appropriate] English words.
9. For each blank choose the most suitable [fitting] word from below.
10. Insert into each sentence a suitable adverbial from the list below.

〈発展的表現〉

11. What word do you think should go into this blank? Put in the word which you think is the most suitable.
12. The same word goes into the blanks of these two [three] sentences. What is the word?
13. Some words are missing in the next story [passage]. Read the whole story [passage] first. Then choose the best [most appropriate] word for each blank.
14. To make both sentences mean the same in each pair, put the right word into the blank of the second sentence.
15. Fill in the blanks in the second sentence with the proper words so that both sentences have the same meaning.
16. Choose the most suitable word [verb] for each blank and change its form if [where] necessary.

―――――― **Interaction** ――――――

| | |
|---|---|
| T： さあ，下線部分を書き換えて下さい。 | Now I'd like you to rewrite the underlined part(s). |
| S： 何かヒントありませんか。 | Give me some hints. |
| T： いいよ，じゃあ5語で書き換えてごらん。（空欄を5つ書いて）空欄を埋めてみよう。 | O.K. You can rewrite it in five words. Now fill in each blank. |

| | |
|---|---|
| S： to が入りますか． | Is the word 'to' part of the answer? |
| T： はい，最初の空欄に入りますよ． | Yes, 'to' goes into the first blank. |
| S： じゃあ，わかった． | Then I've got it. |

## d.　文の転換・結合　Conversion and combination

### ア．　文の転換　Conversion

1. Turn the sentences into negative forms [question forms / exclamatory sentences / imperative sentences / declarative sentences].
2. Change the voice (of each sentence).
3. Turn the active form into the passive form.
4. Change it into the narrative form.
5. Put the verbs in brackets into the future tense.

〈発展的表現〉

6. Make these sentences (a) negative and (b) interrogative, using *do*.
7. Put the following into indirect speech.
8. Turn the direct narration into the indirect narration.
9. Change each sentence into a simple sentence [a compound sentence / a complex sentence] (by using 〜).

**Notes:**　文法用語を避けるとしたら例を挙げて指示をすることになる．例えば4であれば，Change the sentences in quotation marks, using *that* [*what* / *if*, etc.]．直接[間節]話法を direct [indirect] narrative とするのは口語表現としてはわかりづらい．(☞ p. 176)

### イ．　文の結合　Combination

1. Put the two sentences together.
2. Fill in each bracket with a suitable relative pronoun.
3. Put the two sentences together, using such words as *which*, *who*, *that*, etc.
4. Put the two sentences together, using words like *but*, *because*,

*though*, etc.
5. Connect the two sentences with words like *where, when, how*, etc.
6. Combine the two sentences (into one sentence) by using relatives [to-infinitives].

〈発展的表現〉

7. Join the following pairs of sentences to form complex sentences with relative clauses. Use commas where necessary.
8. Use a suitable joining word such as *and, but, so, then, therefore*, etc., and make each pair of simple sentences into a compound sentence.

**Notes:** ☞ p. 178(文型練習の場合)


④ 言語活動　Performance Activities


a. 聞くこと　Listening

1. Listen and repeat.
2. Listen to the greeting between two old friends.
3. Check your answers by listening to the tape [CD] again.
4. Look at these questions before listening to the interview.
5. Listen to the instructions for a Bingo game and follow them with your partner.

〈発展的表現〉

6. When you hear the /r/ sound, put up your right hand. When you hear the /l/ sound, put up your left hand.
7. When [If] you cannot tell the difference between /r/ and /l/, you don't have to put up your hands.
8. I will give you three words. One word sounds different from the other two words. So listen to me carefully and tell me which word

sounds different by saying the numbers 1, 2, or 3.
9. You will listen to five pairs of words. If the words are just the same, say 'same', and if they are different, say 'different'.
10. Let's do 'Odd Man Out'. I'll give you six groups of words. Each group has five or six words, but one word is different from the other words in the group. Now listen and tell me which word is different.
11. I'll read some words from this lesson for [to] you. Listen to me carefully and write them down in your notebooks. Later we'll check the spellings.
12. I'll give you six simple sentences. If my sentence is true, say "True," and if my sentence is false, say "False." O.K.? The first sentence is "Spring comes after summer".
13. You have four pictures on your desk. I'll talk about one of them. Listen to me carefully and choose the picture I'm talking about [describing].
14. You have the same story as in Lesson 3, Part 1 on your sheet. But some words are not on the sheet. Now I'll turn on the tape [I'll read the story]. So listen carefully and write those words [fill in the missing words] on your paper.

**Notes:** 6〜9は音の識別．13は絵を用いた活動で，絵の違いを微妙なものにすると難易度が高くなる．

〈少し高度な活動〉
15. You have a set of five picture cards. Those pictures make a story. Now I'll tell you the story, so listen to me very carefully and put the cards into the right order.
16. Look at the chart on your sheet. There are some blanks. Now I'll give you the information you need to fill in the blanks. Listen carefully and fill in the blanks.
17. Let's draw a picture. First, I'll describe the picture [I'll tell you what the picture looks like]. So listen to me carefully and draw the

picture in your notebook.

18. Let's make a town. Look at the map on your sheet. There is a town on it, but it is not complete yet. It needs more shops, parks, schools, and other buildings. I'll tell you their locations [where they are]. So listen to me carefully and mark them down on your map.
19. Let's do 'Where Am I?' Look at the map on your paper. Now I am standing at Sakuramachi Station. Listen to me carefully and follow me to the place I'm going to.
20. I'll talk about a person [thing] (in this lesson). Listen to me carefully and tell me who the person is [what it is].
21. I'll talk about one student in this class. Listen carefully and guess who the student is.
22. Listen, everyone. I'll give you two sentences. After you hear the two sentences, put them together using the words *which* [*who / that / whom / because*].
23. We will have a dictation test. Listen to me carefully and fill in the blanks in the sentences [story] on your sheet. I'll repeat each sentence [the story] three times.
24. Now you'll listen to a song. After listening to the song, tell me any words, that you hear. Listen carefully and try to catch as many words as you can.
25. First write down the numbers from 1 to 6 in your notebooks. Now, I'll read six sentences. If the sentences are true of the story (of this lesson), circle the numbers; if not true, cross them out [put an × over them].
26. You're going to listen to a short conversation [story / passage] now. After that I'll ask you some questions about it, and you will answer them in English. So listen very carefully.

**Notes:** 15 ではストーリーを変えて同じカードを何回でも用いることができる．16 は表，図，グラフなどを作成する作業を目的とする聞く活動になるが，教科書の内容をまとめる活動としても使える．17 では絵を描かせたあと，生徒同士

で比べさせるとよい．教師が同じことを言いながら，黒板に正しい絵を描いて提示する．18のような活動では，地図だけでなく，家，台所，居間など，身近なものを描かせることができる．19で使う地図は18で作成した地図でよい．22は文と文の関係に注意を喚起するのに有効．24では，適当なところで生徒が聞き取った単語の確認をやめ，教師が歌詞を再生すればよい．あるいは最初から穴埋めの形式にする．(☞ p. 256)

## b. 話すこと　Speaking

1. Repeat after me; I like apples. (生徒: I like apples.) Oranges. (生徒: I like oranges.) Snakes. (生徒: I like snakes.)
2. What fruit do you like, Mieko? ... (生徒: Strawberries.) Now everyone; Mieko likes strawberries. (生徒: Mieko likes strawberries.) How about you, Yuji?
3. What is this in my hand? ... Yes, I have a cup in my hand. Repeat after me, everyone; you have a cup in your hand. (スプーンを手にして) Now what do I have in my hand? Yes, I have a spoon in my hand.
4. There are six animals on the board. Which animal do you like best? Ask each other in your pairs [groups].

〈発展的表現〉

5. Now you have twenty cards in your hands. Everyone, stand up with the cards and choose one card. The members of this group will read their cards [make a sentence with their cards]. If you have the same cards, you may sit down.
6. Find a friend with the same card [who has the same card]. You have to move around the class and ask your friends the question 'Do you have ～?' ['Are you ～?'].
7. Look at the picture on the board. What is this? (生徒: Car. Book.) No, it is not a car, and it's not a book. (絵をさらに詳しく書いて) Now what do you think this is?

**Notes:** 1 は substitution drill であるが，snake などのキューを突然言って，活動をおもしろくする．5 はカルタ形式にしてグループ活動にしてもよい．6 ではカードの代りに簡単な文や文章を使ってもよい．

〈少し高度な活動〉

8. There are several questions on the board. Now I'll ask you all these questions. Michiko, what . . . ? . . . Thank you, Michiko. Now in your pairs [groups] you'll ask all these questions.

9. Now ask your friends to do some actions. First think up the actions in your pairs [groups]. Then you'll ask the other students to do the actions.

10. You have a list of questions on your paper. Ask other students those questions. When your friend says 'yes', write that person's name and circle it. When your friend says 'no', write his or her name and cross it out.

11. Look at the picture [chart] on your paper. I'll ask several questions about it. Please answer my questions in English.

12. Look at the picture [chart] on your paper. Now make some questions about it, and ask your partner the questions.

13. There are five differences in the two pictures. Find them with your partners. Ask each other questions like 'Is there ∼?' or 'Does the man have ∼?', or 'Where is ∼?'

14. We will all start from the school on the map. Each person, mark on the map where you are going and how you are going there. Now, in pairs, give each other directions and find out where your partner is going.

15. I have a person in my mind. The person is a man. You know him very well. You often see him on TV. Now ask me some questions about him and guess who he is.

16. Now it's time for you to make and ask questions about section 2 [today's part]. First make the questions in pairs, then ask other

pairs your questions.
17. Let's play [have a game of] 'Show and Tell'. Today, Yoshiko will show us something and talk about it. Yoshiko, come here and show us what you've brought. Listen to her carefully and ask her questions about it.

**Notes:** 8では，このあと聞き出した内容を何人かの生徒にクラスで発表させる．9は，他の生徒が見えない状態にある誰かの動作を，もう1人の生徒が描写するという形式にするとおもしろい．10では結果を何人かの生徒にクラスで発表させる．15は guessing game であり，生徒に I have a person [a thing] in my mind. の部分をやらせてもよい．その際には教師も guessing に参加して，質問のコツを提示する．16は教科書の内容確認にとどまらず，内容に関連しての質問や意見を求めさせる．(☞ p. 254)

## C. 読むこと　Reading

1. Read the story [passage] and answer the questions about it.
2. Draw a picture according to the story you are going to read.
3. Match the English words on the left with the Japanese words on the right.
4. Match the groups of words on the left and the right to make sentences.
5. Read five different sentences and choose the right picture for each sentence.
   〈発展的表現〉
6. Look for words which have almost the same meanings. They will give you important hints about what you're reading.
7. The following words [sentences] talk about familiar things [people]. Read them carefully and choose [write] the English word for the thing [the person].
8. Look for connecting words and tell me how they help to connect sentences or ideas together.

9. I'm afraid the underlined words in the next story are not familiar to you. Read the story and guess the meanings of those words from the context [situation].

   **Notes:** 1〜5は理解の成否を簡単にチェックしようとするもの．6, 8, 9は文章読解におけるストラテジーを示すもので，6は重要な単語，8は接続語句に注意を喚起し，9は語句の意味推測を求めている．

〈少し高度な活動〉

10. Read the following story and fill in the eight blanks with the (connecting) words [phrases] below.
11. You will read a short story, but there is one sentence in the story which doesn't belong to [is not necessary in] it. Find and underline the sentence.
12. Read the following short passage and two sentences. Decide where the sentences belong [should come] in the passage.
13. The sentences in the next paragraph are not in the correct order. Read each sentence carefully and put them in the right order.
14. There are five titles and five paragraphs. After you've read the paragraphs, match the titles and the paragraphs.
15. The following story is made up of four paragraphs, but they are not in the right order. Read each paragraph and put them in the correct order.
16. There are some blanks in the chart on your sheet. Fill in the blanks, after reading the following passage.
17. Read the following story and fill in the blanks in the summary (of the story) with the most suitable words in the story [below].
18. How do you think each of the characters felt at the end of this story? Match the characters with their feelings.

   **Notes:** 10〜18は課題に答えようとすることで内容理解を深める読む活動．13〜15はパラグラフを意識してのもの．16はインフォメーション・トランスファーで内容理解を図，グラフ，表，絵などに置き換えている．17はクローズテスト

の形式. 18 はスタンダードな課題.

## d. 書くこと  Writing

1. Fill in this form.
2. Write your number and name.
3. Write your Sunday diary in English.
4. Read the story and write your answers to the questions about it.

〈発展的表現〉

5. Look at the board. There are 10 words, but one letter is not written [missing] in each word. Come to the board and write the missing letters.
6. I will give you spellings of words. Listen and write down each word in your notebooks. Then read the words aloud.
7. I will give you five Japanese words [phrases]. Listen and write the English words [phrases] for those Japanese words [phrases].
8. You will write the first two paragraphs in your notebook. Write them very quickly. Let's see how many minutes you need.
9. Put the words in each group into the right order to make a sentence. Write each sentence in your notebook.
10. Look at the pictures on the board. Write English sentences which describe the pictures (in the present tense / in the past tense / in the present progressive / in the past progressive).

**Notes:** 5〜7 は主に単語レベルでの書く活動. 8 は書写の活動. 9, 10 は文レベルでの書く活動.

〈少し高度な活動〉

11. There are seven sentences and they make a paragraph, but they must be put together with some connecting [joining] words to make a good paragraph. Use the list of words to put them together and write the paragraph.

12. Write the names of the people in this lesson and how the people are related to each other.
13. Let's summarize this lesson. Think of 5 WH's (when, where, who, what, why) and 1 H (how). Then make a short story [passage] which summarizes this lesson.
14. Please listen to a short story [passage] three times. Then write it in your notebooks. You don't have to use the same words you hear. You can use your own words.
15. This dialog is between Bob and Louisa, but Louisa's part is missing. As you read Bob's part, write Louisa's part.
16. The dialog [story] is not complete [completely ended]. So write and finish the dialog [story] with your own words [in your own way].
17. Read the dialog [letter / story] and write the same kind of dialog [letter / story] in your own words.
18. Let's make a story about Dick. In each group one student after the other writes a different sentence about Dick. See what is written and add your own sentence.
19. Now you write a letter to Mr. or Ms. X. Someone in this class will read your letter and the reader will write a letter in reply. You can write your letter like the example.
20. You will make a speech in front of your classmates. Your speech will be about your school life [anything you like]. Before you make [give / deliver] the speech, you have to write it.

**Notes:** 11はパラグラフ単位で書く活動であるが，この前段に来る活動として，「文の転換・結合」(p. 223) の活動を入れるとよい．12は文章中の人物や出来事，物事に焦点を当てて，その関係を書き出す活動．14は dicto-compo の形式であるが，文章を読ませてそれを生徒自身の言葉で再生させる方法でもよい．15〜18は guided composition の形式である．15〜17はペアやグループ活動で行ない，結果を発表させるとよい．18, 19では，教師が具体的な状況や使用する語句や構文の条件を与えることもできる．

# 6. 終　了
## Consolidation

### ① 残り時間　Remaining Time

**a.　短い場合**　Little time left

**ア．急いで進む**　In a hurry
1. It's 11:53 now.
2. It's seven (minutes) to twelve now.
3. It's almost lunch time [time for the lunch break].
4. Only a few minutes to go [spare].
5. We have only a few minutes to go [spare].
6. We're running out of time.
7. Let's hurry up.
8. You have ten minutes to do this.
9. Let's hurry up and finish Exercise D.
10. Let's get the last thing done.
11. We still have one more thing (to do) for today's schedule.
12. There's almost no time (left).
13. It's almost time to stop [finish].
14. The bell is going to ring in a moment.
    〈発展的表現〉
15. All right. Let's do the rest of the exercises in the next lesson.
16. I don't think we have time to read further [to go through these items / to practice it again].
17. There's not enough time. We'll have to finish now.

18. We don't have enough time to do any conversation practice.
19. I'm afraid we don't have time to do this activity [to start a new exercise].
20. Let's have a quick look at the example again [let me explain the example again quickly] before finishing today.

> **Notes:** 1〜7 までのいずれかの表現だけでも状況によっては急いで作業を進めるように促す意味にもなるが，8〜11 の表現を付け加えると意図がより明確に伝わるようになる．1, 2 では各校の時間割により，授業終了時間の少し前の時刻を代入して使う．3 の time for the lunch break はアメリカ人により多く使われる表現である．4 の spare は自由にできる余分な時間がそれだけある，という意味．12〜19 では時間がないから本日はこのあたりで終了する意味になる．16 で否定を表わす not は文頭近くのこの位置に置く．I think we don't have 〜 とは言わない．

> **Student Response**
> 授業終了　Let's stop now. / Let's finish. / We're tired. Whew! / Good!

## イ．生徒を呼び止めて　Asking students to wait

1. (Please) wait.
2. Just a moment, please.
3. Wait a moment.
4. Don't go rushing off.
5. (Please) stay in your seats.
6. One more thing before you go.
7. No, no, no. The bell hasn't rung yet.
8. It isn't time to finish yet.
9. Go back to your places [seats].
10. Sit quietly. The other classes are still working.

〈発展的表現〉

11. Wait a moment. Let's finish the last question before you go.
12. Don't go rushing off. Why don't we check your answers now?
13. Please wait. Let me explain a little more about No. 3.

14. Where are you going? We haven't finished yet.
15. Don't go away. We need to finish this passage.
16. Just a moment. You're supposed to stay here for two more minutes.
17. Wait. You're not supposed to leave yet [now].
18. There're three more minutes to go. Go back to your seats.
19. We haven't said good-bye yet. I have something to tell you before you go.

**Student Response**
帰宅　Let's go. / Let's go home.

## b. 長い場合　Much time left

### ア．予定外の活動を入れる　Using the final minutes of class
1. It's only ten to twelve.
2. There's five minutes until the bell rings.
3. The bell hasn't rung yet.
4. We have a few more minutes to go.
5. We have a few extra minutes today. Any questions?
6. It's a little too early to finish our lesson now.
7. It's too early for you to leave the class.
8. We (still) have another five minutes left.
9. You finished that quickly.
10. That was a quick job. We still have ten minutes left [ten more minutes].

〈発展的表現〉
11. Let's do an extra activity.
12. Why don't we practice the last dialog again?
13. Why don't you finish your remaining exercises [finish off your exercises] now?
14. Let's have a quick look at the chart on page 25.
15. What do you say to playing a game?

16. Would you like to have one more round [another go]?

   **Notes:** 1～10 の表現に発展的表現 11～15 を付け加えると，余った時間で予定外の活動を行う旨を述べることができる．16 はゲームをやっているときに使える．Student Response の Oh, sure. / Great idea. / That's what I want. はうんざりした表情と口調で言えば，言葉の表面の意味と裏腹に「いやみ」になる．

   ┌─ **Student Response** ─────────────────────────────
   │ 肯定的反応　A good idea. / Why not? / Sure. / Oh, sure. / Great idea. /
   │ 　　　　　　That's what I want.
   │ 不定的反応　No kidding. / Let's stop here. / Let's not do that.
   └──────────────────────────────────────────

**イ．早めに終わる**　Finishing earlier than planned

1. Can we finish now?
2. Do you want to stop now?
3. It's not a bad idea to call it a day.
4. Great! You finished your tasks earlier than usual.
5. We seem to have finished a little early.

〈発展的表現〉

6. Quiet, please.
7. Go out quietly(, please).
8. Not so much noise, please.
9. Don't make any noise as you leave.
10. Ssshhhhh! Other classes are still working.
11. You can go now. But don't forget your assignment.

   **Notes:** 6～10 は他のクラスへの配慮を伝える．

## C. 予定の変更　Change of schedule

1. Let's do this activity next time.
2. Please finish Exercise B at home.
3. Let's put it off till next time.
4. Let's leave out Exercise D.

5. Why don't we skip page 45?
6. I'm not going to give a quiz today.
7. We can do an extra activity.

〈発展的表現〉

8. We will finish the rest of these exercises next time.
9. We'll stop here and do the rest of these next week.
10. I've decided not to give an assignment today.
11. I don't think we have enough time to have a quiz. Let's make it your homework instead.
12. Today, we were going to cover from page 34 to 37. But we'll leave the last page for next week.
13. I think it's better to stop here rather than to read through the chapter.
14. What do you say to playing Bingo until the bell rings?
15. Don't you think it's a good idea to have an extra activity?
16. Why don't you do your homework now and hand it in as you leave?

**Notes:** 7のあとには理由が続くのが自然である．13のit's better to...および15のit's a good idea to...の代わりにyou had better...を使いたくなるかもしれないが，had betterにはそのアドバイスを受け入れないと何か悪いことが起きる，との含みがあって脅迫めいている．16は生徒にYesと言ってもらいたい，という含みが入る．

### d. 次回の予告　Announcement for the next class

1. Please bring your dictionary [cassette tape / CD] next week (class).
2. Do bring your photograph next time.
3. Don't forget your reading record next time.
4. Don't forget your file [folder]. We need them next week.
5. Be sure to hand in your essay [composition / writing] next Monday.

〈発展的表現〉

6. You were supposed to hand in your composition by today. Bring it

next week.
7. You're requested to bring your personal record next week.

**Notes:** 3は今週までに「読書記録」を準備できなかったのなら，来週こそは持って来るように，との意味．4は本日お知らせするので，来週必ず持って来てほしい旨を伝えている．6は今日までに提出することになっていたのに提出できていない，との意味である．7.「個人記録表」を持って来させるのは教師ではなく学校側の要請であるという含み．

---
**Interaction**

| | |
|---|---|
| T: 今日は「世論調査ゲーム」をやって終わりにしたかったのですが... | I wanted to finish our lesson by conducting an 'Opinion Poll' today. But... |
| S: もう終わりにしようよ． | Let's call it a day! |
| S: そうだ，そうだ． | Yes, let's. |
| T: でもあと5分ありますから． | Come on. We have five more minutes. |
| S: 数学のテストで疲れているんです．もう終わりたいなあ． | We're tired after the math exam. It would be nice if we could stop now. |
| T: 結構でしょう．では来週までにそのゲームに使う自分の意見を考えてきて下さい． | Fair enough. Prepare your opinions for the activity by next class, then. |

---

## e. チャイム　Bell

1. Oh, no! The bell!
2. There goes the bell.
3. It's time to stop now.
4. Let's stop here.
5. We have to stop working now.
6. That's all for today.
7. Let's call it a day.

8. Well, that's it.
  〈発展的表現〉
9. Class dismissed.
10. You can go now.
11. Time is up.

**Notes:** 6は授業の終わりを告げる最も一般的な表現．9は日本の教科書では馴染みがうすい表現ではあるが，英米では一般的な表現である．ただし教師側の権威を感じさせる表現であるので使えるのは小学校・中学どまりである．11は時間内に終わらせるように言っておいた作業やゲームなどの最中に使える．

## ② 宿題の指示　Homework / Assignment

### a.　教科書の該当箇所　Where in the text

**ア．宿題の指示**　Directions for homework

1. Page 14. This is [It's] your homework.
2. Look at the chart on page 34. This is your homework.
3. Turn to page 15. Exercises A, C, and D are your homework.
4. Turn back to page 4. Your homework is from the beginning of this page to the end of page 6.
5. Open your books to page 16. From line 10 to line 23 is your homework.
6. Read the introductory conversation on page 34 at home.
7. Review the key sentences on pages 13 and 14 at home.
8. The upper [lower] half of this page is your homework for today [next time].
9. Complete the chart [list / dialog] at home.
10. We have done only part of the exercises today. Finish them off at home.

〈発展的表現〉

11. Topics are given on page 45. Pick out [Choose] one of them and write an essay at home.
12. Read the story on pages 50–55. Write [Give / Make] a summary of it in English. Try to use your own words.
13. Prepare the short story given at the end of Unit 5. There's no need to put everything into Japanese. [You don't have to put everything into Japanese.]
14. The article on pages 101 and 102 is your homework. Don't translate every word. Just get the gist (of it).
15. Pick out one of your favorite stories. Read it and write a book report by the end of this month. Try not to use your dictionary when reading.
16. Write your impressions of this book by next week.
17. I'm not going to give [set] (you) any homework today.

**Notes:** 15の a book report は本の批判・分析を含むもので，感想文としては 16の impressions よりレベルが高い．

イ．**指示の確認** Are the directions clear?

1. Is it clear?
2. Do you get it [understand]?
3. Did you follow that [me]?
4. Can you follow this?
5. Any questions?

〈発展的表現〉

6. Okay?
7. Right?
8. All right?
9. Got it?
10. Are you with me?

**Notes:** 6〜10 は informal.

## b. 暗唱文の指定　For recitation

1. Memorize these set phrases [examples / expressions].
2. Learn these expressions by heart.
3. (You can) leave out No. 7.
4. Forget No. 9.
5. You should memorize the expressions in the box.
6. You don't have to memorize anything after No. 5.
7. Memorize the five lines on the handout I gave you today.

〈発展的表現〉

8. Note these five lines on the blackboard and copy them down to memorize.
9. Memorize [Review] the dialog so that you can act it out next week.
10. I don't expect you to memorize the whole chapter. Just the model sentences in these boxes will do.
11. I don't want you to spend too much time on this. Just memorize the examples on page 13.
12. Don't try to memorize everything. Just learn the underlined new expressions.
13. It's unnecessary to learn the whole section by heart. Try to understand the story by reading it as many times as possible.

**Notes:** 3, 4 は暗唱しなくてもいい文を指定している。6 は「1〜5 だけを覚えればよい」との意味。

宿題の指示でよく使われる表現：

| | | |
|---|---|---|
| the sentence | at the top of | page 34 |
| these sentences | in the center of | this page |
| these expressions | in the middle of | this handout |
| these model sentences | at the bottom of | this work sheet |
| these examples | | the blackboard |

## C. 単語の予習・練習　Checking the new words and phrases

### ア. 予習　Preparation
1. Preparation is a must.
2. Use your dictionary regularly.
3. Prepare a word book and put every new word in it.
4. Look up the new words in your dictionary.
5. Consult your dictionary when you study [work] at home.
6. Get all the new words ready before you come to school.
7. You can check the vocabulary at the back of the textbook.
8. Try to guess the meaning from the context.
9. You're supposed to prepare for the lesson.

〈発展的表現〉

10. Check the meaning of the new words at the bottom of each page for Monday.
11. Make a list of the words you find unfamiliar and look up their meanings in your dictionaries.
12. Put all the new words in your notebooks. And find their meanings in the dictionaries.
13. You don't have to consult your dictionary. Use the glossary in the back.
14. First, just read through the text to get the important points of the text. Use your dictionary only when you have to. Guess the meaning from the context.

**Notes:** 1 の must は口語的表現で，絶対に必要なものの意味．3 の word book は単語帳．13 の glossary は教科書などの後ろに付いている単語リスト・用語リスト．7 の vocabulary もここでは同様の意味．8, 14 は多読・速読などで辞書を引き過ぎない指導をするとき．

### イ. 練習　Practice
1. Practice the new words at home.

2. Go through the word list and write the new words in your notebooks.
3. Learn to spell these words correctly.
4. Put [Write] each new word in each box on your Bingo sheet.
5. Put [Write] those words on your work sheet [cards]. One word in one box [on one card].

〈発展的表現〉

6. Study the word list carefully at home so that you can spell them correctly.
7. Write sentences, using every new word on pages 23 and 24.
8. I want this practice done in your notebooks [on a sheet of paper / on a writing pad].
9. The idea of this homework is for you to be able to use those words in communicative situations.
10. You must finish this by next Monday.

**Notes:** 4, 5 は Bingo game などのマス目に単語を埋めさせるときに使う. 5 での card は単語カードを意味する.

## d. プリントの配布　Handout

1. These are the handouts for today [tomorrow / next time].
2. (Please) take one and pass them on.
3. Pass these to the back.
4. Now I have a handout for you.
5. Help yourselves to the handouts.
6. Take one as you leave.
7. Pick up one sheet before you go.

〈発展的表現〉

8. Could someone help me give out these handouts?
9. Could somebody in your group come up here and help?
10. Would you like to pass these around?

11. You should write your name and student number at the top.
12. Has everyone got two pages?
13. Are there enough to go around?
14. Pass your paper(s) to the front(, please).

> **Notes:** 5, 6, 7 は教室から出るときに各自プリントを持って行くように，との指示．5 では生徒がプリントを取るのは帰り際だけとは限らない．8〜10 はプリント配布を手伝ってもらいたいときの丁寧な表現．11 は紛失するといけないから，との気持ち．12, 13 は配布物が指定枚数ずつ全員に行き渡ったかどうかを確かめる表現．14 はプリントやテストの解答用紙を回収したいときに言う表現．

---

**Student Response**

プリントをもらう　Could I have one? / Can I have one? / There are no handouts at the back. / Three more, please.

---

**Interaction**

| | |
|---|---|
| T：2種類のプリントを用意しました．似た地図ですから，混ぜないように1枚ずつ取って下さい．これがAで，これがBです． | I have two different maps today: A and B. They look quite similar. So please don't mix them up when you take one. These are for Student A's, and these for Student B's. |
| S：この列だけですか． | Are these only for this row? |
| T：そうです． | Yes, they are. |
| S：足りません． | There are no handouts at the back. |
| T：Aですか，Bですか． | A or B? |
| S：Aです． | A. |
| T：何枚ですか． | How many would you like [do you need]? |
| S：3枚です． | Three, please. |

## e. 小テストの予告　Announcement of a quiz

1. There will be a quiz next week.

2. You're going to have a quiz in the next lesson.
3. I'm going to give a dictation in the next lesson.
4. Don't forget that you are taking a test next Monday.
5. The quiz next week covers from Part 1 to Part 2 of Lesson 5.
6. I'll give you a quiz on Lesson 5 next week [this coming Friday].

〈発展的表現〉

7. I'm thinking of giving a quiz sometime.
8. I'm planning to give a series of quizzes next month.
9. You should expect a quiz sometime next week.
10. The results of the quiz will be included in your grade.

**Notes:** 5, 6は小テストの範囲を示している．7は小テストの実施は考えているものの具体的には案はまだまとまっていない段階である．8は一連の小テストの実施を計画していてそのための作業が進行中であることを意味する．Student Response で，現在進行形と always が一緒に使われると，「いつも〜して嫌だ，困る」という非難めいた感情がこもる．(☞ p. 283)

---
**Student Response**

生徒の不満　Oh, no! / Again! / So soon! / We have quizzes all the time. / Mr. Tanaka is always giving quizzes.

---

**Interaction**

T: 来週の今日は小テストです．
S: えー！　また？
T: 心配はいりません．範囲は16課と17課の単語だけです．日本語で言った単語を，英語で書いてもらいます．
S: スペリングはちゃんと書けなかったら駄目なんですか．
T: 当然です．みなさんのためですよ．頑張って下さいね．
S: あーあ．来週はテスト3つだ．

I will give a quiz this day next week.
On, no! Again?
There's nothing to worry about. It's just a word quiz on Lesson 16 and Lesson 17. You will write the English as I say the Japanese.
Are we supposed to spell those words correctly?
Yes, of course. It's for your own benefit. Try your best.
Ugh! Three tests next week.

## ③ 終わりの挨拶　Closing Remarks

### a.　一般的な挨拶　Departing

1. Good-bye, class [everybody / everyone].
2. See you tomorrow [later / soon].
3. I'll see you tomorrow.
4. Good-bye till tomorrow.
5. Good-bye for now.
6. Bye-bye.
7. Bye now, Ken.
8. Take care.

〈発展的表現〉

9. Watch out for the traffic.
10. Be good on the train [bus].
11. Behave yourself on the train.
12. Don't speed. / Take it easy.

**Notes:** 6, 7 は informal. 8〜12 は家へ帰る生徒に言う表現.

┌─ **Student Response** ─────────────────
生徒の挨拶　Good-bye, Miss [Mr. / Mrs. / Ms.] Thompson.
(Take care. と言われて)　Yes, I will. / Yes. Thank you.

### b.　来週まで　Until next week

1. See you next week.
2. Good-bye and see you next week.
3. I'll see you next week.
4. Have a nice weekend.
5. Enjoy your weekend.

6. 終　了　247

〈発展的表現〉
6. Good luck in [with] the baseball game [football match / piano contest / speech contest].
7. Have a good rest.
8. Try to get rid of your cold by next week.
9. Get your work done over the weekend.

**Notes:** 6は週末に試合などがある生徒に幸運を祈る言葉．7は1週間の疲れが出ている生徒を気遣う場合．8は具合が悪いのに無理して出て来ていた生徒を気遣っている場合．9は課題がまだできていない生徒を促す場合．

## C. 次時まで間が空きすぎる場合　When the next class is far ahead

1. I won't see you until next month.
2. I won't see you next week. So, make sure your assignment is finished.
3. Don't forget your assignment.
4. (Please) try to study English [listen to the tape / CD] every day.
5. You should study English a little every day.
6. Enjoy the break. But be sure you're ready for the next class.

〈発展的表現〉
7. It's a good idea to watch English programs on TV.
8. You should read an English newspaper [English newspapers] every day.
9. Don't work too hard.
10. The national holiday falls on our next class day.
11. I'll have to be absent from school next week. Enjoy an unexpected break. But be sure you get your work done.

**Notes:** 5の You should 〜 はアドバイスを与える際の一般的なパターン．10は次時まで間が空きすぎてしまう理由．そのあとになんらかの指示やアドバイスが続く．

## d. 長期休暇の前　Before a vacation

1. See you in September.
2. I'll see you all again after the Christmas holidays [vacation].
3. Good-bye, class. Enjoy your vacation.
4. Good-bye, everyone. Have a nice [good] vacation.
5. Good-bye, everybody. I hope you'll have a great [wonderful] holiday.

〈発展的表現〉

6. This was the last class before the summer vacation. Have a nice vacation and enjoy yourselves.
7. Enjoy your holiday(s) and I'll see you in two weeks.
8. Oh, you are going for a homestay in Los Angeles. Have fun. [Have a good time].
9. It might be enjoyable to see some English movies on TV.

**Notes:**　長期休暇に入る前に生徒との人間関係ができているので，しばしの別れの挨拶も長めの発話になるのが自然である．2で holidays を使うのはイギリス英語，vacation を使うのはアメリカ英語である．いずれも冬休みのこと．8 の Have fun. は informal. これらに対する Student Response は，"Thank you (very much). (You too!)"

---

**Interaction**

| | |
|---|---|
| S：先生，夏休みにはまた外国へ出られるんですか． | Miss Tanaka, are you going abroad this summer, too? |
| T：ええ，今度はケンブリッジに行って来ようと思っています．イギリスの夏は最高ですから． | Yes, I'm visiting Cambridge this time. Summer in England is just great. |
| S：いいなあ． | Sounds nice. |
| T：聡君はどこかへ行くの？ | Are you going somewhere, Satoshi? |
| S：アメリカの叔母さんのうちへちょっと行ってきます． | Yes. I'm staying with my aunt in the United States. |
| T：あら，すてき．どのくらい | Great! How long will you be staying |

|   |   |
|---|---|
| 行っているの？ | there? |
| S： 2週間です． | Two weeks. |

## e. 時間割変更の予告　Change of schedule announcement

1. School starts at 8:40 from next week.
2. We'll have shorter periods next week.
3. School will be over at noon.
4. One period will be 40 minutes.
5. Break time will be reduced [shortened] to five minutes.
6. All the afternoon classes will be cancelled from Monday through Friday.

〈発展的表現〉

7. Everything will have to be ready for Sports Day [the School Festival].
8. There will be the mid-term [final] exams next week.
9. A general meeting of the PTA is going to be held this Saturday.
10. Teachers are scheduled to visit your homes to have a talk with your parents.

**Notes:**　1は夏時間（summer time）のとき．2～6は短縮授業による時間変更．7～10は短縮授業になる理由．なお，10のような教師の家庭訪問という慣習は英米にはない．

## f. 後片づけ　Clearing the classroom

1. Clean the board [Switch off the air-conditioner / Turn off the lights], will you?
2. (Please) turn off [switch off] the main switches in your booths.
3. Tidy up your desks and chairs before you go.
4. I need your help with this heavy machine.
5. Who would like to help me with these (piles of paper, etc.)?

〈発展的表現〉

6. Would you help me with this tape recorder [CD player]?
7. Could you help me carry this OHP [video] to the storage [AV] room?
8. Would you mind returning this tape recorder [CD player] to the administration [business] office?
9. Have you got everything [your things]?

**Notes:** 2はLL教室で．9を日本語で言うと「忘れ物をしないように」となり，発想が逆である．

---
**Student Response**

（先生の注意に対して） Yes, sir, I will. / Sure. / Okay. / Why not? / No problem.

---

# 授業のバリエーションとテスト
# Variation of Teaching and Testing

第Ⅲ部

# 1. オーラル・コミュニケーション
Oral Communication

## a. 日常会話　A daily conversation

**ア．緊張をほぐす**　Relaxing
1. Now, class, please relax.
2. Take it easy, Noriko.
3. You look nervous. Just relax.
4. Let's loosen up a little, everyone. You must relax and be ready to speak out [up], O.K.?
5. Everybody, please breathe in deeply. You are too tense.
6. Before starting the lessen, let's sing together to relax a little bit.

〈発展的表現〉

7. Don't be too quiet, class. I'm not going to bite you. Just speak out [up], please.
8. Please follow my directions, class. You need some exercise to loosen up. Ready? Now stand up, sit down, bend, look up . . .

**Notes:**　オーラル・コミュニケーションの授業は，スピーキングが中心で生徒が過度に緊張しやすい．授業の導入時に緊張をほぐさせることを念頭に例を示した．6はクラスでいっしょに歌を歌うよう指示した．8は教師がTPR（動作を入れた活動）を用いて実際に生徒を動かすための指示．（☞ p. 180）

---
**Interaction**

T:　なるほど，緊張しているのですね．そんなに心配しなくてもいいですよ．かみつきませんから．

I see, you are all tense. Don't worry too much. I'm not going to bite you.

| | | |
|---|---|---|
| (生徒は笑う) | | |
| T： | ちょっと体操をしよう．命令文を言ってその動作の反対をやってみよう．最初は私が言いますから，そのあと順にやってください．いいですか．練習してみます．「目を閉じて」 | Well, let's do an exercise. When you hear the commands, you do the opposite action. I will give the command first. Then you take turns, O.K.? Let's practice first. Now close your eyes |
| (生徒は目を開ける) | | |
| T： | さあやってみよう．君から後ろへ． | Okay. You first. Then go on. |
| S₁： | 「座れ」 | Please sit down. |
| S₂： | 「右手を挙げよ」 | Raise your right hand. |
| S₃： | 「立って」 | Stand up. |
| T： | 結構でした．さあ，リラックスできましたか． | Very good. Now, have you loosened up? |

イ．**自分のことを語らせる**　Talking about oneself

1. Now please tell the class a little about yourself.
2. Please tell (us) about yourself in three sentences.
3. What did you do yesterday after school? Please tell us.
4. Yesterday was Sunday. Did you go anywhere? Please tell the class.
5. What are your plans for summer vacation? Please tell us.

〈発展的表現〉

6. What do you want to be after you graduate from high school? Please tell us.
7. What kind of job do you want to find in the future?
8. What do you like to do when you have time [in your spare time]?

**Notes:** 　1，2の一般的指示は6〜8のような発話の場面を限定した指示を伴うことが普通である．3以下は生徒が自己表現できるように，身近なことを語る機会を想定し，そのための発問を例示している．

## ウ．ペアワーク　Pair work

1. Please do the next activity in pairs.
2. Please pair off and ask your partner the ten questions you have prepared.
3. Please pair off and ask each other what you did yesterday. At the end, I'll ask some of you to report on what you have found [discovered / learned].
4. Please pair off and exchange your notebooks with your partners and write down each other's comments.
5. Make a pair with the student who is sitting behind you. Then please practice reading the dialog aloud.
6. Please pair off and solve the questions I have given you. At the end, I'll ask one of the pairs to report to the class.

〈発展的表現〉

7. First please pair off. Then use the maps I have given you. One of you chooses a place to visit and shows where you are and gives directions to the place. The other should tell where they want to visit.
8. Now I will give two pictures to each pair. Ask each other questions and decide which picture should come first.

**Notes:**　ペアワークのうち，7は一方にインフォメーション・ギャップがある場合を想定した指示．8はペアの両方にインフォメーション・ギャップがあり，双方で情報を交換しながら問題を解決してゆく場合の指示．ここでは2枚の続きマンガの順序を決めさせる活動を想定した．

## エ．グループワーク　Group work

1. Please make groups of three [four / five] students each and practice the skit.
2. Form groups of four people each and practice acting out the skit.
3. Form groups of three students each and write a short skit. When you have finished, please bring it to me.

4. Get into groups of four and arrange the desks so two people can face the other two and practice pronunciation together.

〈発展的表現〉

5. Please form groups of six students each. Then sit in a circle and practice the skit, first just by reading. After a while, practice acting it out.

**Notes:** グループワークはスキットの創作や練習を中心に例文を示した．5 は始めは音読の練習，次に身振りを付けて練習するよう指示している．

## b. リスニング　Listening

### ア． テープ [CD] を利用する　Using tapes [CD]

1. Listen to the tape [CD].
2. Listen to the tape [CD] first.
3. Don't write anything down. Just listen.
4. Listen and repeat after the tape [CD].
5. Listen to the tape [CD] and tell me what it is about.
6. Listen to the tape [CD] and answer the questions.

〈発展的表現〉

7. While listening to the tape [CD], you may take notes (if you want).
8. Listen to the tape [CD] twice before you answer the questions.

**Notes:** 4 はテープ・CD を聞いてそのあと復唱させる．6, 8 はテープ・CD を聞いたあと質問に答えさせる．7 はテープ・CD を聞きながらメモを取ってもよいという指示．

### イ． 教師が音読して聞かせる　Listening to the teacher's reading

1. I'll read the text. Please listen.
2. I'll read the passage twice, first slowly, the second time at a natural speed.
3. Please listen to the paragraph I am going to read. I'll ask you several questions afterward.

〈発展的表現〉
4. Mr. Johnson and I will read the skit. Tell the class what we are talking about afterward.
5. Mr. Johnson, would you read the paragraph to the class?

**Notes:** 3は教師が音読したあと質問に答えさせる．4はALTと教師がスキットを読み，そのあと，何について話していたか答えるよう指示している．5はALTにモデル・リーディングを依頼している．

## ウ．作業を行わせる　Giving tasks
1. Look at the picture on page 7. I am going to give you the names of ten things. Circle them and tell me where they are.
2. Listen to the interviews and fill in the chart.
3. Now you are going to draw a picture by listening to the directions on the tape. Listen carefully, please.
4. You are going to listen to five recorded samples. They are all real speeches. Tell me what they are about.
5. Complete the chart by listening to the weather forecast. Then exchange the chart with your partner to see if they are the same.
6. Listen to the tape and tell me briefly what the story is about.
7. Here are five messages. Listen and find out who(m) they are addressed to.

〈発展的表現〉
8. Listen to this open-ended story. Conclude it by using your imagination. You may speak in English or in Japanese.
9. I'll give you ten questions. Please answer as quickly [promptly] as possible.
10. Now let's practice dictation. I'll read a short paragraph three times. First, just listen. From the second time on, write what I say. Ready?

**Notes:** 1は絵の中のものを聞き取って発見し，その位置を伝えるリスニングとスピーキングを合わせたタスクの指示．2はインタビューを聞いて表を完成するタスク．3はテープの指示に従って絵を描かせるもの．4は生の録音を聞き，

何のことについて話されているか当てさせる．5は天気予報を聞き，チャートを完成させる．6は物語を聞いて要約させる．7はメッセージを聞いて誰に宛てているものであるか当てさせる．8はオープンエンドの物語の結びを完成させる．ただし，この際，答えは生徒の負担を軽くするため英語でも日本語でもよいという指示を加えている．9は教師の質問に対して速やかに応答させる．1〜9はリスニングの言語活動で，補助的に教材を作成したり，教師が問題を作ってその場で聞かせ作業をさせる場合を想定して例文を挙げた．10はディクテーションの指示．（☞ p. 224）

## c. スピーチ・討論　Speech and discussion

### ア．意見を求める　Asking for opinions

1. Now what do you think?
2. Do you think so?
3. I want to know your opinion.
4. Tell me what you think about it.
5. Do you have any suggestions?
6. What's your view about this problem?
7. Would you like to tell us your idea?
8. Do you agree with her [him]?
9. Do you agree or disagree with this opinion?

〈発展的表現〉

10. If you don't agree, what don't you like about his [her] opinion?
11. If you agree with him [her], can you tell us why in your own words?

  **Notes:**　8, 9は賛成か反対かについて尋ねている．10, 11は単に賛否を尋ねるだけではなく，自分の意見として表現させたいとき．

### イ．スピーチ　Speech

1. Now you are going to make a short speech to introduce yourself. I'll give you ten minutes. Please write your rough draft.
2. In the next class you are going to make a short speech about this essay. Don't make it too long or too short. Please write it within

100 words.
3. Today Toshio and Kazuko are going to make their speeches. Toshio and Kazuko, are you ready?
4. In giving [delivering] your speech, don't read from the paper. You must memorize your speech.
5. In delivering your speech, speak loudly enough so (that) everyone can hear you. Nothing is so boring as to listen to quiet, weak speeches.

〈発展的表現〉
6. In making your speech, first write the introduction, then the body and the conclusion. Don't skip any of the three.

**Notes:** 4, 5 はスピーチを行う際の注意を喚起している. 5 の that は口語では省略されることが多い. 6 はスピーチの書き方を指導している.

## ウ. 暗唱 Recitation

1. Today we are going to practice recitation.
2. Here is the paragraph [letter / poem] you are going to recite.
3. Try to understand the feelings of the person who wrote this.
4. It is important for you to understand the situation in which this was written.
5. You must think who said what and why he [she] said so [and how he [she] said it].

〈発展的表現〉
6. Listen to the speech (by Martin Luther King Jr.). Try to understand in what situation it was delivered and how he felt while he was speaking. You are going to practice his speech later.
7. Here is a short play for a readers' theater. You choose the roles of the characters in the play. We need seven people. Make a group of seven and choose your role and practice.
8. Listen to two nursery rhymes read by a famous British actress. Later you are going to recite them in front of the class, O.K.?

9. Why don't we have a recitation contest at the end of the first term. I will give you three different pieces for recitation, one a narrative, another a monolog, and the last a poem. You may choose whichever [the one] you like.
10. I will read a short monolog. While listening, watch carefully how I read it, my face and my gestures. Also pay attention to the tone of my voice. Take notes. We'll discuss your observations later.

**Notes:** 3～5 はレシテーションのテクニックについて言及している。6 は名演説の朗読でデクラメーション (declamation) と言われるものである。7 の readers' theater はいわゆる劇の朗読で、ここではグループに分かれて練習する指示を与えている。10 は教師がモノローグのモデル・レシテーションを行い、生徒に音調や表情や身振りに注目させ、内容を理解(解釈)させ、あとでそれについて話し合うことを意図している。

## エ. 討 論　Discussion

1. We're going to have a discussion today. Make groups of ten students each. Sit in a circle, will you?
2. In each group, please select a discussion leader and a reporter.

〈発展的表現〉

3. Today I will let you listen to a short speech about air pollution. We are going to discuss the problem later. Now how much do you know about it?
4. The discussion topic for this week is natural resources in Japan. Please read the paragraph at home and talk about it in small groups in the next class. You must reach a consensus at the end of your discussions.
5. First you analyze what the problem is. Then you think about its causes, propose solutions and evaluate them. At the end select the best solution.

**Notes:** 1. ディスカッションのグループ編成に対する指示を与えている。2. ディスカッションのリーダーとレポーターを決めるよう指示している。3 はディス

カッションしようとする話題について，どれほど知識を持っているかどうか確認している．5 はディスカッションの進め方の説明を英語で行っている．

---- **Interaction** ----

| | |
|---|---|
| T： さあ，これからテープで聞いたモノローグについて話し合ってみましょう．どんな感じがしましたか．加寿子さん． | Now let's talk about the monolog you have just listened to on the tape [CD]. How did it sound? Kazuko? |
| $S_1$： とても悲しそうでした． | Very sad. |
| T： みなさん，そう思いますか．私も同感です．さあ，この男の人はどこで話しているのでしょう．友美さん． | Does everybody agree? I think so too. The man sounded very sad. Now where did the man speak to himself? Tomomi? |
| $S_2$： 彼の部屋です． | In his room. |
| $S_3$： 庭だよ． | In his yard. |
| T： はい，どちらでもいいようですね．家のどこかにいますよね．ところでなぜそんなに悲しんでいるのでしょう．誰か？ | Yes, I think you are both right. He is at home somewhere. Why was he sad, by the way? Anyone? |
| $S_4$： 親友が死んでしまったからです． | His best friend had just died. |

## 2. 歌とゲーム
### Songs and Games

### a. 歌　Songs

**ア．曲を聴く**　Listening to songs
1. Listen to this song.
2. Do you know this music?
3. Today I've brought a pop song. First just listen.
4. Let's listen to the tune first.
5. You already know this tune, don't you?
6. The tune is very familiar to you, isn't it?
7. Listen to the words of the song.
8. Try to follow the tape.
9. Here's a song by Stacie Orrico called "I Could Be the One".

〈発展的表現〉

10. Today I want you to listen to this song. It is by the Beatles. And it is very famous. Let's enjoy it.
11. This is "Let It Be." Have you ever heard this before? How do you like it?
12. The song is, as you know, "Yesterday Once More". Did you catch the phrase "Yesterday Once More"?

---
**Student Response**

もう1回聴きたい　I want to hear that song once again. / I like this very much. Will you repeat it please?

もう1曲聴きたい　One more song, please. / Do you have another song? / We have enough time to listen to another song.

---

## 2. 歌とゲーム

### イ．歌う　Singing
1. Let's sing a song.
2. How about singing a song?
3. Do you want to sing a song?
4. I'll explain the words to you.
5. Say the words after me.
6. Once again, all together.
7. Join in the singing, Taro.

〈発展的表現〉

8. When you lose the words, just hum along [follow the melody by humming (la-la-la)].
9. Sing along with the children on the tape [CD].
10. Let's sing a little louder this time.
11. I'll accompany you on my guitar.

**Notes:**　4は歌詞を説明するとき．11はギターなどで伴奏したいとき．

> **Student Response**
> 歌詞がわかりません　I can't understand the words. / Can you tell us the meaning of the words? / Please explain more about the words.
> 誰の歌ですか　Whose song is this? / Who sings this song? / Who wrote the song? / Who set the song to music?

## b．ゲーム　Games

### ア．ゲームの開始・終了　Beginning and ending games
1. Let's play a game.
2. Now it's (the) time for a game.
3. How about playing a matching [counting] game.
4. Now we'll play a guessing [interview] game.
5. What about a game of words [letters / pictures]?
6. Do you feel like playing a game?
7. O.K., let's stop now! Well done.

8. That'll do for now(, thank you).
9. That's enough. That was good.
10. Did you enjoy [like] it?

〈発展的表現〉

11. Do you remember the game we played [enjoyed] last week? Let's do it again.
12. For this game, you need a red pen and a blue pen. Put them on your desks.
13. This is a matching [interview] game. I'll give you a card for the game. But there are four different cards. So don't show your card to others.
14. I want you to enjoy the game. But remember that you must not speak Japanese. Only English!

**Notes:** 1～6が開始．7～9が終了．11は復習として，前に行ったゲームをもう一度やるような場合．

---
**Student Response**

始めていいですか　Can we start the game? / We know the rules very well. So let's begin. / May we stand up and ask each other?

もっと時間をください　Give us a little more time, please. / We need a bit more time to finish.

---

イ．ゲームの説明　Explanation of games

1. The idea of this game is to find the right word as quickly as you can.
2. For this game you have to score as many points as possible.
3. What you have to do is to choose the picture that best fits what I say.
4. This is to test your memory [speed] in ～.
5. Your task is first to ～, then to ～, and to end up with ～.

〈発展的表現〉

6. Look at the (OHP) screen. You can see the shadow of something. Now guess what it is.

7. There are five different cards in the bag. One of you can choose a card. But don't tell anyone which card it is. Then the rest of you have to ask questions to find out which one it is.
8. Someone has to think of an object, a thing or an animal for "Twenty Questions". Then everyone else has to guess what it is by asking Yes/No questions.
9. There are two kinds of cards. Don't show your card to your partner. It's your secret. The cues to fill the blanks are in your partner's card. Ask questions and find out what's different from yours.

**Notes:** 6, 7 は一般的な guessing games. 8 は「20 の扉」. 9 は matching games.

> **Student Response**
> もう一度説明して　Please explain once more. / I don't understand it well. / Would you mind explaining the rules again?
> 席を離れていいですか　Can we leave our seats? / Are we free to move?

## C. チーム分け　Grouping for games

1. Let's form two teams.
2. Get into five teams of four or five.
3. These two rows make one team.
4. I want you in groups of three.
5. Move up and make six groups.
6. I'm going to divide you in half.
7. We're going to work in pairs.
8. Turn around and face your neighbor.
9. Can you face the people behind [in front of] you?

〈発展的表現〉

10. Murayama-kun, you can choose your own team.
11. Kaneko-san, will you keep the score?
12. Yamada-kun, you are the leader of this team.

13. Get into groups of four and put your tables together. / Move your desks and form a big table for four students.
14. Don't you have anyone to work with? Why don't you turn around and join them?
15. Oh, dear. You are alone, aren't you? Would you mind moving over there and working with them?
16. We are going to work in teams of four. And each team must be mixed with boys and girls.

**Notes:** 14, 15 はあぶれた生徒のために．16 はチームが男女混合であることを明示したいとき．(☞ p. 27)

---
**Student Response**

男女混合ですか　Should we have both boys and girls in [on] each team? / Girls only? [Boys only?] / The team should be mixed with boys and girls?

机[椅子]は？　Do we move our desks [chairs]? / Must we rearrange the desks [chairs]?

---

## d. 順番　Taking turns

1. It's Satoshi first.
2. Are you next, Sachiyo?
3. Now it's your turn, Team A.
4. Jiro's first. Then it's your turn next.
5. Whose turn is it? Quickly!
6. Come on! Wasn't it your turn, Team B?
7. Have you all had a chance [turn] now?
8. Who hasn't had a turn yet?

〈発展的表現〉

9. I know you want more time to do this. But that's enough [all].
10. Which team can answer [do what I say] first? Well, Team C, you go first.

11. Now we'll have a team competition. For this, go from front to back [from left to right].
12. We have five teams for this game. 1, 2, 3, 4, 5. Now, Team 5, you are the first team to go. Next, Team 4, and ...
13. Your guess was right, so now you come over here. You can make a question and ask it to others.

   **Notes:** 5, 6 は急がせるとき. 13 は guessing game の途中で.

   ---**Student Response**---
   私たち[私]まだです　Not us [me] yet. / We [I] haven't had a turn yet. / You skipped our [my] turn.
   私たち[私]の番ですか　Is it us [me] now? / Is it our [my] turn next? / Whose turn is it next?

## e. 順位決定法　Deciding winners

### ア. 得点　Scores
1. One point for Team 2.
2. Two points for the boys.
3. The one who answers first will get a point.
4. The first one to guess right gets a point.
5. O.K. Now add up all your points.
6. How many points did you get altogether?
7. How about counting up the points?
8. What was your final score?
9. You lose a point if you guess wrong.

〈発展的表現〉
10. The first team [group] with ten points is the winner.
11. The first one to write the right word on the board scores two points.
12. You won't lose any points even if your answers are wrong. So never mind your mistakes. [So don't worry about mistakes.]
13. The first student who finishes the task will score five points. The

second one will get four . . .
14. When you come and write the correct answer on the board, you will be given a point.
15. During this activity, you must not use Japanese. If you use Japanese, you will lose three points.
16. For this game, you can answer in Japanese when you don't know how to say it in English. But in such a case, you will get only one point. When you answer correctly in English, you can get two points.

> **Student Response**
> 減点ありますか　Is this a bad point system? / Will we lose points when we guess wrong?
> 何点ですか　How many points for each question? / How many points can we get when our answers are correct?

イ．勝敗　Winning and losing
1. The winner(s) of the game!
2. The winning group is . . . !
3. This team has won.
4. Team 5 [Michiko] is the winner.
5. Team A is the winner. Congratulations! The second place goes to Team C . . .
6. It's a draw [tie].
7. It was a close finish.

〈発展的表現〉
8. Give the winning team a big hand.
9. Give three cheers for the winner.
10. Your team was the last this time, I'm afraid. Better luck next time! [Stick to it!]
11. You've done very well, everyone. You've enjoyed the game and practiced hard. That's wonderful, isn't it?

**Notes:** 10 は「頑張れ」と励ますとき．11 は勝敗決定後の慰め．

---
**Student Response**

誰が勝ったの？　Who is the winner? / Which team has won?

勝った　We did it. We are No.1, I think.

私たちの順位は？　Please tell us our ranking. / Where are we placed? / How did we finish?

---

**Interaction**

| | |
|---|---|
| T： このゲームは新出単語の発音を当てるというものです．誰でもいいから，発音を思いついた人は挙手をして，それをはっきりと言って下さい．正しかったら，その人がいるチームに2点あげます． | The idea of this game is to guess the pronunciation of new words. Anybody who thinks they know the pronunciation of the word, raise your hand. And tell us loud and clearly. If it is correct, I'll give two points to the group you belong to. |
| S： 面白そうだな． | That sounds fun. |
| T： 始めるよ．1番．この単語の発音は？　f-o-r-e-i-g-n という綴りです．（板書） | Shall we begin? No. 1, how do you pronounce this word? It is spelled 'f-o-r-e-i-g-n'. |
| S： /fɔ́regin/（など） | /fɔ́regin/, etc. |
| T： 違うなー． | No. |
| S： /fɔ́ːrən/ | /fɔ́ːrən/. |
| T： それだ！　このチームに2点． | That's right. Two points for this team. |

## 3. 教育機器の利用
### Using Teaching Aids

#### a. 操作　Operation

ア．テープレコーダー　Tape recorders
1. This cassette-tape recorder is very light.
2. Insert a cassette this way.
3. This tape recorder has seven buttons: play, stop, forward, rewind, record, eject and pause.
4. Press this button to rewind the tape.
5. This machine stops at the end of the tape automatically.
6. This recorder is powered by rechargeable batteries.
7. Before inserting a cassette, tighten the tape with a pencil.

〈発展的表現〉

8. If your tape is normal [Type I], set it to NORMAL.
9. You can adjust the volume with the VOL control.
10. When the battery is weak, the playback sound is distorted.
11. Clean the tape head after 10 hours of use.
12. Set the counter to 000 by using the reset button.
13. For private listening with an earphone [a headphone], plug it into the earphone [headphone] jack [socket].

イ．CD
1. Take the CD out of the case.
2. Turn on the CD player, open the lid and slide the CD in.
3. Choose the sound track you want to hear and press the play button.

4. Adjust the volume.
5. The track number and the elapsed playing time of the current track appear during play.
6. To keep the CD clean, handle it by its edge. Don't touch the surface.
7. Don't expose the CD to direct sunlight or heat sources.

**Notes:** 5. elapsed playing time は「経過時間」.

### ウ. ビデオ　Video cassette [tape] recorders
1. Are you going to use the video recorder today?
2. This is a very small VCR (= video cassette recorder).
3. You can record a TV program by connecting this VCR to that TV set.
4. The camera has a built-in microphone.

〈発展的表現〉

5. Can I operate this video camera in normal lighting conditions?
6. Press this button for smooth power zooming between wide-angle (W) and telephoto (T) positions.
7. To focus the lens, turn the focus ring while looking through the viewfinder.
8. If you use the remote control, you can stop or start it without being near the machine.
9. You can edit by copying the sections you want onto another tape.
10. If you have two VCRs, you can copy [dub] video recordings.

### エ. DVD
1. Today I'll show you a movie on DVD.
2. What is 'DVD'? — It's a 'Digital Video Disk' which is recorded by a digital system.
3. Can I play DVD movies on this computer?
4. Keep DVDs away from heaters, direct sunlight, and small children?

オ．**OHP**　(Overhead Projectors)
1. Please carry this overhead projector to our classroom.
2. Could you draw [close] the curtain so that we can see the letters more clearly?
3. Now I'm going to project five words on the screen.
4. Write your answers on this transparency.
5. I'll show you the intonation pattern of this sentence by using the OHP.

〈発展的表現〉
6. Read the green part of the dialog.
7. The stressed syllables are shown in red letters.
8. Takao, please come here and write the missing words on the sheet.
9. Rearrange the sentences on the sheet so that they form a paragraph.

**Notes:**　6は対話文を色別で表記した場合．7は強勢のある音節を赤で表示した場合．8は cloze test の解答を TP シートに書かせる指示．9は段落構成文を細長い TP シートに書き，正しい段落構成になるように個々の文を並べさせる練習．(☞ p. 138, 189)

カ．**スライド投映機**　Slide projectors
1. Please look at the screen [picture].
2. How many birds can you see in this picture?
3. Describe what the man is doing in this picture.
4. Today we're going to write the script for our slide story.
5. I can't see the picture well. Could you make it larger?

〈発展的表現〉
6. I'll show you four (pictures on) slides. Tell a story using the past tense as [while] you look at the pictures.
7. Here are slide sequences of four pictures. What kind of story can you think of?
8. These are slide pictures of your town. Can you explain what they

are about?
9. Takao, please help me carry the projector and slide sets (back) to the audio-visual room.

## キ. LL (Language Laboratory)
1. The next class will be in the language lab(oratory).
2. Sit in your booth according to the seating chart.
3. Now put on your headsets.
4. Set your tape counter to zero.
5. If you have any trouble, please push the intercom button.

〈発展的表現〉
6. Rewind your tape to zero on the tape counter.
7. First listen to the dialog from the console.
8. Insert your tape and check if your machine works all right.
9. Practice the dialog twice by repeating after the tape.
10. Listen carefully, first to the model, and then to your speech.
11. When you push the instant repeat button, you can listen to the same sentence as many times as you want.
12. In four-phase tapes, students (1) listen to the cue, (2) make the desired response, (3) hear the correct model, and (4) repeat the correct model.

## ク. CALL
1. CALL is Computer Assisted [Aided] Language Learning.
2. Nowadays a variety of good CALL programs are available either online or on CD [DVD].
3. Computer-adaptive TOEFL is administered in many countries.
4. Distance learning can be more effective if it is combined with CALL programs.
5. The computer is very useful for word-recognition drills because word forms can be changed, contrasted or highlighted in an instant.

6. Vocabulary CALL program prints a word on the screen which then disappears, asking the learner to type the word.
7. To master spellings, one useful CALL technique is an alphabetical jumbling program.
8. In Sentence Building, the learner is presented with a contextualized sentence, followed by randomly ordered chunks, which have to be restored to their original form.
9. There are also various computer programs for listening, speaking, reading and writing practice
10. Software piracy is a crime. Beware! You should never do it.

ケ．インターネット　Internet
1. Do you have a PC (personal computer)?
2. What does "www" stand for? It stands for "World Wide Web".
3. I often use a computer to play games.
4. I use my notebook computer to read and watch BBC World News.
5. Our family uses a (desktop) computer to get access to the Net.
6. There are a lot of good websites for learning English.
7. There is plenty to see on the Web, so it is important to know how to find it or where to look (for it). Search engines are very useful for that purpose.
8. What search engine(s) do you use most often?

〈発展的表現〉
9. The internet is often used as a term to describe the World Wide Web otherwise known as the Web.
10. The Internet is often shortened to the Net. It is a multi-faceted communication medium.
11. Many famous persons have their own homepages. Some novelists write their digital novels on their homepages.
12. If you have any questions about software or hardware, FAQs will help you.

13. FAQs are 'frequently asked questions'. Before you ask your own questions, first check FAQs.
14. World-wide news agencies have their own websites, where you can see or read most up-to-date news on your PC.
15. It is interesting to make a website for your school, your class, your community, and so on.
16. If you want your own website, at first you must learn how to use software to build a homepage.
17. Homepages are written in Hypertext Mark-Up Language (HTML).
18. When you finish building your homepage, the next step is to upload it. Nowadays good freeware is available to do it.

コ. E メール　email

1. Email is electronic mail. It's easy and fast.
2. Do you know the word 'netiquette'? It's the etiquette of Internet usage.
3. It is impolite to write email all in CAPITALS.
4. It is also impolite to send email without deleting a long list of the old email.
5. The term 'chat' means real-time communication between two or more people.
6. You can send your assignments by email, but meet the deadline of July 5.

〈発展的表現〉

7. If you get an attachment you're not expecting, it's safest to delete it before you open it. It may have a virus in it.
8. If you have virus protection software on your machine, it'll protect your machine against viruses.
9. If you keep getting 'junk' mail, just ignore them.
10. Some people may get angry if they receive attachments they don't ask for [request], because they have to pay for their online time.

## b. セットの仕方　Setting up

### ア．カセット・CD　Cassette recorders and CD players
1. Turn on [off] the power [switch].
2. Push the power button on [off].
3. Push the eject button.
4. Put the cassette [CD] in the machine.
5. Put the cassette [CD] in.
6. Close the lid of the compartment.
7. Take out the cassette [CD].
8. Put your headset on.
9. Take off the headset. Push the reset button.

〈発展的表現〉
12. Now you'll hear the tape [CD]. Are you ready?
13. After you record the tape, listen to it first and then repeat after it.

---------------- **Interaction** ----------------

| | |
|---|---|
| T: では，ヒアリング練習をしましょう．用意はいいですか． | Well, let's begin the listening practice. Are you ready? |
| S: 待って下さい．プリントがまだです． | Just a moment, please. I haven't got the handout yet. |
| T: 急いで下さい．時間がありません． | Hurry up. We don't have much time. |
| S: 受け取りました．いいですよ． | O.K., I've got it now. |

### イ．ビデオ・DVD　Video and DVD
1. Push the open [close] button.
2. Push the playback button.
3. Put the video cassette tape [DVD] in.
4. Push the stop button.
5. Push the rewind button.
6. Take out the video cassette tape [DVD] from the machine.

〈発展的表現〉
7. Now let's watch the video [DVD]. Please turn on the monitor.
8. We'll watch the video [DVD] today. Can anyone use this remote control?
9. Take the video [DVD] to the classroom and put this video cassette tape [DVD] in.

## ウ. OHP
1. Open the head mirror.
2. Put the OHP sheet on the glass top.
3. Switch on the lamp.
4. Switch on the cooling fan.
5. Select the most suitable lens out of the three.
6. Focus the picture [figure] on the screen with this knob.
7. Take off the OHP sheet from the glass top.
8. Turn off the lamp.
〈発展的表現〉
9. Open the head mirror, but don't touch the face of the mirror.
10. Don't turn off the cooling fan until the lamp becomes cold.
11. Please take away the OHP after the lamp gets cold.

## エ. スライド  Slide
1. Turn on the lamp.
2. Turn off the power.
3. Set the slides in the case.
4. Set the slide case in the changer.
5. Put the slide projector on the table.
6. Focus the lens on the screen.
7. Take the slides out of the changer.
8. Switch off the lamp.
9. Shut [close / draw / pull] the shades.

10. Open [release / roll up] the curtains.

〈発展的表現〉

11. Operate the slide changer with the remote control.
12. Pull down the screen with the hooked stick.
13. Take care not to set the slide upside down.
14. Don't handle the projector roughly when the lamp is hot.
15. Don't touch the cooling fan while the projector is going.

---- **Interaction** ----

| | |
|---|---|
| T：今日はスライドを見ます． | Today you can enjoy a slide show. |
| S：やった！ | Wow! Wonderful! |
| T：これは... | This is the scene of... |
| S：先生，絵が逆さまです． | Mr. Ito. The picture is upside down. |
| T：あれ．では，これで． | Oh, sorry. Well, how about this? |
| S：今度は左右逆です． | This time it is backwards. |
| T：あれ．裏表を間違えた． | Aha, I mistook the outside for the inside. |

オ．LL

1. Push the fast forward [the rewind] button.
2. Push the reset button of the selector.
3. Listen to these questions and responses.
4. Are you ready to take part in the conversation?
5. Lab work is an integral part of your English language course.
6. Push the number in the answer selector which you think correct.

〈発展的表現〉

7. Now you'll hear the dialog. Are you ready?
8. Repeat after the tape, and practice with the tape.
9. This time say the part of B in the dialog.
10. Now listen to each line of conversation. You will hear it twice. Then repeat it during the pause.
11. When you have something to ask me, please push the call button.

---
**Interaction**

T: 発音練習をします．みなさん，ブースに座りなさい．
S: はい，先生．
T: 対話をテープに録音したら，各自テープにならって練習しなさい．
S: 何回ですか．
T: 少なくとも3回．では，始めます．

T: Let's practice the pronunciation. Everybody, sit at a booth.
S: Yes, Miss Kato.
T: First record the dialog, and then practice after the tape.
S: How many times?
T: At least three times. Now start.

---

## c. 機器の故障　Out of order

### ア．カセット・CD　Cassette recorders and CD players

1. This cassette recorder isn't working.
2. This cassette tape [CD] is broken.
3. The tape isn't going round.
4. I can't turn up [down] the volume control knob.
5. I can't put the cassette [CD] in.

〈発展的表現〉

6. Did you turn it on? / Have you turned it on?
7. This cassette recorder [CD player] is out of order. Use another one.
8. There isn't any sound coming from the speaker. I can't record anything.
9. Look at the cassette tab. Is it all right?
10. If the cassette tab is broken, you should cover the tab with cellophane tape.
11. You put the cassette in upside down. You should put it in the right way.

---- **Interaction** ----

| | |
|---|---|
| S: 佐野先生，テープが動きません． | Miss Sano! My tape isn't going round. What shall I do? |
| T: 電源，入れましたか． | Did you switch it on? |
| S: はい．でも，動きません． | Yes. But it still doesn't work. |
| T: 電池のチェックをしてごらん． | O.K. Then check the batteries. |
| S: あっ．電池がだめです． | Oh, they are dead. |
| T: では，この電池を使いなさい． | Well, use these new ones. |
| S: ありがとう，先生． | Thank you, Miss Sano. |

イ．**ビデオ・DVD**　Television monitors and DVD players
1. The colors are strange.
2. The picture is fluttering [jumping].
3. I can hear both Japanese and English.
4. This video-tape [DVD] isn't recorded on at all.

〈発展的表現〉
5. Turn the picture-control knob to the right.
6. Press the color balance button to get a better picture
7. Slowly turn the horizontal control (knob) either clockwise or anti-clockwise.
8. Press the audio-monitor button to check the sound quality.
9. When you record, you should push the recording button last.

ウ．**OHP・スライド関係**　OHP and slide
1. This lamp is broken [isn't working].
2. The cooling fan isn't working [is out of order].
3. The slide changer is jammed.

〈発展的表現〉
4. After the machine gets cold, change the lamp with a spare one.
5. The slide projector is too hot. So stop using it.
6. That auto slide changer is out of order. You should operate the

changer by hand.

## エ. LL 関係　Language laboratory
1. I can't hear anything.
2. The tape is slipping.
3. I can't run the tape.
4. Please fast forward the tape.
5. Can't you rewind the tape?
6. I can't open the lid of the cassette compartment.

〈発展的表現〉
7. My headset buzzes. I can't repeat after the tape.
8. Your headset is out of order. Move to another booth.
9. Oh, the tape has snapped. You'll have to use another cassette.
10. This playback button is broken. Go to another booth.
11. This machine is faulty. Use No. 10 booth.
12. Oh, the tape is wrapping around the pinch-roller. Stop the machine.
13. This microphone doesn't work well. Use this one.
14. There is something wrong with this headset. I'll have it repaired later.

**Interaction**

| | |
|---|---|
| S: 先生, ちょっと. | Excuse me, Mr. Ito. |
| T: どうしたの. | What's wrong? |
| S: セレクターのライトがつきません. | The light for the program selector is out. |
| T: どれ. ランプが切れてるね. 大丈夫. セレクターは作動してますよ. | Really? Let me see. Oh, the lamp is out. But don't worry. The selector is still working [all right]. |

## d. 聞こえますか・見えますか　Checking equipment

1. Can you hear me?
2. Can you hear the tape clearly?
3. Can you see the screen?
4. Can you see the picture clearly?
5. Can you see the letters on the screen clearly?
6. Can you hear the sound from the speaker clearly?

〈発展的表現〉

7. If you can't hear me clearly, turn the volume control knob clockwise.
8. If you can't hear the tape, please push the call button.
9. If you can't see the screen, please move to another place [booth].
10. If you can't see the picture clearly, I'll turn off the room light(s). All right?
11. If you can't see the letters clearly, I'll enlarge them some more.
12. If you can't see the words on the screen clearly, raise your hand and I'll show them in close-up.

> **Student Response**
>
> 聞こえない　Pardon (me). I can't hear you. / Excuse me. Please speak louder. / Pardon. Speak clearly and slowly, please. / Hey, the rest of you, could you be quieter? / I can't hear the tape. Please be silent.
>
> 見えない　Excuse me. I can't see the screen. Please move to the left. / Can I move my seat next to Kenji? / We can't see the screen clearly. May I turn off the lights? / The letters on the screen are too small. Please make them bigger [larger].

# 4. テスト
Testing

## ① 小テスト  Quizzes and Short Tests

### a. 問題配布時に  Handing-out papers

1. Now, time for a quiz.
2. Let's write them down.
3. Show me how hard you have worked.
4. Let me give you a simple quiz to check it [your understanding].
5. Let me see how hard you have prepared.
6. We'll make sure of what we've learned by writing it.

〈発展的表現〉

7. I'll give you a test sheet.
8. Who has not got this one yet?
9. You must have the answer sheets as well.
10. Everyone, take this sheet. One (for) each.
11. Is there anyone who hasn't got this paper?
12. There are two kinds of quiz sheets. Did all of you get both?
13. I gave out a question sheet and an answer sheet. Did you get both of them?
14. Today, I'll write the questions on the board. So take only this answer sheet.
15. If there are some sheets left, give one of them to Akira. Return the rest to me.
16. If there are any badly printed sheets, give them back to me. I'll

give you a new one.

**Notes:** quiz を「小テスト」(a small informal test) の意味で使うのは主として米国の用法で，英国では a short [small] test と言う．1〜6 は小テスト前のひとこと．15 は問題用紙が余ったとき．16 は印刷の不鮮明な用紙のあったとき．(☞ p. 244)

---
**Student Response**

まだもらっていない　I haven't got one yet. / Will you give one more to this row?

---

## b. 机の上を片づける　Putting away textbooks and notebooks

1. Clear your desktops.
2. Put your things away.
3. Put your books inside your desks.
4. Get all the things out of the way.
5. Put your books and notebooks away.
6. Take your books [notebooks] off your desk.
7. Put [Tuck] them away into your desk drawers.
8. Makio, close your textbook and put it away.

〈発展的表現〉

9. It's time for the quiz! Don't look at your textbooks.
10. Some of you still have your books opened. You can't do that.
11. You have only an answer sheet and a pencil on your desk, don't you?
12. You need only some pencils and an eraser. Nothing else, please.
13. Put your book and notebook in the top right corner of your desk. Hurry up.
14. I don't think any of you will cheat in this quiz. But will you put your things away?

**Notes:**　7 の tuck は「しまいこむ」の意．どちらかというと「押し込む」，「〜の端を突っ込む」の感じ．

> **Student Response**
> 教科書見てもいい？　Can we look at the textbooks? / Must we do this without the textbook?
> ノートは見てもいいですか　Can we use [refer to] our notes?

## c.　辞書の使用　Using a dictionary

1. You can use a dictionary. / Dictionaries are okay.
2. You can use [look in] your dictionary.
3. If necessary, you can look up the words in the dictionary.
4. In this quiz, you must not use a dictionary.
5. You can consult the dictionary for the meaning [usage] of a word.
6. Don't use dictionaries. Try to guess the meanings of the words.

〈発展的表現〉

7. For this composition quiz, we need Japanese-English dictionaries. Do you already have them?
8. Translate these Japanese sentences into English. Some are a little difficult. So you can look them up in a Japanese-English dictionary.
9. In this quiz, you can refer to English-Japanese dictionaries, but not to Japanese-English ones.
10. Do you know how to use a dictionary? This is a quiz for using one. I have brought twenty dictionaries. One for every two persons.
11. Now we'll have a 'speed' game. Who can find the meaning of this word in your dictionaries the quickest? Let's go!
12. In this test, you must write a paragraph of more than ten sentences. But do it without using your dictionaries.

**Notes:**　6 は内容から単語の意味を予想させたいとき．10, 11 は辞書を使い始めたときの練習のために．

> **Student Response**
> 辞書を引いてもいいですか　Can we use [look at] our dictionaries? / Must we do this without a dictionary.

## d. 自己採点　Self-marking

1. Mark your own quiz paper.
2. Check your answers by yourself.
3. Give yourself one point for every correct answer.
4. Grade your own sheets. The right answers are on Page 29.
5. The answers are somewhere in your textbook. Find them by yourself.
6. How about marking them by yourself today? Don't be over-generous, though.
7. Correct your own mistakes. The answers are on the blackboard.

〈発展的表現〉

8. People in this row, will you take turns giving the answers to No.1 through No.6? Everyone, mark your answers.
9. Each question is worth two points and ten in all. Eight or more points is a pass.
10. Now, count your mistakes. Less than six mistakes is a pass.
11. In this quiz, spelling [punctuation] is very important. Check it by yourself again.
12. When you mark papers, don't erase your mistakes. Correct them with a colored pen.

**Notes:** 6は「甘い採点をしないように」と注意するとき．

---
**Student Response**

これ間違ってますか　Is my answer correct or not? Please look at it. / I wrote 'the' instead of 'a' here. Is it wrong?

---
**Interaction**

T: はい，やめて．今日は隣と答案交換をしましょう．
S: 自己採点がいいな．

OK, stop. [Stop now.] How about changing papers with your neighbors today?
We want to mark them ourselves.

| | |
|---|---|
| T: みんなそう思ってるみたいだね．それじゃ，自己採点．甘くつけちゃダメだよ． | Everyone seems to think so. O.K. Mark your own papers. But don't be an over-generous marker. |
| S: わかりました． | I see. [Okay.] |

### e. 答案交換　Exchanging papers with neighbors

1. Exchange [Swap] papers.
2. Hand it to your neighbor.
3. Exchange papers with your partner.
4. Give your quiz sheet to your neighbor.
5. Show your notebook to your friend.
6. Exchange your notebook with your partner's.

〈発展的表現〉

7. If you don't know how to mark them, come and ask me.
8. If you find mistakes in your partner's sheet, not only check them but correct them with a red pen.
9. Check your partner's spelling carefully. If she [he] left something out, add it with a colored pen.
10. Is your neighbor's punctuation all right? Look at your textbook carefully again.
11. I'll show you the answers on the blackboard. Will you mark your partner's sheet? But remember you must be a strict marker.
12. Before you return the sheet to your partner, make sure of what you've checked [make sure that you've checked it].

**Notes:** 1〜6は交換させるときの指示．7〜12は採点をしているときの指示．

---
**Student Response**

点数は？　How many points for each question?

間違いを指摘するだけでいい？　Shall we only check the errors? / We don't have to correct errors, do we?

## f. 後日返却　　Returning papers

1. You'll have the papers tomorrow.
2. I'll give them back in the next class.
3. I will mark your papers and hand them back to you tomorrow.
4. I'll check your answers and return them to you by Friday.
5. Mark your own sheet. Then give it to me. I'll check it again.
6. Collect your notebooks. I'll see how well you've learned it.

〈発展的表現〉

7. I'll mark them. So don't forget to write your names and numbers on them.
8. I want to check any mistakes in your usage. Your notebooks will be returned next week.
9. I'll check the errors by tomorrow. The students in charge of quizzes, come to my office tomorrow and collect them to give back.
10. I am afraid many of you did not work very hard for this quiz. So I will mark your answers and see who did a good job and who didn't.

**Notes:**　9は係を使って返却したいとき．10は注意．

## g. 挙手などによる確認
Checking (answers) by having students raise their hands

1. No mistakes; raise your hands.
2. Those who have no mistakes, raise your hands.
3. Those with more than eight points, put your hands up.
4. Stand up, those of you who got more than six points.
5. Ten points, a perfect score; put up both your hands.
6. Who got more than eight points? Raise your hands.

〈発展的表現〉

7. Ten points, put your hands up. Then nine points, put your hands up. Most of you have already put up your hands. So nine should

be the pass mark.
8. If you got eight to ten points, put up both hands. Five to seven, put up your left hand. Less than that, (put up) your right hand.
9. Those who got more than six correct answers, raise your right hand. Those who didn't, raise your left hand.
10. Today's quiz is True-or-False. I'll read out the seven sentences one by one. If you think they are true, show your palms. If they are false, show your clenched fists.
11. Lean your body to the right if you think the answer is 'Yes'. Lean to the left if it is 'No'.
12. There are three choices from ア to ウ in each question. If you think ア is correct, show your thumb. If イ is correct, show your forefinger. If ウ is correct, show your little finger.

**Notes:** 8, 9 は得点によって挙手の種類を変え，合格点など決めるとき．10, 11 はいわゆる T-F を挙手や身体の向きで反応させたいとき．12 は三選択を挙手の種類で反応させるとき．

---
**Student Response**

混乱しちゃった　It's confusing. / Pardon, please. / Which is which? It's too difficult. Tell us how to do it again. / I'm confused.

---

## h.　正答読み上げ　Giving correct answers orally

1. Listen. The answer to No. 1 is ... No. 2 is ...
2. I'll read out the correct answers.
3. Listen carefully to what I say.
4. What's the answer to No. 3, Yuta?
5. How does the second one go, Suzuki-kun?
6. What have you got for No. 4, Yukari?
7. What do you have for question No. 9?
8. And the next one, please, Jiro.
9. What about the last one, Sachiko?

〈発展的表現〉

10. It's spelled 'c-r-u-e-l'.
11. Its pronunciation is very difficult. Do it once again.
12. I didn't count it as a mistake if you put 'the' here.
13. I didn't take any points off if you only spelled something wrong.
14. Your answer is a little different from this, but it is also correct.
15. Could somebody read out what he [she] put as an answer? Don't worry about the mistakes.
16. What did you write for the first question, Tsuyoshi? Not yet?

**Notes:** 1～3, 10～13は教師が読み上げるとき．4～9, 14～16は生徒に読み上げさせるとき．

## ② テストの解説　Comments on the Test Results

### a. 成績概評　General comments

1. Well done.
2. Great!
3. You did a good job.
4. That wasn't very good.
5. You'd better try harder.
6. You need to make a bit more effort.
7. You can do better than this.
8. There's room for improvement.
9. Why don't you work a little (bit) harder?

〈発展的表現〉

10. The average score is 62.
11. The average mark of this class was 59.
12. I was disappointed to find a lot of simple mistakes.

13. I'm glad most of you cleared the pass mark in the term-end [midterm] exam.
14. There is a difference of about sixty points between the highest score and the lowest.
15. In your report cards your performances are indicated on a five-point scale.
16. I marked your tests based on a point-off system. [I took one point off for each mistake.] The perfect score is 100. 100 minus the number of your mistakes equals your scores.
17. Look at your question sheet and your answer sheet carefully again. Some of you misunderstood the meaning of question No. 3.
18. I don't think there are any marking mistakes. But if you can't understand your score [the scoring], come to the office later.
19. I may have made mistakes. If you think some items were checked wrong, please say so [see me after class].

**Notes:** 1〜3は全体的によくできていたとき．4〜9はやや不満の残るとき．10, 11は平均点．13は合格点．14は最高点，最低点．15は5段階評価．16は減点方式．

---
**Student Response**

平均点は？　Will you tell us the average score? / What's the average mark?

私もがっかり　I'm not happy, either. / I'm disappointed, too.

---

## b. 問題ごとの解説　Specific comments

1. The tense is important here.
2. The idea here is to put the verb into the correct tense.
3. The idea behind this is to rewrite the sentences, using the passive.
4. Here you are to combine these sentences using relative pronouns.
5. I wanted you to rewrite the verbs into their correct forms.
6. What No. 4 asks of you is to choose the best verb that fits the

sentence.
7. The point of the third question is to change all nouns into pronouns.
8. Is it clear [Do you understand] what you had to do in the test?

〈発展的表現〉
9. I said you would be tested on this many times.
10. We did the same exercise in the class again and again.
11. You should've had a look at the idioms much more carefully.
12. Did you learn by heart the key sentences and the new vocabulary?
13. If you'd looked at the textbook regularly, you could have answered these questions very easily.
14. In this case, 'found' is not the past tense of 'find'. This 'found' has a different meaning.
15. This 'made' is not the past tense. It's the past participle and explains the word preceding it.
16. In this sentence, a relative pronoun is left out. Can you guess what it is?

Notes: この部分を英語で解説しようとすると，どうしても英語は複雑になる．部分的に語句のみを英語で言うというのも1つの方法であろう．1〜7は設問全体の大まかな解説．8は多くの生徒が問題の趣旨を取り違えているとき．このあとどうすべきだったかの説明がくる．9〜13は注意，14〜16はやや細かい解説．

― Student Response ―
問題集のどこ？　Which page of the exercise book should we do? / Where can I find it in the exercise book?

## c. 個々の解答の仕方でほめる
Rewarding comments on each test item [students' performance]

1. You did well here. (here が特定の設問であることがわかる状況で)
2. You wrote a fine composition, Akane.

3. You understand well how to use the prepositions, Natsuko.
4. Taro, you rewrote all the sentences correctly. Very good.
5. Yuta, you remembered all the key sentences. Well done.
6. You found that 'to be' should be used here. Very good.
7. It's good you used your own words to describe the scene.

〈発展的表現〉

8. Yukio, you know how to rewrite these sentences into indirect speech. Tell us how to do that.
9. Jun made a good sentence to show he understood the meaning of 'through'. Will you write it on the board?
10. In this case, we can't use the present tense. Ryo knows why. Will you tell us the reason?
11. The idea of this question is to give a title to the paragraph. There are some good examples. Koji, Noriko..., come and write your suggestions on the blackboard.
12. The substitution of 'too-to-' for 'so-that-' seems difficult. But some of you did quite a good job.

**Notes:** 1, 2 は例えば 〜 but you didn't do so well in the grammar questions. などと続ける. 8〜12 は生徒の解答を例として全員に示しながらほめるとき.

---
**Student Response**

決まり文句ですか　Is that a set phrase? / Must we remember that as a ready-made expression?

まだわかりません　I still don't understand. / Your explanation is too difficult.

# ALTとの対話
# Interaction with ALTs

第Ⅳ部

## a. スピーチの依頼　Requesting a speech

### ア．自己紹介　Self-introduction
1. Please introduce yourself to the class.
2. Say a few words to the students to introduce yourself.
3. First take a few minutes and tell the class about yourself.
4. Will you introduce yourself to the students?

〈発展的表現〉

5. Please tell the students who you are, where you are from and so on to help the class know you better.
6. Would you introduce yourself a little [just a bit] so that the students can get to know you?
7. The students are interested in knowing about you. Can you tell them just a little about yourself?
8. Please greet the students and say a few words about yourself. Will you accept a few questions at the end?
9. I'll introduce you to the class first, then you tell them about yourself. Would that be all right?

**Notes:**　一般に ALT (Assistant Language Teacher) に何かを依頼する際には，なるべく丁寧な言い方を用いるのが無難である．Would you mind 〜? / Will you 〜? のほうが，How about 〜 / Why don't you 〜? よりも当りが柔らかい．また音調もぶっきらぼうにならないような配慮が欲しい．6 の just a bit は a little と同意で会話でよく用いられる．9 は日本人教師があらかじめ簡単に ALT の紹介を行ったあとでさらに自己紹介を依頼するという手順の説明をし，同意を求める．

### イ．日常生活の話　Everyday life
1. Can you tell the class how you spent the weekend?
2. You went to Nikko over the weekend. Can you tell the class about it?
3. Would you tell the students about what you did during the holi-

days?
4. What're you going to do next Sunday? Can you tell the class a little about it?

〈発展的表現〉

5. Did you do anything special over the weekend? Would you mind telling the class a little about what you did?
6. How was your trip to Nikko? Can you tell the class about your trip?
7. Have you been enjoying your life in Japan? Could you tell the class about your new experiences here?
8. Are things very different here from what they are in your own country? If so, please tell us about them.
9. Could you tell us about the differences and similarities between your home country and Japan?
10. What do you think about this school and the students? Please tell us.

**Notes:** 1~3, 5, 6 は ALT が週末や休日に行ったことについて生徒に話すことを依頼する．4 は ALT の週末の予定を話してくれるよう依頼する．週末を祝日，夏休み等に変えて利用できる．7 は着任後日の浅い ALT に日常生活について話してくれるように依頼する．8, 9 は ALT に自国と日本の相違点，類似点を話してくれるよう依頼する．10 は生徒の印象について話すよう依頼する．

## b. モデル・リーディングの依頼　Requesting a model reading

### ア．音読の依頼　Asking for reading aloud

1. Please read this sentence.
2. Will you read this passage?
3. Read this dialog aloud, please.
4. Please read these sentences one at a time.
5. Now I want you to read the whole page twice.

〈発展的表現〉

6. Now this time can you read the whole passage twice, the first time,

slowly and the second time, a little faster.
7. Will you pause a little at the end of each sentence so that the students can think about what it means?
8. First explain the vocabulary and then read the passage aloud, please.
9. Let's read the dialog for the students. You take A's part. I'll take B's. Shall we begin?
10. Please read each sentence twice. After the second reading, let them [get them to] read after you.
11. Ask the class to read aloud after you. Please correct their pronunciation mistakes at the end.
12. Will you read what you've written on the board and have the students repeat it in chorus?

**Notes:** 〈発展的表現〉には具体的な読み方の指示まで含むものもある．9は日本人教師とALTが掛け合いによってモデル・リーディングを行うようにという指示．10はALTのモデル・リーディングのあと，生徒にコーラス・リーディングをさせる指示の依頼も含む．11は10に加え，さらに読みの訂正依頼も含む．10と12で生徒に「～させる」でmakeを用いると，強制の意が入るのでlet, have, getのほうが無難である．

## イ．音読方法の指示　Indicating how to read aloud

1. Will you read this slowly and clearly?
2. A little more slowly, please.
3. More loudly, please.
4. Read this dialog dramatically, please.
5. Please read it at a natural speed.
6. Will you pause between sentences?

〈発展的表現〉

7. The class doesn't seem to understand. Will you read it again more slowly and clearly?
8. I don't think they can follow you. Can you read a little more slowly?

9. I want you to read this passage at a natural [normal] speed, but please give a little pause between paragraphs.
10. It's a little noisy outside. Will you read it again a little louder?
11. As this is a dialog, could you please read it again a little more dramatically?

**Notes:** 1, 4〜6, 9 はモデル・リーディングの前に行う音読法への注文. 2, 3, 7, 8, 10, 11 は再度読み直しの注文であるから依頼が音調や顔の表情などにより命令的にならないように注意すること.

## C. 板書の指示　Directions for work at the board

1. Please draw it on the board.
2. Show us by drawing it on the board.
3. Will you write the word on the board?
4. Can you spell the word out on the board?
5. Please draw a rough picture to explain the situation.
6. Would you draw a simple map on the board, please?
7. Will you write the word both in block letters and in script?

〈発展的表現〉

8. The students would understand what you're talking about better, if you explained it by drawing. Please use the board.
9. Before you read, please write the names of the people and places on the board to make it easier for the students.
10. Please use colored chalk as well as white chalk, if you like. Then the drawing will be more interesting.
11. Please don't speak with your back to the class. It's difficult for them to understand what you are saying.
12. Can you wait a few minutes until they finish copying what you have drawn [written] on the board?

**Notes:** 9 は物語などのモデル・リーディングに生徒の理解が進むよう，あらかじめ板書して予備知識を与えるよう依頼している. 11, 12 は板書の際の具体的

注意を含む. 11 では生徒に背を向けたまま話さぬよう依頼. 12 では生徒にメモを取る時間を与えてくれるよう注文する.

## d. 生徒への対応　Directions concerning students

### ア. 個別指導の依頼　Working with individual students
1. Please walk around and help the students.
2. Can you walk around a little and give assistance to individual students?
3. Let's monitor the students and see what they're doing.
4. Please look at the students' notebooks, and correct any mistakes you find.

〈発展的表現〉

5. Why don't we walk around to see how the students are doing? Will you help the students who need assistance?
7. Will you walk around and check the students' pronunciation?
8. Can you walk around and ask the students if they have any questions?
9. Let's see how they wrote the sentences. Will you correct any of their mistakes?
10. Please monitor the class and help the students who're having problems. At the end will you tell the class the points they must remember?

　**Notes:**　4, 9 はノートを見て誤りがあれば訂正を, 7 は発音の訂正を依頼する. 10 は個別指導の結果, 共通の問題点を事後指導してくれるように依頼する.

### イ. 生徒への指示を依頼　Indicating how to direct students
1. Please tell the students to pair off and practice this.
2. Ask some students to come to the front and perform [demonstrate it].
3. Will you ask for volunteers?

4. Please pick five boys and two girls for the skit.
5. Can you choose one student in each row?
6. Will you tell the class to stand up and practice?
7. Please tell the class to go back to their seats.

〈発展的表現〉
6. It's time for practice. Let's divide the class into eight groups of six. Would you like to explain it to the class?
7. Will you divide the class into two by splitting them down the middle and having them face each other for the dialog?
8. Please ask the class to pair off and spend ten minutes writing a dialog for the skits.
9. Ask the class to divide into groups of four and have them discuss the problem.
10. Will you assign one reporter for each discussion group and let him [her] report back at the end?

**Notes:** 7～10は形態の指示とそれに伴う言語活動についても言及している．

### e. 授業の流れについて　Directions concerning teaching procedure

#### ア．活動の中断を求める　Interruption of activities
1. May I stop you for a second?
2. Can I interrupt you a second?
3. May I stop you here?
4. Okay, could you stop now?
5. Would you mind stopping for a moment?

〈発展的表現〉
6. Excuse me, may I interrupt you for a second? The students do not seem to understand what you're talking about.
7. Do you mind if I interrupt you for a second? There are some students who don't seem to understand what you mean.
8. Can I stop you a second? I want to explain it in Japanese.

9. Sorry, can you give the class a little (more) time to think?
10. Will you stop a second and check if they're following you?
11. Sorry to interrupt you, but would you mind writing the word on the board?

**Notes:** 1〜5を用いる場合は，活動中に中断を求める理由をはっきりさせてALTに不快感を与えぬよう配慮すること．事前に了解を求めておけば，これらは中断のための単なる合図となる．8〜11は生徒の理解を助けるために中断してなんらかの手だてを加える方法も示している．

## イ．時間調整　Schedule

1. Time's up. Let's stop here.
2. There goes the bell. We must finish up.
3. Time's running out. Let's do it next time.
4. We've got only five more minutes. Why don't we do it next week?
5. We have ten more minutes. Any suggestions?
6. There's a little time left. What should we do?
7. Will you give me the last three minutes? I want to tell them about their homework.

〈発展的表現〉

8. We're running out of time. We should stop this activity today. Would that be O.K.?
9. Sorry but time's running out. Do you mind if we do this next time?
10. We're behind schedule today. I'm afraid we must give up the final activity. Would that be all right?
11. So far, we've got fifteen more minutes. Why don't we give the students a little more time for discussion?
12. Oh, we have five more minutes today. Will you read the passage aloud before we finish [end]?
13. Everything's gone smoothly today. We still have five minutes. Why don't you ask the class what activities they've enjoyed most?

**Notes:** 授業進行の関係で時間調整が必要になったときは，ALTの了解のうえで

その場で計画の修正を行うのがよい。1～4, 8～10 は時間不足が生じた場合の例。5, 6, 11～13 は時間が余ってしまった場合の例。

## f. 指導案作成　　Making teaching plans

1. October 20 is our demonstration day. I'd like to make a teaching plan with you.
2. What are the teaching objectives of this lesson?
3. The objectives are, first, to understand Section 1 of Lesson 8, and, second, to use the important language functions in it.
4. What kind of extra materials should we prepare?
5. I think we need a skit and OHP pictures.
6. I want to make a skit which includes the use of this language function.
7. That's a good idea. I also have some good tasks for applying that function.
8. OK. Then, let's first demonstrate the task so that the students can see how to do it.
9. What activities do you think are good to check their use of the language function?
10. That's a crucial point. We need a kind of activity which challenges the students.

**Notes:**　3. language function は、説明する (explaining)、質問する (asking (questions))、謝る (apologizing) などの「ことばの働き」。

## g. ティーム・ティーチングの評価　　Evaluation of team-teaching

1. Do you think our objectives were clear?
2. Could you evaluate the students' speaking ability?
3. I'll interview the students, and why don't you check the points you think are important?

4. As a part of the final examination, I want to administer a listening test. Could you record the script onto the audio-tape?
5. In the coming term-end test, I'll mark the reading comprehension items.
6. I'd appreciate if you could mark the writing section of the coming test?
7. The English Teachers' Association in this district has decided to administer an achievement test in February. Could you help us make the objective reading test items with four options?
8. Three students are going to make a three-minute speech as warm-up activities today. Could you sit at the back of the room and evaluate them from the viewpoint of their attitude?
9. Did the students have a positive attitude toward communicating?
10. I think the activities were effective and we could finish what we planned to do.

**Notes:** 3. Why don't you〜? は「〜したらどうですか」。4. script はリスニングテストの「(録音用)台本」。6. I'd appreciate〜は「〜してもらえたらありがたい」という丁寧な依頼。7. The English Teachers' Association は中・高等学校教員などの「英語部会」。7. four options は「4つの選択肢」。8. from the viewpoint of attitude は「態度の観点から」。

## h. 授業環境の説明　General announcement about English classes

1. We will have a shorter class hour of 45 minutes due to the PTA meeting in the afternoon.
2. We will have visitors in the first ten minutes of our class. But their purpose is not to evaluate our teaching.
3. Tomorrow is the Open Day [Open House]. You will notice several parents observing our class. They are not so much concerned with our teaching as their children's performance in the class.
4. There might be a sudden interruption of a few minutes in the

fourth class hour. That is part of annual fire drill.
5. Yamada has told me that he will be late for our class by ten or fifteen minutes. He visits the hospital once a month for a regular check of his respiratory condition.
6. Since this is the last class before our term examination, we have to cover the textbook up to page 101. We should [had better] leave several minutes for the students to ask their questions at the end of the class.
7. You don't have to stick to the original. As far as the "communication" stage is concerned, you can modify the plan as you like.
8. We had better pay particular attention to Yamada. He is somewhat mischievous.
9. Let's give Tanaka a chance or two to speak up during the class. Otherwise she is awfully shy and rarely speaks up [gives] her opinions.

**Notes:** 授業環境について事前に ALT に知らせておく必要のある指示を挙げてみた。1～7はクラス全体に関わることであり，8～9は特定な生徒への配慮を求めている指示である。1. shorter class hour は「短縮授業」。3. Open Day（英），Open House（米）は「授業参観日」。are not so much concerned with A as B は「AよりもBに関心がある」。5. respiratory conditions は「呼吸器官の状態」。7. 'communication' stage は「'コミュニケーション'の(指導)段階」。on your own initiative は「自分の自発的な考えで」。

## i. 小学校での「英語活動」　Q & A's about "English Activities"

1. Q: What is the status of "English Activities" in the elementary school curriculum?
   A: "English Activities" have been created, as one of the activities of the Period for Integrated Study, to address to international understanding focusing on "foreign language conversation," particularly "English conversation."

2. Q: What are the aims of Elementary school "English Activities"?
   A: "English Activities" amount to experiences that expose children to other cultures as means of promoting contact with people from other countries, so their primary purpose is to foster interest and desire, not only to teach a language.
3. Q: Why is spoken English emphasized in "English Activities"?
   A: It is too much to ask elementary school children to communicate, using both spoken and written means, and doing so may cause them to develop a dislike for English.
4. Q: What contents and activities are included in "English Activities"?
   A: You can choose any content and activity if they interest children, meet their expectations and development, and promote their participation. There are no fixed contents and activities.
5. Q: Who will teach "English Activities"?
   A: Basically the Homeroom Teacher (HRT) is responsible for the academic and moral instruction of students because s/he knows his/her students best, but the HRT can work together with the Assistant Language Teacher (ALT), the Japanese Teacher of English (JTE) or local volunteers such as Guest Teachers (GTs), Volunteer English Teachers (VETs), and English Activity Assistants (EAAs).
6. Q: What kinds of teaching methods are available for "English Activities"?
   A: Don't hold on to a single teaching method. Try to use many kinds of ideas and activities. Start with methods that are not overly demanding but are appropriate to the level of the students and the circumstances of each school.
7. Q: How long is one lesson unit of "English Activities"?
   A: It may be flexibly set depending upon learning activities. There are examples of short activities lasting five minutes or 20–25

minutes and long activities lasting 90 minutes, half a day, or even a full day although most lessons are allotted 45 minutes per unit.

8. Q: How should a lesson be designed?
   A: Lesson structure will differ depending upon the person(s) conducting the lesson, the teaching materials, the length of each lesson, the teaching tools and equipment used, and the number of times lessons will be provided.

9. Q: How is student progress to be measured?
   A: It should be based not on test scores but on descriptive assessment about learning conditions, students' degree of participation in activities, and their enthusiasm and attitude towards learning.

10. Q: What should we keep in mind when we teach "English Activities"?
    A: There are several Dos and Don'ts in teaching "English Activities":

    Dos:
    1) Focus on spoken English.
    2) Introduce what students want to say and do.
    3) Introduce items found in students' daily lives.
    4) Select basic and useful expressions.
    5) Include familiar topics with new perspectives.
    6) Have students become aware of cultural differences through expressions and gestures used by people in other countries.
    7) Use topics, materials, and subjects matching students' developmental stages.

    Don'ts:
    1) Don't translate everything into Japanese.
    2) Don't force students to memorize.

3) Don't correct small mistakes.
4) Don't use only whole-class teaching; apply various learning formats.

**Notes:** 2. as means of 〜は「〜の手段として」. 10. whole-class は「(対面式)一斉指導」.

## j. 日本の教育事情　Q & A about education in Japan

1. Q: How long do Japanese children attend school?
   A: Kindergartens admit children aged 3, 4 or five and provide one-to-three year courses. After kindergarten, they have to attend nine years of compulsory education from age 6 to age 15. Attendance is mandatory for elementary and lower secondary school (or lower division of secondary education school).
2. Q: What is required if they want to enter school beyond the compulsory school level?
   A: They have to pass an entrance examination to enter upper secondary school.
3. Q: How many courses are available for them?
   A: General courses are for those who wish to advance to higher education, specialized courses are intended to provide vocational or other specialized education, and integrated courses are a mixture of the two where students can independently select subjects from among a variety of classes covering general and specialized subjects.
4. Q: How are physically or mentally handicapped children educated?
   A: They go to special education schools where the type and degree of their disability are taken into consideration. The educational programs for them are equivalent to standard kindergartens, elementary schools, lower secondary schools and up-

per secondary schools.
5. Q: Do the students change classrooms for each lesson?
   A: They don't change rooms except for science, music, industrial arts and homemaking, and physical education. In upper secondary school they change rooms more often, because they have more choices in selecting subjects.
6. Q: How is local educational administration conducted?
   A: Prefectural boards of education administer and operate schools (mainly upper secondary schools and schools for physically or mentally handicapped) and the cultural and social education institutions (lifelong learning centers, libraries, museums, etc.) are established by prefectures.
7. Q: Who serve as members and personnel on boards of education?
   A: The members of prefectural or municipal boards of education are appointed by the governor or mayor with the consent of the assembly concerned.
8. Q: How is primary and secondary education financed?
   A: Most school expenditures (94.4%) are from public funds; however, the percentage of distribution differs between local public and private schools.
9. Q: To what curriculum standards should elementary and lower secondary schools conform?
   A: Curriculum standards for elementary and lower secondary schools are prescribed in the Courses of Study issued by the Ministry of Education, Science, Sports and Culture (MESSEC).
10. Q: How are textbooks published and distributed?
    A: Textbooks for elementary and lower secondary schools must follow the procedure of the application for authorization from the publishers, authorization by the MESSEC, adoption by local boards of education, and free provision by the Government.

11. Q: How is the in-service training of teachers conducted?

    A: Various systematic programs are conducted at national, prefectural and municipal levels so that teachers can pursue consistent in-service training in order to maintain their competence and quality appropriate to their professional responsibilities as teachers.

    **Notes:** 1. 幼稚園及び小学校・中学校(義務教育)を年齢と通学期間で説明したもの. 2. 義務教育が修了した後, さらに勉強したい場合は高校進学への道がある. 3. 高等学校のコースの概略. General courses は普通課程, Specialized courses は専門課程, Integrated courses は総合課程. 4. 心身に障害がある子どもに対する教育. 5. 授業形態の説明. industrial arts and homemaking は「技術・家庭」. 6. 教育委員会の役割. 7. 教育委員の任命. 8. 初等・中等教育の経費. 9. 教育課程と学習指導要領. 10. 教科書の検定・採択. 11. 教員の現職研修.

# 教室英語歳時記
# Seasonal Terms for Warm-Up

第Ⅴ部

# 1. 季節・祝日
## Holidays and Festivals

### a. 日本の祝祭日　National holidays and festivals

1. We have fourteen national holidays. We also have many national and local festivals. (Dates in parentheses depend on each calendar year)

   | | | |
   |---|---|---|
   | Jan. 1 | New Year's Day | 元旦 |
   | Jan. (12) | Adults' Day [Coming of Age Day] | 成人の日 (1月の第2月曜日) |
   | Feb. 3 | Bean-Throwing Ceremony | 節分 |
   | Feb. 11 | National Foundation Day | 建国記念の日 |
   | Mar. 3 | Girl's Festival | ひな祭り |
   | Mar. (20) | Vernal Equinox Day | 春分の日 |
   | Apr. 8 | Buddha's Birthday Festival | 花祭り [灌仏会] |
   | Apr. 29 | Greenery Day | みどりの日 |
   | May 3 | Constitution Day | 憲法記念日 |
   | May 5 | Children's Day | こどもの日 |
   | July 7 | The Star Festival | 七夕祭り |
   | July (19) | Marine Day | 海の日 (7月の第3月曜日) |
   | Sept. (20) | Respect for the Aged Day | 敬老の日 (9月の第3月曜日) |
   | Sept. (23) | Autumnal Equinox Day | 秋分の日 |
   | Oct. (11) | Health-Sports Day | 体育の日 (10月の第2月曜日) |
   | Nov. 3 | Culture Day | 文化の日 |
   | Nov. 15 | Celebration for Children of 3, 5 and 7 Years of Age | 七五三 |
   | Nov. 23 | Labor Thanksgiving Day | 勤労感謝の日 |

|      | Dec. 23 | Emperor's Birthday　天皇誕生日 |
|---|---|---|
|      | Dec. 31 | New Year's Eve　大晦日 |

2. We have three national holidays and one Sunday from April 29 through May 5.
3. We have a holiday-studded "Golden Week" from Greenery Day (April 29th) through Children's Day (May 5th).
4. If a national holiday falls on Sunday, we have a holiday the following Monday.
5. Is it true that Japanese office workers have little chance for daily contact with their families? — Yes. That's why they take their children to amusement parks on holidays.

## b.　英米の祝日　National holidays in the U.K. and the U.S.A.

(Dates in parentheses depend on each calendar year)

### ア．米国の祝日　National holidays in the U.S.A.

| Jan. 1 | New Year's Day　元旦 |
|---|---|
| Jan. (19) | Martin Luther King Jr.'s Birthday (3rd Monday in January)　キング牧師誕生日 |
| Feb. 12 | Lincoln's Birthday　リンカーン誕生日 |
| Feb. (16) | Washington's Birthday / Presidents' Day (3rd Monday in February)　ワシントン誕生日／大統領の日 |
| Apr. (9) | Good Friday (Friday before Easter)　聖金曜日 |
| May (31) | Memorial Day (Last Monday in May)　戦没者追悼記念日 |
| July 4 | Independence Day　独立記念日 |
| Sept. (6) | Labor Day (1st Monday in September)　労働祭 |
| Oct. (11) | Columbus Day (2nd Monday in October)　コロンブス記念日 |
| Nov. (2) | General Election Day (1st Tuesday after the 1st Monday in November. Observed usually only when presidential or general elections are held.)　総選挙日 |

| | | |
|---|---|---|
| Nov. 11 | Veterans Day | 復員軍人の日 |
| Nov. (25) | Thanksgiving Day (4th Thursday in November) | 感謝祭 |
| Dec. 25 | Christmas Day | クリスマス |

イ．**英国の祝日**　National holidays in the U.K.

| | | |
|---|---|---|
| Jan. 1 | New Year's Day | 元旦 |
| Jan. 2 | Bank Holiday (Scotland only) | 一般公休日 |
| Mar. 17 | St. Patrick's Day (N. Ireland only) | 聖パトリックの祝日 |
| Apr. (9) | Good Friday (Friday before Easter) | 聖金曜日 |
| Apr. (12) | Easter Monday (England, Wales and N. Ireland only) | 復活祭明けの月曜日 |
| May (3) | May Day Bank Holiday (1st Monday in May) | メーデー |
| May (31) | Spring Bank Holiday (last Monday in May) | 春の一般公休日 |
| July 12 | Orangeman's Day (N. Ireland only) | オレンジ党員の日 |
| Aug. (2) | Bank Holiday (Scotland only, 1st Monday in August) | 一般公休日 |
| Aug. (30) | Summer Bank Holiday (England, Wales and N. Ireland only, last Monday in August) | 夏の一般公休日 |
| Dec. 25 | Christmas Day | クリスマス |
| Dec. (27) | Boxing Day (1st weekday after Christmas) | クリスマスの贈り物の日（かつて使用人などに贈り物をした） |

c．**エイプリルフール**　April Fools' Day

1. April 1st is April Fools' Day.
2. On April Fools' Day you can play a trick on another person.
3. Be careful. Today is April Fools' Day.
4. Last Monday was April Fools' Day. What trick did you do [pull] on your brother [sister]?

**Notes:** 英国ではエイプリルフールのいたずらができるのは正午までで，正午が過ぎてからいたずらをすると，その人が「馬鹿」ということになる．

## d. 花見　Cherry blossom viewing

1. The cherry blossoms in the park are at their best this evening.
2. The cherry trees in our school are in full bloom today.
3. Let's go to Ueno Park to see the cherry blossoms.
4. Many groups are having parties under the cherry trees.
5. Many people enjoy eating and drinking rather than viewing the cherry blossoms.
6. Some groups sing along with a tape recorder [*karaoke*] in a cherry blossom viewing party.
7. Cherry blossom petals fall on the people drinking below (them).
8. The cherry blossom is the national flower of Japan.
9. *Sakura* or the cherry blossom is the symbol of Japan.
10. All parks with cherry trees are crowded with people who have cherry-blossom viewing parties under the trees.
11. The cherry blossom 'front' is approaching Asahikawa in Hokkaido.
12. When did this custom start? It started as a Buddhist ceremony in the twelfth century.
13. Why is it that cherry blossoms symbolize the *samurai* spirit? The *samurai* wished that, if they had to die, they would die 'beautifully' like falling cherry blossoms.

**Words & Phrases:**　八重桜 double cherry blossoms,　垂れ桜 weeping cherry blossoms,　夜桜 cherry blossoms at night [in the evening]

## e. 梅雨　Rainy season

1. It's depressing when it rains. Few people like this kind of weather. Do you?

2. The rainy season has finally set in. We are at the northern end of the Asian monsoon belt.
3. We are having another wet day [spell]. How long has it been raining?
4. It's been raining for a week. The ground is soaking wet with rain.
5. Gee! Such heavy rain! Do you know the English expression, "It's raining cats and dogs"?
6. Do you know we had a really heavy rain [a rainstorm] last night. I was awakened by the rain beating against the windows.
7. It's raining very heavily up in the mountains. We are getting concerned about a possible flooding of the low lands.
8. Did you read the news about yesterday's flood in southern Japan?
9. It has stopped raining, but the clouds are still threatening another shower.
10. Although it isn't raining now, it is still very humid and uncomfortable.
11. It seems the rain has passed, finally. We'll see sunshine for the first time in a week. [This will be the first sunshine for a whole week.]

*Words & Phrases*:　梅雨前線 a seasonal rain front,　梅雨入り［明け］ the setting-in [end] of the rainy season

## f.　夏至　Summer solstice

1. What do you call [How do you say] 'geshi' in English? — It is the Summer solstice.
2. When does the summer solstice occur? — It occurs about June 21st.
3. Where is the sun in the summer solstice? — It is in the most northern position.

*Words & Phrases*:　不快指数 discomfort index [DI],　避暑地 summer

resort, 夏休み summer vacation, 入道雲 gigantic columns of clouds, 海水浴 sea bathing, 登山 mountaineering, キャンプ camping

**Notes:** 夏至の太陽の位置は厳密には over the Tropic of Cancer という.

### g. 七夕　Star Festival

1. *Tanabata* is celebrated on July 7th. It comes from an ancient Chinese legend. There are two stars, Altair and Vega. They love each other, but they can meet only once in a year. That is July 7. However, if the weather is bad, they can't meet.
2. There is a legend that the Herdboy Star and the Weaver Star were separated by the Milky Way.
3. The *Tanabata* Festival is held on the 7th day of the 7th month of the lunar calendar.
4. People in earlier times [ages] prayed for fair weather, offering sweets and food to the two stars.
5. Members of the family wrote wishes or poems on strips of colored paper and decorated bamboo cuttings in the garden with them. This may remind you of Christmas trees.
6. The *Tanabata* Festival is slowly disappearing from big cities. It's not easy for city dwellers to have gardens in which to decorate bamboo cuttings.

**Words & Phrases:** 短冊 a strip of fancy paper for writing a short poem on, 色糸 colored threads, 機織り weaving, 裁縫 sewing / needlework, 習字 penmanship

### h. 花火　Fireworks

1. We can watch fireworks this evening by the river banks.
2. Can we watch fireworks at the lakeside?
3. I bought fireworks for my sister.

4. I like fireworks because they display brilliant flashes of light and colors.

**Words & Phrases:**　花火大会　a fireworks display [exhibition],　線香花火　sparkler,　仕掛花火　a set piece of fireworks

## i.　お祭り　Festivals

1. In Japan we have festivals in every season.
2. Which festival in this area do you like best?
3. In festivals of shrines we often see *mikoshi* or a portable shrine, that is, "temporary dwelling places of the gods".
4. Most festivals in Japan are related to agriculture. Even a small village has its own autumn festival to thank the local god for the crop.

## j.　秋分　Autumn(al) Equinox

1. Tomorrow is Autumn Equinox and we have no classes.
2. We have two equinox days. One is about March 21st and the other is about September 23rd.
3. On equinox days daytime and nighttime are equal in length all over the earth.
4. Where is the sun on equinox days? It is directly above the equator.
5. "Higan" which comes twice a year at the spring and autumnal equinoxes, means "the other side" in Buddhism. Our life is considered to be on "this side".

**Words & Phrases:**　彼岸の入り　the beginning [the first day] of the equinoctial week,　彼岸の中日　the autumn [spring] equinox,　暑さ寒さも彼岸まで　No heat or cold lasts over the equinox.

## k.　月 見　Moon viewing

1. *Tsukimi* or moon viewing takes place on the full moon in autumn.
2. When is *tsukimi*? ― It is observed on August 15th of the lunar calendar.
3. What do you do in *tsukimi*? ― We offer *tsukimi-dango* (rice dumplings), fruits and vegetables in season to the full moon, together with *susuki* or Japanese pampas grass.
4. People living in the earlier days of Japan had moon viewing parties in Autumn.

　**Words & Phrases**:　十五夜 a full moon night（行事としては 2, 3 の文で説明する），十三夜 a moon thirteen days old（行事としては moon viewing on September 13th of the lunar calendar），祭壇 a tiny altar（この場合は運搬可能な小さい祭壇）

## l.　菊　Chrysanthemum

1. The Chrysanthemum Festival this year is from October 25th to November 10th.
2. You can see a lot of chrysanthemums in the park during the Chrysanthemum Festival.
3. Look at the chrysanthemum figures! How beautiful!
4. The chrysanthemum is the symbol of the Japanese Imperial crest.
5. There are lots of chrysanthemum contests in Japan in late autumn.

　**Words & Phrases**:　菊の御紋 the Imperial chrysanthemum crest

## m.　紅 葉　Red and yellow leaves / Colored leaves

1. The maple leaves in the school yard have turned red. Winter is coming soon.

2. The mountains look red. The maples up there must have turned red.
3. I want to go to Kyoto just to see the red maple leaves in a temple garden.
4. I saw on TV last night that there were lots of cars in Nikko. People went there to see the red leaves at their best.

**Words & Phrases**:　紅葉狩り　a maple-viewing / an excursion for viewing autumnal tints

## n.　木枯らし　A cold [chilly] wind

1. The chilly wind stopped [died away] at last.
2. Can you hear the whistling of the cold wind through the tree-tops?
3. This cold wind may be a sign that winter is coming soon.

## o.　冬至　Winter solstice

1. What is the English for the Japanese *toji*? Toji is the day when daytime is shortest.
2. *Toji* is "the winter solstice" in English. It is said to have the shortest daylight.
3. When does the winter solstice occur? — It occurs about December 22nd.
4. Where is the sun on the winter solstice? — It is in the most southern position.

**Notes**:　冬至のときの太陽の位置は厳密には over the Tropic of Capricorn という.

## p.　クリスマス　Christmas

1. It's already Christmas time. You can hear Christmas songs in many

shops downtown.
2. Did you believe in Santa Claus when you were in the first grade?
3. Are you going to have a Christmas party with your friends?
4. Do you have a Christmas tree in your home?

**Words & Phrases**: クリスマス・プレゼントを入れてもらう靴下 Christmas stocking, クリスマスの祝儀 Christmas box (召使い, 郵便配達人などに与える. その日を Boxing Day という), キリスト降誕日(12月25日) Christmas Day

## q. 正 月　New Year

### ア. 挨 拶　Greetings

1. (I wish you a) Happy New Year!
2. How many New Year's cards did you get?
3. Did you go somewhere during the New Year holidays?
4. Which shrine did you visit on New Year's Day?
5. We get *otoshidama* as a New Year's present.
6. *Otoshidama* is a gift of money given to children by their parents and relatives.

### イ. 飲食物　Food and drink

1. We celebrate the New Year by drinking *o-toso* and eating *o-zoni*.
2. *O-zoni* is a sort of broth containing *mochi* (rice-cakes or paste) and vegetables.
3. New Year's dishes are symbolic of happiness and prosperity.
4. We eat *kazunoko* or herring roe because it symbolizes "many children."
5. We also eat black beans and pieces of lotus root.
6. What does the lotus root symbolize? — It symbolizes "sacredness" because it has a straight stem and puts forth a pure-white flower.
7. What is *o-toso*? — It is a sweet *sake* flavored with Japanese spices.

8. We drink *o-toso* on New Year's Day because *o-toso* is said to have preventive powers against sickness.

## ウ. 遊び　Games

1. During the New Year holidays we enjoy flying kites, card games, and *hanetsuki* or battledore and shuttlecock.
2. More and more families spend their New Year holidays at some hot spring resorts.
3. Young people go abroad or go skiing during the New Year holidays.

## エ. 飾り　Decorations

1. What is that straw rope? — It is *shimenawa*. It is said to bring good luck to the house and keep evil out.
2. At the entrance to the house are decorations which usually consist of two pine trees and three stalks of bamboo.

**Words & Phrases**:　御幣 little angular strips of white paper / an emblem supposed to represent offerings of cloth to the deities of a Shinto shrine

## r. 梅　A plum (tree)

1. The plum blossoms in the courtyard are at their best.
2. Do you like *umeboshi* or pickled plums?
3. Kairakuen in Mito City is famous for its plum blossoms.

## s. 節分　Bean-throwing ceremony

1. *Setsubun* or the bean-throwing ceremony is observed on Feb.3. We throw roasted beans in and around the house, shouting "Devils out, fortunes in!"
2. Why do you throw beans? — Because they are supposed to scare off evil spirits [demons] from our household.

3. *Setsubun* is literally the end of winter or the first day of spring.

**Words & Phrases**: 年男 a lucky-bean scatterer at the *setsubun* rites

## t. 雛祭り　Girls' [Doll's] Festival

1. The Doll's Festival is celebrated on March 3.
2. What is the meaning of the Girls' Festival? — It is to pray for the happiness of the girls in the family.
3. Why is that festival called *hinamatsuri*? — Because a set of dolls called "hina-ningyo" are arranged on a stand.

## u. 花言葉　Language of flowers

### ア. 誕生花　Birthday flowers

1月　**snowdrop** (雪の花)　hope; fortune (希望，幸運)

2月　**violet** (すみれ)　sympathy; modesty (同情，謙遜)

3月　**daffodil** (すいせん)　friendship; sincerity; kindness (友情，誠実，親切)

4月　**primrose** (さくらそう)　love and envy (愛とねたみ)

5月　**Madonna lily** (フランス百合)　chastity (清純)

6月　**rose** (ばら)　true love; passionate fidelity (真実の愛; 情熱的な貞節)

7月　**carnation** (カーネーション)　kindness, consideration (思いやり)

8月　**heather** (ヒース)　[白] best fortune (最高の幸運)，[紫] solitary love (孤独の愛)

9月　**golden rod** (あきのきりん草)　luck; success (好運，成功)

10月　**rosemary** (まんねんろう)　reminiscence, remembrance (追憶) **chrysanthemum** (菊)　sincerity (誠実)

11月　**ivy** (つた)　foundation of friendship and love (友情・愛情の素地)

12月　**Christmas rose** (クリスマスローズ)　gentleness; sympathy;

mercy（優しさ，同情，慈悲）

## イ．日本の花の花言葉　Language of Japanese flowers
注 1)　ここでいう日本の花とは，「日本でよく見かける」という意味であって，日本原産という意味ではない．また，季節ごとの花の種類は，比較的馴染みのあるものに限定した．
2)　花名のあとに挙げてある(花言葉の)意味は主なものに限定した．なお，日本と英米とで意味が異なる場合は「ただし書き」を付けた．
3)　季節による分類は大まかなものであり，南北に長い日本列島では，地区によって季節のずれている所もあるであろう．
4)　英米の花言葉については Jean Marsh, *The Illuminated Language of Flowers*（Macdonald and Jame's, 1987）に拠ったが，見出し語として載っていないもの(つまり，英米であまり見かけないもの)には，英名の最後に * を付した．

[春]

**amaryllis**（アマリリス）　chatterbox（おしゃべり）．ただし英米では pride; splendid beauty（誇り，素晴らしい美しさ）．
**cape Jasmine**（くちなし）　great happiness（とても幸せ）
**cherry**（桜）　innocence（純潔）．ただし英米では fraud（欺瞞）．
**Chinese peony***（しゃくなげ）　shyness（恥じらい）
**dandelion**（タンポポ）　parting（別離）．ただし英米では the message of love（愛の神託）．
***hitorishizuka****（ひとりしずか）　hidden beauty（隠れた美）
**iris**（アイリス）　love message; good [welcome] news（恋のメッセージ，吉報）
**Japanese apricot***（梅）　faithfulness, devotion; elegance（忠実，気品）
**lily-of-the-valley**（すずらん）　purity; modesty（純潔，謙遜）．英米では "Happiness returns."（「幸福が戻ってくる」）．
**peony**（ぼたん）　shyness（恥じらい）
**rose**（バラ）　love; beauty（愛情，美）．英米ではバラの種類によって 30 以上もの花言葉がある．
**tulip**（チューリップ）　[赤] confession of love（愛の宣告），[黄] hopeless

love（望みなき恋）
***yamabuki*****（やまぶき） nobility（崇高）

[夏]

**cactus**（サボテン） greatness; passion（偉大，熱情）．ただし英米では passion のみ．

**clover**（クローバー）［4枚葉］a good luck（幸運），［3枚葉］promise; hope（約束，希望）．ただし英米では四葉は Please become my love.（私のものになって），赤が diligence（勤勉），白が Please think of me.（私を思ってね）．

**dahlia**（ダリア） grace; brilliance（優美，華麗）．ただし英米では uncertainty（不安定）．

**four-o'clock**＊（おしろい花） cowardice（臆病）

**bindweed**（昼顔） bond, knot（絆）

**hydrangea**（あじさい） coldness; caprice（冷淡，移り気）

**lily**（ゆり）［白］purity; lusciousness（純潔，甘美）．[黄]は英米では deceit; cheerfulness（偽り，陽気）．

**lotus**（はす） eloquence（雄弁）

**morning glory**（朝顔） frail love（はかない恋）．ただし英米では pretension（気どり）．

**rhododendron**（しゃくなげ） dignity; solemnity（威厳，荘厳）．ただし英米では danger（危険・要注意）．

**snapdragon**（金魚草） presumption（でしゃばり）

[秋]

**bush clover**＊（萩） thoughtfulness（物思い）

**chrysanthemum**（菊） nobility（高貴・高潔）．ただし英米では赤が be in love（愛しています），白が truth（真実），黄が neglected love（無視された愛）．

**cosmos**＊（コスモス） maiden sincerity; harmony（乙女の真心，調和）

***higanbana*****＊（彼岸花） sad memory（悲しい思い出）

**maple**（もみじ） modesty; reservation（慎み，遠慮）

**monkshood**（とりかぶと） revenge（復讐）．ただし英米では chivalry（騎

士道).
***ominaeshi*** *（おみなえし） frail love; beauty（はかない恋，美人）
**saffron**（サフラン） joy; Don't waste（歓喜，濫用するなかれ）
**thistle**（あざみ） revenge; strictness（報復，厳格）

[冬]
**begonia**\*（ベゴニア） kindness（親切）
**cabbage**（葉ぼたん） interest（利益）
**camellia**（椿）［赤］modest virtue（控えめな美徳），［白］supreme sweetness [loveliness]（最高の愛らしさ）
**fir**（樅） time（時間）
***fukujuso***\*（福寿草） invitation of happiness（幸せを招く）
**Japanese silver leaf**（つわぶき） Revive, love.（愛よよみがえれ）
**poinsettia**\*（ポインセチア） My heart is filled with love.（私の心は燃えている）
***sasanqua***\*（さざんか）［赤］modesty（謙譲），［白］agreeableness（愛敬）

> ***Words & Phrases***： 国花（national flowers）は，England が rose，Scotland は thistle（あざみ），Wales は leek（にら），Canada が sugar maple（さとうかえで）．英国の場合，行政区分では「連合王国」(the United Kingdom of Great Britain and Northern Ireland) が正式な国名であるから，米国の「州花」(state flowers) に準じて考えるべきであろう．

## 2. 学校行事
### School Events

### a. 遠足 Outing

**ア． 遠足の前** Before an outing

1. We're going to have a picnic [an outing / an excursion / a day trip] tomorrow, aren't we?
2. We'll go on an outing [a hike / a long walk] tomorrow.
3. You [Your legs] will get good exercise tomorrow.
4. Tomorrow is the day for our spring excursion.
5. We'll surely have fine weather for our outing.
6. Which will you bring tomorrow, a sandwich or *onigiri*?
7. How long do you think you will walk?
8. You must wear sports shoes.
9. You won't come in skirts, will you?
10. I'm sorry the outing was cancelled. (中止された場合)

> **Words & Phrases**: 天気予報 a weather forecast [report] (on TV / radio), おやつ snacks (または biscuits, cookies, candies など具体的に), 軽快な服装で dressed in sports clothes / dressed in light clothes good for exercise, 水筒 a canteen / a flask / a thermo / a water bottle (主としてイギリス)

> **Notes**: 「遠足」については an outing が最も一般的である．歩くことが中心であれば hike や a long walk, 行楽の要素が多ければ(バス旅行なども含めて) a picnic, an excursion が適当であろう．また自然観察など勉強の要素が多ければ a field trip なども使えるであろう．10. 野球の試合などが雨によって延期された場合には The game was rained out. という表現があるが，それに準じて米語では「晴れの日にあらためて」の意で So you had to take a rain check.

と言うことがある(この rain check は次回の試合に有効な入場券の意味).

### イ． 遠足のあと　After an outing

1. Are you tired [exhausted]?
2. Did you have a good rest last night?
3. Your legs must hurt even now.
4. Are your legs all right now?
5. All your faces are well [slightly] tanned.
6. It was an ideal [a perfect / a fantastic] day for an outing.
7. We couldn't have hoped for better weather.
8. The sight from the top was just wonderful [marvelous].
9. It was a hard climb, wasn't it?

***Words & Phrases***:　疲れた　be tired [exhausted]，　足が痛い　legs hurt / have a pain in one's legs，　中止される　be called off [cancelled]，　延期される　be rescheduled on ～ [put off till ～]

**Notes**:　疲れた原因を言うときは I'm tired from the long walk. (最近は with よりも from を使うことの方が多い)．exhausted は tired より強意で，体力を消耗しきった感じ．fatigued でも代用できるが，これは主として書き言葉であり exhausted ほど意味が強くない．

## b.　写生会　Sketch outing

### ア．　写生会の前　Before the sketch outing

1. We'll go sketching along the Arakawa River.
2. We're going to the park to draw [paint] pictures.
3. Tomorrow we are going out to draw [paint] in the fields.
4. Do you want to paint in watercolors or draw with pastels or color pencils?
5. I can't go with you, but have a nice day at the park.
6. I am fond of painting pictures. I wish I could go with you.
7. Don't forget to bring a drawing board or something you can draw

your picture on.

***Words & Phrases***: （水彩）絵の具 (water) colors [paint], パレット a palette, 絵筆 a (color) brush, 画板 a (drawing) board, 風景画 a landscape (picture / painting)

**Notes:** sketch は日本語の「スケッチ」と同じく，おおまかな写生のこと．原則的には，paint は多色の絵の具を使い，draw は単色で描く場合であるが，教室英語としてはあまり神経質になる必要はない．

### イ．写生会のあと　After the sketch outing
1. How were your pictures?
2. How did your picture come out, Takeko?
3. Did you finish painting it?
4. Where did you go?
5. How many hours did you stay in the park?
6. Did you go there by bus or did you walk?
7. Do you think you did a good job?
8. What did you draw, the bridge, the buildings, or the trees?

***Words & Phrases***: うまくいかなかった didn't do it very well, 絵が下手 poor [not very good] at painting / not very artistic, 張り出される go on exhibition (at the School Festival)

## C. 校内球技大会　Sports events (intraschool)

### ア．大会の前　Before the sports events
1. Tomorrow is our ball-game day [Sports Day].
2. Everybody, do your best.
3. Which (ball) game will you join?
4. Do you play volleyball or softball?
5. Which team are you on, volleyball or softball?
6. Who is the best player on your team?
7. Which class do you think is the strongest this year?

***Words & Phrases***: 優勝候補 the best bet for the championship / the class which is most likely to win, 組み合せる match A against B / pair A with B, 試合する play with [against] B, 球技 a ball game

## イ．大会のあと　After the sports events

1. You won the championship.
2. You came a close second.
3. Were you excited during the semifinal?
4. Everybody did very well. I was impressed.
5. It was a very close game. It was exciting.
6. What score did you get against Class B in the finals?
7. I didn't know you were such a good basketball player.
8. Your class won because everyone did his or her best.

***Words & Phrases***: いい試合 a close game, 惜しい試合 a game almost won, 準優勝 second best, 最下位になる get the lowest score / be in the lowest rank / be in the basement / be at the very bottom

**Notes**: 英米ではホームルーム単位で団体戦を行うということはあまりないので，2位や3位まで賞状 (certificate for the second [third] prize) を教室に張って誇示するという状況はあまりない．

## d．対外試合　Sports events (interschool)

### ア．試合の前　Before the sports events

1. Tomorrow you're going to have the municipal [prefectural] interschool tennis [basketball / baseball, etc.] game [match / tournament].
2. You will play football [soccer] with [against] Yamada High School.
3. We are to have [hold] the judo match for the prefectural title.
4. You will have a practice match [game] with Takada Junior High School.
5. The spring tennis tournament will be held tomorrow at Nishi High School.

6. Our school team will join [participate in] the prefectural kendo tournament this coming Sunday.
7. I'm sure you will do your best to win the game.
8. Give them a hand and cheer them on [root for them].

**Words & Phrases:** 頑張れ Cheer up! / Do your best. / Hold on., 予選 an elimination / an eliminating match [contest], 地区予選 a regional elimination / a district contest, 決勝戦 the finals / the final round [game / match], 練習試合 a practice match [game] / a workout

**Notes:** 「試合」の意味ではアメリカで game, イギリスでは match が多く用いられる．また game は主として -ball のつく競技で使われ，tournament は通例選手権を争う勝ち抜き試合のことである．8の root for 〜（盛んに声援する）は主として米口語．

## イ．試合のあと　After the sports events

〈勝った生徒に〉

1. That was a good game.
2. I'm happy you won the game.
3. Your victory pleased the principal.
4. You won the trophy [the cup].
5. I didn't doubt that the game would end in our victory.

〈負けた生徒に〉

6. You played fair.
7. You played on courageously.
8. I'm sorry the game ended in a draw.
9. You held your ground [stood out fast].
10. That wasn't very bad. You did a fairly good job.
11. Don't be discouraged. You'll have another chance next year.

**Words & Phrases:** 全力で戦う do one's best in the game [match], 引き分け a draw (game), 雪辱する get even with 〜, 優勝杯 trophy, 優勝旗 championship pennant

**Notes:** 9.「最後まで頑張った」という意味．

## e. 修学旅行　School trip

### ア．修学旅行の前　Before the trip

1. You're going on your school excursion tomorrow.
2. Tomorrow is (the day for) the trip all of you have been waiting for.
3. You are excited about the trip, aren't you?
4. Will you travel by bus or by train?
5. Have you ever been to Nara?
6. Is this your first time to visit Kyoto?
7. What are you planning to see at Odawara?
8. How many days will you be away from school?
9. Did you read the guide for the trip carefully?
10. Have a nice trip. And tell me what you've seen when you come back.

### イ．修学旅行のあと　After the trip

1. Welcome back (to school).
2. How was the trip?
3. Did you enjoy the school [field] trip [excursion]?
4. How did you like the field trip to Hokkaido?
5. You must have seen many interesting things. What was the most interesting?
6. What did you buy for souvenirs?
7. What did you buy for your parents?
8. What did you do on the bus [train]?
9. Do you want to visit Kyoto again?

***Words & Phrases***: バス旅行 a bus [coach] tour, 夜行列車 a night train, 旅行日程 an itinerary, お小遣い pocket [spending] money, 日帰り旅行 a day trip

**Notes**: 英米の学校には修学旅行という制度そのものがないから，旅行の内容に合わせて trip, excursion, tour などを使い分けるのがいい．

## f.　弁論大会　Speech contest

1. Yamada will join an English speech contest tomorrow.
2. You have a speech [an oratorical] contest in Japanese.
3. Who represents your class in the inter-class debate?
4. The District English Speech Contest will be held at the City Hall.
5. The speech contest is sponsored by the city.

## g.　文化祭　School festival

### ア．文化祭の前　Before the school festival
1. What is your club [class] planning for the school festival?
2. Will you put on a play in English this year, too?
3. You'll have your pictures on display [view].
4. We're going to hold a bazaar. Please contribute something to it.
5. Last year we earned 25,000 yen in [from] the bazaar. I hope we'll be just as successful this year.
6. Are you going to set up a refreshment booth? What are you going to sell?
7. Do you intend to join the *karaoke* contest?

### イ．文化祭のあと　After the school festival
1. I enjoyed your band performance most.
2. I was impressed by the show your club jointly produced.
3. I found the artistic level of your paintings quite high.
4. I was very happy to find another of your talents.
5. What part of the show were you most interested in?
6. Who of [from] your family came to see your work?
7. What did you eat at the food stall they opened?
8. Did you find something interesting in the bazaar?
9. How many days did you spend making that robot you displayed?

***Words & Phrases***: 展示物 an exhibit, 生け花 (a) flower arrangement, 工作 a handicraft, 習字 a calligraphy work, 刺繍 an embroidery work, 上演する put on a play / present a play on the stage, 役柄を演じる play the part of, 講演を聞く have a lecture, 合唱[カラオケ]コンクール a chorus [*karaoke*] contest

**Notes:** 学校を開放して父母や地域に日頃の活動を紹介する行事は open house とか open day とか呼ばれ, 出し物に応じて drama day とか speech day とか言われる. また資金集めのためのバザーを中心にしたものに school fete と呼ばれるものがある. いずれにせよ, 文化祭に対応するようなものは英米の学校にはないから, 教室英語としては school festival でいいだろう.

### h. 運動会　Sports Day

#### ア. 運動会の前　Before Sports Day

1. You're excited. Tomorrow is our Sports Day.
2. We'll have our athletic meet tomorrow.
3. I hope the weather will be [is] good.
4. Which race are you in?
5. What events are you going to take part in?
6. What's your best time for the 100-meter dash?
7. Who are the runners for the inter-class 400-meter relay?
8. I'm very excited to see what you're going to do in the cheering competition.
9. Everyone plays some part in managing the Sports Day. Are you in charge of timekeeping?

#### イ. 運動会のあと　After Sports Day

1. How many medals [ribbons] did you get?
2. Which event were you most excited about?
3. I didn't know you were such a fast runner.
4. Who was the hero [heroine] for the class yesterday?
5. I was amused by the costume parade [procession].

6. The relay was very exciting. I was very happy to see you win it.
7. You have a hoarse voice. You must have been very excited when you were cheering. [You must have been cheering very excitedly.]
8. Sports Day was such a success. Everybody did a very good job.

***Words & Phrases***: 100 メートル競争 a 100-meter dash, 400 メートル競争 a 400-meter race, 400 メートルリレー a 400-meter relay, 二人三脚 a three-legged race, 騎馬戦 a piggy-back fight, パン食い競争 a bun-snatching race, 大玉送り an earth-ball relay, 玉入れ tossing balls, 応援合戦 cheering competition, 組み体操 a human pyramid, アトラクションのレース a fun [special / amusing] race

**Notes**: 「運動会」は sports day, field day, athletic meet, sports-and-fun day などどう訳しても，その雰囲気はうまく伝えることができない．飴食い競争，風船割りなどを英語に（たとえば searching-for-candy race, sitting-on-balloons など）訳して英語授業の雰囲気を盛り上げるのもおもしろい．

## i. 定期試験　Term examinations

1. We're going to have the term [mid-term] examinations next week.
2. How many tests do you have on the first day?
3. Do you study late in the night or early in the morning?
4. What subject are you most concerned about?
5. Do you still have club activities? You must be very short of time.
6. Everybody must have crammed for the test.

***Words & Phrases***: 平均点 the average (score), 合格点 the pass mark, 一夜づけ cram for the test overnight, 最高［低］点 the highest [lowest] mark [score], 満点 the perfect score, 数学で落第点をとる flunk math

## j. 入学試験　Entrance examination

1. Good luck with your entrance examinations.
2. The entrance examinations to prefectural high schools are coming

soon.
3. You have exactly a month until the first round of entrance examinations to national colleges [universities] begins.
4. Miss Ando was admitted to B College on the school's recommendation.
5. How many entrance examinations are you going to take?
6. I know Mr. Yamada is absent because of his entrance examination to C School. I wish him success.
7. It's only natural that everyone is getting pretty nervous. The examinations are drawing near.

**Words & Phrases**: 推薦状 a recommendation, 推薦入学 admitting students on recommendation, 推薦入試 an examination for candidates recommended by their school principals, 入試センター試験 the preliminary [first-stage] entrance examination to colleges, 面接試験 an interview, 入試科目 a subject of the entrance examination, 入学願書 an application form

**Notes**: 日本の大学入試センター試験に最も類似したものといえば，アメリカの諸大学入学申請に際して要求される SAT (The Scholastic Assessment [Aptitude] Test) と ACT (The American College Test) があるが，これは合否判定の一部でしかないとか，何回でも受験できるなど多くの点で異なっていることに注意．

## k. 生徒会活動　Students meeting

1. Which committee do you belong to?
2. You are going to elect the (vice) president of the student council.
3. You're a member of the executive committee.
4. He was elected to the chair [as the chairman] of the student council by a vote of 120 to 40.
5. We have the general meeting [assembly] of the student council this afternoon.

6. What are the major subjects you're going to discuss at the meeting?
7. Very few students are concerned with the rules of the student council.
8. The welcome [farewell] party is sponsored by the student council.

**Words & Phrases**: 選挙管理委員会 an election committee, 総会運営委員会 a steering committee of the general assembly, 実行委員会 a working committee, 中央委員会 a central committee, 予算を票決[可決]する vote [adopt] the budget, 決算 settlement of accounts (☞ p. 360)

## l. 給食　School lunch

1. Did you enjoy today's lunch?
2. Which dish do you like best?
3. What dish don't you like?
4. What is your most favorite dish [food]?
5. What is the dish you don't like [you like least]?
6. We'll have a surprise for today's lunch. Guess what.
7. Do you prefer the lunch your mother prepares?
8. Would you like to have a school lunch program at our school?

**Words & Phrases**: あげパン a fried bun, ハンバーガー hamburger (英国では beefburger とも言う), サンドイッチ sandwich (3枚のパンを使った二段重ねのものは double-decker, 米国では club sandwich という。また、1枚のパンの上に卵・野菜などをのせたものを open sandwich という), ソフトめん soft noodle, 酢豚 sweet-and-sour pork, 焼きそば chowmein, 肉じゃが boiled meat and potatoes, おでん fish cakes and vegetables in broth, 豚汁 miso soup with pork and vegetables, 先割れスプーン a spoon with a fork-like tip

## m. 掃除　Cleaning

1. We're going to be sweeping and dusting today.

2. 学校行事　341

2. Today is Spring Cleaning (Day).
3. Today we'll do spring cleaning.
4. Nobody loves cleaning, but nobody likes dirty rooms either.
5. Which room [part of the school ground] are you assigned to clean?
6. I see lots of trash [dust] in the room. You should sweep the floor more carefully.
7. Can you tidy up the teacher's table? It's just a mess.

**Words & Phrases**: 掃除当番 a cleaning duty, さぼる goof around [off], 雑巾がけをする wipe (the floor) with a cloth, 黒板消しをはたく clean [dust off] the blackboard eraser, 窓拭きをする clean the windows, はたきをかける dust, 草取りをする weed, ごみ箱 a trash can, 掃除道具 cleaning things [equipment], ちりとり a dustpan, 落書き scrawling / scribbling / graffiti

**Notes**: wipe [swab] the floor という語句は普通モップで拭くことを連想し、日本の伝統的な雑巾がけのスタイルは浮かばない.「ごみ」でも食べかすのような生ごみは garbage, 紙屑・空きびんのようなものは rubbish, trash.

## n. PTA　Parent-Teacher Association

1. Will your parents come to the PTA meeting?
2. Teachers will visit your home this afternoon.
3. We have no class in the afternoon because of the PTA meeting.
4. Several of your parents will be guests today.
5. Don't get nervous about your parents watching you from behind.
6. Your parents will come and we will talk together about the choice of schools after graduation.

**Words & Phrases**: PTA総会 the general assembly of the Parent-Teacher Association, 授業参観 class observation, 進学相談 seek for advice on the choice of schools, 家庭訪問 a home visit, 父母呼び出し summon one's parents

## 0. 入学式・卒業式　Entrance [Graduation] ceremony

1. Today is the entrance ceremony.
2. It was exactly a year ago when you had your entrance ceremony.
3. Do you remember how you felt at your entrance ceremony?
4. You will see your seniors in the graduation ceremony. In just one more year you will be having [in] your graduation ceremony.
5. Do you know what their memorial gift will be?
6. You saw many students with tears in their eyes when they sang "Auld Lang Syne". Are you going to cry, too, next year?

***Words & Phrases***: 卒業記念品 a graduation memorial gift, 祝辞 a speech of congratulations, 卒業証書 a certificate of graduation, 卒業アルバム a year book, 謝恩会 a thank-you party, 予餞会(卒業生を送る会) a farewell party, 新入生 a freshman, 歓迎会 a welcome party

# 3. 社 会
## Social Affairs

### a. 地震　Earthquakes

1. Channel One Morning News says that there was a big earthquake in China.
2. I didn't know that Japan has so many earthquakes.
3. The true center of the earthquake was in the south of the Suruga Bay.
4. Is it true that earthquakes are caused by a giant *namazu* or catfish wiggling its tail under the earth?
5. "Earthquakes, thunder, fires and Dad" are often said to be most dreaded, but I doubt if contemporary fathers still enjoy such a status!

   ***Words & Phrases:***　微[弱/強/激]震 slight [weak/strong/severe] shock, 地震帯 earthquake zone,　震源地 epicenter,　火砕流 pyroclastic flows

### b. 災害　Disasters

1. Typhoon No.12 caused damage of ¥200 million to the crops.
2. I hope this heavy rain will not cause a flood.
3. The cyclone hit Bangladesh and caused many deaths.
4. Typhoons are tropical storms which start in the South Pacific.
5. Last Sunday's flood forced the people of the town to leave their homes.
6. The volcano spewed ash [hot lava] all over the area.

## c. 交通事故　Traffic accidents

1. One woman was killed in the traffic accident near this school.
2. When you come to school by bike, don't forget to wear a helmet.
3. Don't ride two people on one bike; it's dangerous.
4. Be careful when crossing this street because the traffic is very heavy here.

   ***Words & Phrases***：救急車 an ambulance, 応急処置 first aid, 夜間運転 night driving, 横断歩道 pedestrian crossings, 白線［黄色い線］white [yellow] lines

## d. 誘拐　Kidnapping

1. A junior high school girl was kidnapped and ¥20 million was demanded for her release.
2. Be careful of any stranger who offers you a ride. He may be a kidnapper.
3. A boy of ten has been missing for a week. He may have been kidnapped.
4. One of the men who kidnapped a bicycle shop owner asked for ¥100 million in ransom.
5. The man who had been kidnapped was freed in a remote village.

## e. 殺人　Murder

1. In the United States an average of 25 people are killed by guns everyday.
2. A burglar went into the house and, when discovered, murdered all the family.
3. What a horrible crime! He murdered seven young girls, after sexually attacking them.

## f. 外国の出来事　International affairs

1. In this age of broadcasting satellites we can see live what is happening throughout the world.
2. There is always a war somewhere in the world. How warlike human beings are!
3. We must be more sensitive and responsive to what is happening outside Japan.

## g. 環 境　Environment

1. There are a lot of things you can do to save the earth.
2. Is that river clean enough to swim in?
3. The air in the central part of the city is polluted by cars.
4. Let's walk instead of riding in cars. It'll help clean the air.
5. Do you know that even the ice at the poles is polluted?
6. Have you heard about the "greenhouse effect"?
7. In less than two centuries humans have increased the total amount of carbon dioxide by 25 percent.
8. At least three percent of the global ozone layer has already been destroyed.
9. Unless we take action now, no forest will be safe from (pollution by) acid rain in the future.
10. Acid rain destroys plant and animal life in streams, damages forests, and even erodes buildings.
11. More than 90 percent of the world's total supply of drinkable water is ground water.

## 4. スポーツ
### Sports Club Activities

#### a. 陸上競技　Track and field

1. What is your time in the 100 meter dash?
2. You are an anchor in the 400 meter relay, aren't you?
3. You are the pole vault record holder in this district.
4. You won the men's 100 meters with the meet record of 12.31.

***Words & Phrases***:　短距離競争 a sprint [dash]、　短距離走者 a sprinter、同記録 a tie、バトン baton、フライング・スタート a premature start、フライングをする jump the gun、ラップタイム lap time、大会新記録 the meet record, a new record (in the inter-high-school athletic meet)

#### b. サッカー　Soccer

1. Your team won again. What was the score?
2. Do you know the formal name of soccer? It's Association Football.
3. Which position do you play, forward, midfielder or defender?
4. You drew 1–1 with Minami High School. That's not too bad.

***Words & Phrases***:　インステップ・キック an instep kick、オーバーヘッド・キック an overhead kick、ストライカー a striker、ゴールキーパー a goal keeper

#### c. 野球　Baseball

1. You hit a home run in the seventh inning. We were all excited.
2. You did a wonderful job as the shortstop [left fielder, etc.]

3. How many batters did you strike out in yesterday's game?
4. You hit a two-run homer which led our team to a 7–2 victory over Higashi High School.

**Words & Phrases**: コールドゲーム a called game, スクイズ・プレー a squeeze play, デッドボール hit by a pitch, バッテリー a battery, ブルペン a bull pen, ボーク a balk, 救援投手 a relief pitcher, 暴投 a wild pitch, 公式試合 a pennant race, アウトコース outside, ゴロ a grounder

## d. バレーボール　Volleyball

1. The blocking of your team was very effective.
2. Your team displayed wonderful combinations of toss-and-spike.
3. You are an all-round player — good in attack as well as defense.
4. You were one point behind [ahead] at that time.

**Words & Phrases**: アンダー[オーバー]ネット under [over] the net, ホールディング holding, ドリブル dribble, スパイク spike, 回転レシーブ (a) rolling receive, サービス・エース a service ace, 時間差攻撃 a time differential spike, 変化球サーブ a change-up service, フェイント a feint

## e. バスケットボール　Basketball

1. Your team showed very good defense techniques.
2. It was too bad that he missed the free throw.
3. How many baskets did you score in the first half?
4. You made a twenty-foot jump shot just before the final buzzer.

**Words & Phrases**: 30秒ルール thirty-second rule, バイオレーション violation, ピボット a pivot, フォーメーション・プレー a formation play, フリースロー a free throw, マンツーマン・ディフェンス man-to-man defense, ジャンプシュート a jump shot

## f. 卓球　Table tennis / Pingpong

1. Your pingpong team was seeded this season, wasn't it?
2. Your loop-drive was wonderful. You went as far as the semifinal.
3. It was a close game. You won it by 3–2 after a long rally.

**Words & Phrases**: エッジボール　an edge-ball, オープンハンド・サービス　an open-hand service, サンドイッチ・ラバー　sandwich-rubber, ボレー　a volley, トップ打法　a top-attack, ループ・ドライブ　a loop-drive, フォールト　a fault, ラリー　a rally

## g. バドミントン　Badminton

1. The net play was really exciting to see.
2. Your overhead stroke was very powerful [impressive].
3. You did wonderfully well. You must have practiced hard.

**Words & Phrases**: シャトルコック　a shuttlecock [bird], スマッシュ　a smash, バックハンド［フォアハンド］ストローク　a backhand [forehand] stroke, ヘアピン・ショット　a hairpin shot

## h. テニス　Tennis

1. You really have a powerful service.
2. That was a close game. You went to deuce in the final set.
3. What was your score against Higashi High School?
4. You advanced to the final with a 6–2, 6–4 victory over Kita High School.

**Words & Phrases**: スマッシュ　a smash, フォールト　a fault, ボレー　a volley, ロビング［ロブ］　lobbing [a lob], ジュース　deuce, シングルス　singles, ダブルス　doubles, 混合ダブルス　mixed doubles

## i. スキー  Skiing

1. I'm a very poor skier. I cannot even turn my skis.
2. I love skiing, but the ski competition must be different from skiing for pleasure.
3. You made a magnificent jump. How far did you jump?

*Words & Phrases*: シャンツェ a ski jump (独 Schanze), ゼッケン a (race) number (独 Zeichen), ビンディング binding (独 Bindung), アルペン種目 the Alpine events, ノルディック種目 the Nordic events, 直滑降 a straight descent, 滑降競技 a downhill race, 大回転競技 the giant slalom

## 5. 生　徒
### Students

### a. 誕生日　Birthday

1. When is your birthday?
2. Did you get anything for your birthday this year?
3. Do you do anything special on your birthday?
4. How do you celebrate birthdays in your family?

### b. 病　気　Illness / Sickness / Disease

1. Takada is sick in bed and cannot come to school today.
2. You look pale. Are you sick?
3. You'd better take a rest in the health room.
4. There are lots of colds about. Be careful not to catch one.
5. Our principal has been suffering from a serious illness since last month. I hope he will recover soon.

　**Notes:**　4. の about は，イギリス英語で in various parts of a place の意味で，「流行っている」とほぼ同じ意味になる．風邪の種類としては a bad [slight] cold, a cold in the nose (鼻風邪), (the) flu [influenza] (流感)等がある．症状としては have a headache, have (a) fever, cough, have a runny nose (鼻水が出る), have a chill (寒気がする)等があげられる．その他，病気に関する主な表現を掲げる．

ア．一般症状　General conditions
発熱　fever
寒気　chill
頭痛　headache

めまい　dizziness
耳なり　ringing in the ear
だるい　tired
肩こり　stiff neck

激痛　sharp pain
鈍痛　dull pain
寝汗　night sweat
発汗　sweat
不眠症　insomnia

胸やけ　heartburn
げっぷ　belch
便秘　constipation
吐き気　nausea
血便　blood stool
軟便　loose stool

イ．循環器系　Circulatory system
　動悸　palpitation
　息切れ　short of breath
　脈の乱れ　arrhythmia
　立ちくらみ　faint

オ．呼吸器系　Respiratory system
　くしゃみ　sneeze
　喉の痛み　sore throat
　鼻水　runny nose
　咳　cough

ウ．外科系　Surgical system
　外傷　external wounds
　切り傷　cut
　骨折　fracture
　脱臼　dislocation of bone
　捻挫　sprain
　打撲　bruise

カ．耳鼻咽喉系　Ear, nose & throat
　かすれ声　hoarse voice
　鼻づまり　nasal congestion
　中耳炎　tympanitis / earache

キ．歯科　Dentistry
　歯痛　tooth pain
　虫歯　tooth decay（状態）/
　　　　a decayed tooth

エ．消化器系　Digestive system
　腹痛　stomachache
　空腹時　when hungry

## C. 怪我　Injury / Wound / Hurt

1. What happened to your leg, Kaneda?
2. One of the first-year students met with a traffic accident and was badly injured yesterday afternoon.
3. How did you get injured?
4. Why do you have [why is] your finger bandaged?
5. Does your wound still hurt?
6. You must have been absent-minded to cut yourself with a knife.

**Notes:** injury と be [get] injured は事故等で怪我をするという意味で，wound と be [get] wounded は刃物等による外傷や戦争での怪我を指す．hurt は injury, injure とほぼ同意で用いられる他に，感情を傷つけるという場合に用いられる．怪我の種類としては break one's leg [arm], sprain [twist]（捻挫する），bruise（打撲），a scrape [abrasion / graze]（擦り傷）等がある．

## d. 選手として活躍　Performance

1. You belong to a baseball club, don't you? Are you a regular (member / player)?
2. What is your position on the team?
3. How did you play in the soccer game yesterday? Did you score any goals?
4. Our basketball team beat Minami High School in the semifinal yesterday.
5. I watched your judo match yesterday. You beat three players, didn't you? Well done!

**Notes:**　トーナメント（tournament）における1回戦は the first round と言う．以下 the second, third と続き，準々決勝は quarterfinals, 準決勝は semifinals, 決勝は the finals となる．

## e. 入賞・入選　Winning prizes

1. Kimura won first prize in the English speech contest.
2. Do you know that an art exhibition is now being held in the City Gallery? Ueda's oil painting was selected as a fine work of art.
3. Our choir was awarded the gold medal in the musical competition yesterday.

**Notes:**　コンクールは英語では competition か contest を用いる．金賞は gold medal [prize], 銀［銅］賞はそれぞれ silver [bronze] で表す．佳作は fine work か work of merit が使われる．

## f. 好き嫌い　Likes and dislikes

1. Are there certain foods that you like or dislike? / Do you have likes and dislikes about food?
2. What is your favorite subject?
3. How do you like your life at this high school?
4. You have good marks in every subject, don't you? What makes you prefer one subject over another?

**Notes:**　preference は「あるものを他よりも好むこと」の意味で使われる．他に好き嫌いを表す表現としては be particular about（えり好みをする），be fussy about（小うるさい）等がある．

## g. 趣味　Hobbies

1. Please tell us about your hobbies, Saito.
2. How do you spend your leisure [spare time]?
3. Let's tell each other about our hobbies. Kasai, you start.
4. I hear that you have a lot of interests. What is your most recent interest?
5. Our ALT, Mr. Norfleet, has long been interested in archaeology, the study of old things. Let's hear him talk about it.

**Notes:**　趣味を表す表現としては他に pastime, recreation 等がある．hobby が余暇を利用して個人が楽しみのために積極的に取り組む活動であるのに対し，pastime, recreation は気晴らしのために行う活動という意味合いを持つ．

## h. 家族　Family

1. How many are there in your family?
2. How many brothers [sisters] do you have?
3. Is your brother [sister] younger [older] than you?
4. Is everyone in your family well?

5. Does your family do anything special (together)?
6. Please tell us about your father [mother]? What kind of person is he [she]?
7. Do you have a pet at home?
8. Do you sometimes go on a family trip?
9. Do all of you in your family live together?
10. When does your family get together?

**Notes:** 1 の How many (people) are, 9 の all (the members) of you は ( ) 内の語句が省略されるのが普通．

## i. 住まい   House

1. In what part of the city do you live?
2. Suzuki, you live in Midorigaoka, don't you? How do you come to school?
3. Do you live in your own house or in an apartment?
4. Does your house have a garden?
5. How many floors does your house have?
6. How many rooms are there in your house?
7. Do you have your own room? How do you like it?

**Notes:** 日本語のマンションは apartment (house), condominium (分譲アパート) のことであり，mansion (大邸宅) とは異なる．階を表すのに a three-storied building (3 階建てのビル) のように story を用いることもある．

## j. テレビ番組   TV programs

1. How long [much] do you watch TV every evening?
2. What kind of TV program(s) do you like?
3. I watched the 'NHK Special' last night. Did anyone else watch it?
4. Some people think TV is good, while others think it's bad. Let's discuss the advantages and disadvantages of television.

**Notes:** テレビ番組の種類としては news, documentary, drama, movie, quiz show, talk show, music program, variety show [entertainment] 等がある．

## k. 友人関係　Friends

1. Do you have many friends?
2. Who is your closest friend?
3. How long have you two known each other?
4. How did you come to know each other?
5. Who do you think is the most popular in this class?
6. Let's introduce ourselves to each other to broaden our circle of friends.

## l. 職業　Jobs / Occupation

1. What do you want to do in the future?
2. What is your father's occupation?
3. Have you ever had a part-time job?
4. Are you planning for your future career?
5. What do you think of first when you try to decide on a job?
6. What is the most important thing [factor] for you in choosing a job?
7. Ishida, I hear you are interested in computers. Are you going to become a computer engineer?

**Notes:** 日本語の職業に最も近い意味の語としては occupation があげられる．job は勤め口の意味の他に職業上の仕事・作業の意味で使われることがある．career は生涯の仕事の意味で用いられることが多い．profession は主に知的な職業，専門的な職業を指す．

## 6. 教育関係用語
### Educational Terms

**a. 教室** Classrooms

**ア. 特別教室** Special classrooms

| | |
|---|---|
| 化学実験室 | chemistry laboratory [lab] |
| 理科準備室 | science teachers' room / science storage room |
| 調理室 | (school) kitchen |
| 被服室 | sewing room / dressmaking room |
| 音楽室 | music room |
| 美術室 | art room |
| 書道室 | calligraphy room |
| 視聴覚教室 | audio-visual room |
| LL 教室 | language laboratory [lab] |
| コンピュータ室 | computer room / CALL room |

**イ. その他** Other rooms

| | |
|---|---|
| 講堂 | auditorium |
| 集会室 | assembly |
| 体育館 | gymnasium |
| 職員室 | teachers' room / staff room |
| 事務室 | administration office |
| 校長室 | principal's office |
| 保健室 | nurse's office / health room |
| カウンセラー室 | counseling room / counselor's office |
| 応接室 | reception room / guest room |
| 会議室 | meeting room / conference room |

6. 教育関係　357

図書館　　　　　　school library

b. 中学校の科目　Subjects for lower secondary school

国語　　　　　　　Japanese
社会　　　　　　　Social Studies
算数　　　　　　　Mathematics (math)
理科　　　　　　　Science
音楽　　　　　　　Music
美術　　　　　　　Fine Arts
保健体育　　　　　Health and Physical Education (PE)
技術家庭　　　　　Industrial Arts and Homemaking
英語　　　　　　　English
総合的な学習　　　Period for Integrated Study
特別活動　　　　　Special Studies
道徳教育　　　　　Moral Education
選択科目　　　　　elective subjects

c. 高等学校の教科・科目　Subjects for upper secondary school

ア．国 語　Japanese
国語表現Ⅰ[Ⅱ]　　Japanese Expression I [II]
国語総合　　　　　Comprehensive Japanese
現代文　　　　　　Modern Japanese
古典　　　　　　　Classics
古典講読　　　　　Reading Classics

イ．地理歴史　Geography and History
世界史A[B]　　　World History A [B]
日本史A[B]　　　Japanese History A [B]
地 理A[B]　　　Geography A [B]

ウ．公 民　Civics
　　現代社会　　　　　Contemporary Society
　　倫理　　　　　　　Ethics
　　政治・経済　　　　Politics and Economics

エ．数 学　Mathematics
　　数学基礎　　　　　Basic Mathematics
　　数学 I [II, III]　　Mathematics I [II, III]
　　数学 A [B, C]　　 Mathematics A [B, C]

オ．理 科　Science
　　理科基礎　　　　　Basic Science
　　理科総合 A [B]　　Comprehensive Science A [B]
　　物理 I [II]　　　　Physics I [II]
　　化学 I [II]　　　　Chemistry I [II]
　　生物 I [II]　　　　Biology I [II]
　　地学 I [II]　　　　Geology I [II]

カ．保健体育　Health and Physical Education
　　体育　　　　　　　Physical Education (PE)
　　保健　　　　　　　Health

キ．芸 術　Art
　　音楽 I [II, III]　　Music I [II, III]
　　美術 I [II, III]　　Fine Art I [II, III]
　　工芸 I [II, III]　　Industrial Art I [II, III]
　　書道 I [II, III]　　Calligraphy I [II, III]

ク．外国語　Foreign Language
　　オーラル・コミュニケーション I [II]　 Oral Communication I [II]
　　英語 I [II]　　　　English I [II]

| | リーディング | Reading |
|---|---|---|
| | ライティング | Writing |

ケ．**家 庭**　Home Economics / Homemaking
　　　家庭基礎　　　　Fundamental Home Economics
　　　家庭総合　　　　Comprehensive Home Economics
　　　生活技術　　　　Life Techniques

コ．**情 報**　Information
　　　情報 A [B, C]　　Information A [B, C]

## d.　組織（教師・生徒）　Organization (staff, students)

ア．**教職員**　Staff
　　　管理職　　　　　management / managerial position
　　　校長　　　　　　principal / headmaster / headmistress
　　　教頭　　　　　　vice principal / deputy principal
　　　事務長　　　　　director of the administrative section
　　　事務員　　　　　school clerk
　　　用務員　　　　　janitor
　　　教務　　　　　　division of school affairs
　　　生徒指導　　　　division of student guidance
　　　進路指導　　　　division of career guidance
　　　健康指導　　　　division of health guidance
　　　渉外　　　　　　division of public relations
　　　渉外主任　　　　head of public relations
　　　学年主任　　　　head teacher of a grade
　　　HR 担任　　　　 homeroom teacher
　　　HR 副担任　　　 deputy [assistant] homeroom teacher
　　　日直　　　　　　day duty
　　　非常勤講師　　　part-time teacher

| | |
|---|---|
| 実習助手 | laboratory assistant |
| 英語指導助手 | Assistant Language Teacher (ALT) |

### イ．生徒　Students

| | |
|---|---|
| 生徒会 | student council |
| 生徒会長 | (student council) president |
| 会計 | (student council) treasurer |
| 執行部 | the executive(s) |
| 体育委員会 | athletic committee |
| 文化委員会 | cultural committee |
| 校紀委員会 | disciplinary committee |
| 学級委員長 | homeroom leader |
| 書記 | secretary |
| ～係 | student in charge of ～ |
| 日直 | day duty |

### e．教務関係　Academic affairs

| | |
|---|---|
| 出席簿 | roll book / attendance book |
| 通信簿・通知箋 | school report (card) / report card / grade report |
| 指導要領 | Course of Study |
| 指導案 | teaching [lesson] plan |
| 指導要録 | cumulative guidance record |

## f．校舎・校庭・運動場
School buildings / School grounds / Playgrounds

### ア．校舎　School buildings

| | |
|---|---|
| 管理棟 ① | administration building |
| 普通教室棟 ② | classrooms building |
| 理科実験棟 ③ | science laboratory building |

|  |  |
|---|---|
| 正面玄関 ④ | main entrance / front door |
| 生徒用玄関 ⑤ | student entrance |
| 茶室 | tea-ceremony room |

**イ． 校 庭**　School grounds / School yards

|  |  |
|---|---|
| 前庭 ⑥ | front yard [garden] |
| 中庭 ⑦ | courtyard |
| 自転車置き場 ⑧ | bicycle shed |

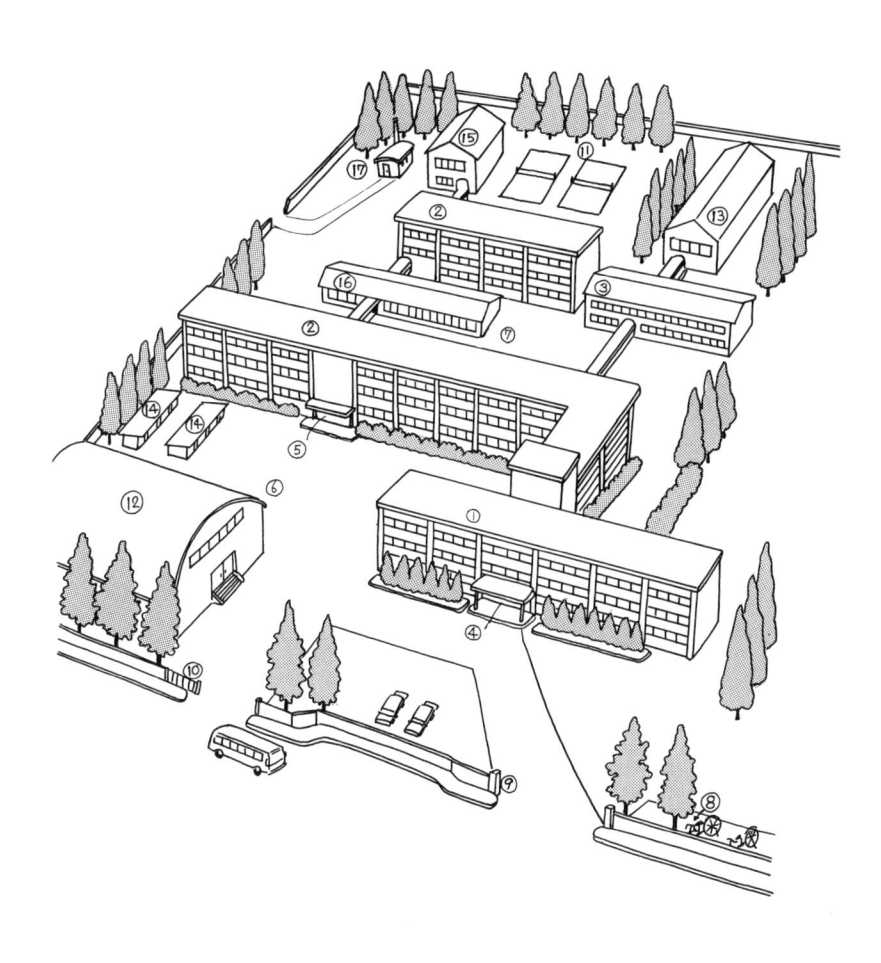

正門 ⑨　　　　　　main gate
生徒通用門 ⑩　　　gate for students / side gate

## ウ．運動場　Athletic fields / Playgrounds
陸上競技場　　　　track / field
テニスコート ⑪　　tennis court
野球場　　　　　　baseball field [ground]

## エ．体育館　Gymnasiums
体育館 ⑫　　　　　gymnasium [gym]
武道場 ⑬　　　　　martial arts hall
部室 ⑭　　　　　　club houses

## オ．その他　Others
生徒会館 ⑮　　　　student hall
食堂 ⑯　　　　　　school cafeteria
焼却炉 ⑰　　　　　incinerator

**編者紹介**
**高梨庸雄**(たかなし つねお)
　ハワイ州立大学大学院修了(英語教育学).高校教諭,教育センター指導主事,国立大学教授を経て,現在,京都ノートルダム女子大学教授.小学校英語教育学会会長.編著書に『英語リーディング事典』,『英語コミュニケーションの指導』,『英語リーディング指導の基礎』(以上,研究社)など.

**高橋正夫**(たかはし まさお)
　新潟大学卒業,ハワイ大学修士課程修了.新潟大学名誉教授,現在,新潟医療福祉大学教授.著書に『実践的コミュニケーションの指導』,『身近な話題を英語で表現する指導』(以上,大修館書店),『高校英語のコミュニカティヴ・プラクティス』(中教出版)など.

**カール・アダムズ**(Carl R. Adams)
　米国カリフォルニア州出身.School for International Training で TESL (英語教授法)の MA を取得.現在,東京国際大学教授.共著書に *Journeys: Listening & Speaking* (Longman).

**久埜百合**(くの ゆり)
　中部学院大学短期大学客員教授・千葉大学非常勤講師.成城学園初等学校英語科講師を 23 年間勤める.NHK学校放送番組「えいごリアン」企画委員.小学校英語教育学会副会長.著書に『こんなふうに始めてみては・小学校英語』(三省堂),『子ども英語救急箱』(ピアソン・エデュケーション)など.

---

きょうしつえい ご かつよう じ てん かいていばん
教室英語活用事典(改訂版)

2004 年 7 月 30 日　初版発行
2017 年 10 月 20 日　8 刷発行

編　者　　高梨庸雄
　　　　　高橋正夫
　　　　　カール・アダムズ
　　　　　久埜百合

KENKYUSHA
〈検印省略〉

発行者　　関戸雅男
印刷所　　研究社印刷株式会社

発行所　株式会社　研究社
http://www.kenkyusha.co.jp

〒102-8152
東京都千代田区富士見 2-11-3
電話 (編集) 03 (3288) 7711 (代)
　　 (営業) 03 (3288) 7777 (代)
振替 00150-9-26710

表紙デザイン:吉崎克美／イラスト:小林裕美子、黒木ひとみ
© T. Takanashi, M. Takahashi, C.R. Adams, and Y. Kuno 2004
ISBN 978-4-327-46149-2　C3052　　Printed in Japan